NEW YORK:
The Centennial Years 1676–1976

Kennikat Press

National University Publications

Interdisciplinary Urban Series

General Editor

Raymond A. Mohl

Florida Atlantic University

Edited by

Milton M. Klein

NEW YORK:
The Centennial Years 1676–1976

The Contributors

Thomas J. Archdeacon
Albert Fein
Kenneth T. Jackson
Milton M. Klein
Bayrd Still
Bruce M. Wilkenfeld

National University Publications
KENNIKAT PRESS // 1976
Port Washington, N. Y. // London

Manufactured in the United States of America

Published by
Kennikat Press Corp.
Port Washington, N.Y./London

Library of Congress Cataloging in Publication Data

Main entry under title:

New York: the centennial years, 1676-1976.

(National university publications: Interdisciplinary urban series)
Bibliography: p.
Includes index.
1. New York (City)—History—Addresses, essays, lectures. I. Klein, Milton Martin, 1917-
II. Archdeacon, Thomas J.
F128.3.N59   974.7'1   76-28325
ISBN 0-8046-9143-6

CONTENTS

Milton M. Klein

INTRODUCTION

Someone remarked recently that one has to be crazy to live in New York City these days; but millions do. It is no less a tax upon sanity to attempt to encompass the city's history in a single book. "Each man reads his own meaning into New York," the *New York Times* columnist Meyer Berger once remarked. "To many it becomes a second home and takes on additional meaning. The defeated go down in it, embittered, or flee from it and curse it."[1] But the city is more than a measure of success or failure. It is too huge, too protean, too many-sided to be encapsulated in any single poem or novel or work of architecture, of literature, or of history. For the historian, the essence of New York is especially elusive, too subject to incessant change to capture in words. One of the city's most distinguished adopted sons, and a professional historian, Allan Nevins, whimsically explained the problem thus:

Over its skyscrapers hangs some demon forever waving a wand and exclaiming "Presto, Change!" At his command the change comes—comes through growth, the successive waves of immigration from abroad and migration from within, the passion for rebuilding engendered by high land values, the want of reverence for the past.

Another chronicler of the city's history put it more simply: "New York gives little time to thinking of its past. Its concern is with the future."[2]

One of New York's recent mayors, John V. Lindsay, agrees: "The City moves too fast to serve as a model for those who would capture its entirety in print."[3] It has, indeed, moved too fast for its inhabitants to savor its past for very long. The monuments of yesteryear are torn down and replaced by architectural tributes to the present. There is little left of old New York for its visitors or its own citizens to enjoy—no early palaces as in Paris or ancient ruins as in Rome or medieval castles as in London. The diarist Philip Hone complained as early as 1839 that "The spirit of pulling down and building up is abroad. The whole of New York is rebuilt about once in ten years."[4]

Despite—indeed because of—its kaleidoscopic character, no American city has been written about more than New York. One of the contributors to the present volume, Bayrd Still, has compiled an engaging history of the Empire City entirely as seen through the eyes of the many contemporaries who have sought to describe it through three centuries.[5] But, as Professor Still himself admits, these observers more often described than assessed or interpreted. Interpretation and assessment are preeminently the task of the historian; but, unfortunately, the historians have thusfar been neither equal to the task nor energetic enough in undertaking the project. The reasons for this deficiency are complex and not always easily comprehended.

The largest cluster of city histories date from the middle to the end of the nineteenth century; they include brief accounts like David T. Valentine's—which carries the story only to 1750—as well as the magisterial volumes of Mrs. Martha J. Lamb which chronicle the city's history to 1880.[6] In between are a variety of works, ranging from the short single-volume penned by Theodore Roosevelt in 1891 to the collectively-authored and multivolume history edited about the same time by James G. Wilson.[7] Despite their variety, almost all these accounts reflect the compelling urge of their authors to justify the city to the nation, as if New York's very existence constituted some kind of aberration from the country's norms. In the process, what was emphasized was the city's contributions to the country's progress; and what was recited was the litany of the city's "firsts": first to draw blood in the Revolution—at Golden Hill in January 1770; first to house the nation's capital; first in commerce, population, higher education, etc. While recognizing the city's own difficulties at times, these historians wrote in so defensive a style that they tended to blur New York's problems in their frenetic effort to insure that it receive "a due share of credit" in the nation's history.[8]

While laudable in its patriotic intent, this approach to the city's history has significant limitations, not the least of which is its failure to recognize the evolution of the city as a city, on its own internal terms. A second deficiency of this line of inquiry is its focus on the nation's dependence on New York rather than the interdependence between the city and the nation. The present volume of essays seeks to redirect interest in the history of New York by stressing its own internal development and the degree to which the city's history mirrored, more than led, the history of the rest of the country.

The selection of the "centennial" years as a thread upon which to hang New York's development is not entirely dictated by the circumstances of the Bicentennial observance. The dates represent seminal points in the city's history. In 1676, New York was still largely Dutch, over 80 percent of the population was still so identified; but the Anglicization following the English conquest was soon to bring Leisler's Rebellion. This uprising was not merely a "futile last grasp" for power by the declining Dutch element but also the beginning of those "interest politics" based on ethnicity, religion, and culture which were to characterize the city's "factious" system of government thereafter.[9] In 1776, the city faced the crisis of revolution, British occupation, and a great fire which (along with another two years later) destroyed one-third of its buildings. More important, the city on the eve of independence had begun to represent the paradigm of social diversity, ethnic complexity, dynamic commercialism, and popular politics that was to become the later United States. During the year of the Centennial, New York was recognizably the capital of the nation, leading all other American cities in commerce, industry, finance, publishing, transportation, and population. It had become by then, too, the gateway to America, through which poured the "wretched refuse" of Europe's teeming lands. In 1876 thoughtful, reform-minded New Yorkers were coming to recognize that if the city—as the nation—was to survive, new urban institutions would have to be created to accommodate the masses which now crowded its streets and buildings. The talents directed to establishing these institutions—libraries, schools, hospitals, roads, and parks—were astonishingly abundant and versatile; they seemed appropriate to the needs of an urbanized democracy. But the reformers were soon confounded by two challenges: the nation proved less interested in establishing institutions which urbanization demanded than was New York; and in the city itself, private interests expressed increasing opposition to devoting public resources to social institutions that would serve the needs of the general community. By 1976 these challenges appeared to be almost insurmountable. In a sense, the crisis of 1976 represents the fruition of the dilemmas of 1876. Increasingly the nation shows unwillingness to support urban social institutions designed to meet the needs of those who cannot serve their own; and New York City's citizens seem reluctant to devote increasing amounts of their own resources to finance the apparatus of public welfare.

There are, then, historic roots to the crisis of bicentennial New York; but they are more than material. Implicit in the long tradition of New York's varied public institutions—social, cultural, recreational, and economic—is an acceptance by wealthier New Yorkers of their social responsibility to their less affluent fellow citizens. The humaneness of New Yorkers has not always been visible to visitors, who were more impressed with the city's bustle, hum, and energy; but it has always been there, less the product of philosophical imperatives than the consequence of life in one of the most heterogeneous communities in the world.

The Dutch brought to the city in the first instance a latitudinarian attitude toward matters of faith and morals which not even the English conquest could eradicate. Hence, English rule assumed a moderation, a spirit of adjustment, and a political liberality which Dutch tradition fostered and which heterogeneity compelled. English and Dutch, Presbyterians and Anglicans, Jews and Protestants, landlords and merchants learned to adjust to each other without necessarily loving each other. This accommodation did not extend to blacks, although the harsh features of southern slavery were moderated considerably in the New York environment. The influx of millions of European immigrants in the nineteenth century made New York a "collection of cities," where people learned to tolerate each other not by formulas but from the force of circumstance. Humanitarianism, acceptance, and an easy friendliness became the real hallmarks of the New Yorker—not always apparent to visitors because New Yorkers made no effort to explain their kindliness and offered no ideological rationalizations to justify it. But New Yorkers understood well enough what they called the "New York mind and character." It was, as one of the city's native aristocracy described it in 1866, "positive, institutional, large-hearted, genial, taking it for granted that all men are not of one pattern, and that we are to live by allowing others to have their liberty as we have ours."[10]

From this concern for others stemmed the altruism and philanthropy which produced a magnificent public library, a splendid institute for mechanics' education, a children's aid society, a traveler's aid society, and numerous hospitals, orphanages, and settlement houses. These social institutions did not represent mere benevolent impulse or humanitarian emotionalism; they reflected rather a hard-headed understanding that the cauldron of nationalities that was New York could survive only with a pattern of government and social action which recognized the humanity of each of the city's inhabitants. Tolerance was the price New Yorkers learned to pay for enjoying the fruits of living in one of the most exciting cities in the world. A visiting Englishman, Charles Whibley, understood the cool, unsentimental reality of New Yorkers' forbearance of each other when he wrote in 1907,

In New York . . . you are met everywhere by a sort of urbane familiarity. The man who does you a service, for which you pay him, is neither civil nor uncivil. He contrives, in a way which is by no means unpleasant, to put himself on an equality with you. . . . [11]

The Irishman Brendan Behan witnessed the same easy, urbane familiarity sixty years later: "We don't come to a city to be alone, and the test of a city is the ease with which you can see and talk to other people. A city is a place where you are least likely to get a bite from a wild sheep and I'd say that New York is the friendliest city I know."[12]

In 1976 some of the conviviality, the friendliness, the tolerance, and the kindliness of the city is gone; but so have these qualities diminished in the nation at large. It is not true, as cynics are wont to say, that the United States begins west of the Hudson, or that New York is not America. The city's history evidences just the opposite. When New York was the capital of the world, so was the United States its leading country. As New York developed urban institutions to meet the challenge of millions of newcomers, so did the nation create similar public institutions. As New York expanded into its surrounding environs, so did the nation commence its suburban sprawl. And as New York has met with rising crime rates, declining reading scores, increasing racial tensions, inflated public payrolls and shrinking private employment, so has the nation. New York was the bellwether of the country when both were in their ascendancy; now they both reel under the weight of fiscal and administrative millstones.

There is reason for cautious optimism that the humaneness and civility which once were the hallmarks of both the country and its greatest city are not irretrievably lost. New Yorkers still revel in a cosmopolitanism that is the wonder of all who visit the city and a source of constant refreshment to those who live in Gotham. The preservation of New York's traditional diversity is rooted historically in the city's ability to respond to its humane instincts, to tolerate those who are different, and to care for those who are in need. New Yorkers managed to make these adjustments to social necessity when they lived in what was little more than a rural trading post. It seems inconceivable that they should be less able to do so when New York is still the financial capital of the nation. What is required is more than material means, but an abiding faith in the capacity of a free people to survive its own frailties. Baghdad on the Hudson is a monument to New York's demonstration of that faith for more than three centuries.

NOTES

1. Meyer Berger, Alexander Klein, ed., *The Empire City: A Treasury of New York* (New York, 1955), pp. xix, xx.
2. Allan Nevins, "The Golden Thread in the History of New York," *New-York Historical Society Quarterly*, XXXIX (1955), pp. 7-8; Bank of Manhattan, "*Mannahatin*": *The Story of New York* (New York, 1929), p. 217.
3. John V. Lindsay, "The Most Diverse, Eclectic, and Changeable of Cities," David G. Lowe, ed., *New York, N. Y.* (New York, 1968), p. 5.
4. *The Diary of Philip Hone*, ed. Allan Nevins, 2 vols. (New York, 1927), I, 395.
5. Bayrd Still, *Mirror for Gotham: New York as Seen by Contemporaries from Dutch Days to the Present* (New York, 1956).
6. David T. Valentine, *History of the City of New York* (New York, 1853); Martha J. Lamb, *History of the City of New York*, 2 vols. (New York and Chicago, 1877, 1880).

7. Theodore Roosevelt, *New York* (New York, 1891); James G. Wilson, ed., *Memorial History of the City of New York,* 4 vols. (New York, 1892-1893).

8. The phrase is in I. N. P. Stokes's monumental *Iconography of Manhattan Island, 1498-1909,* 6 vols. (New York, 1915-1928), I, ix; but the sentiment appears in many nineteenth-century histories.

9. Thomas J. Archdeacon, *New York City, 1664-1710: Conquest and Change* (Ithaca, N. Y., 1976), p. 155; Patricia U. Bonomi, *A Factious People: Politics and Society in Colonial New York* (New York, 1971), pp. 279-286.

10. Dr. Samuel Osgood, quoted in William L. Stone, *The Centennial History of New York City* (New York, 1876), p. 248.

11. Quoted in Still, *Mirror for Gotham,* p. 282.

12. *Brendan Behan's New York* (New York, 1964), p. 12.

Peter Schenk, Nieu Amsterdam, ca. 1673 (courtesy of the New-York Historical Society)

Thomas J. Archdeacon

ANGLO-DUTCH
NEW YORK, 1676

Arnoldus Montanus, view of New Amsterdam, 1671 (courtesy
of the New-York Historical Society)

Imagine a traveler approaching New York City from the sea in 1676. At a distance of three miles, he might have caught his first scent of the New World. The primeval forest was still master of the American continent, and the breezes along the coastline carried the odors of its great trees to the ocean. After half a century of settlement, Europeans had barely begun to change the landscape.

The odors of vegetation must have been welcome to the travelers. Crossing the Atlantic from England required at least six to eight weeks, and the voyage was never easy. Food stocked for the voyage turned bad with the passing days. White peas were boiled in brackish water; thick pieces of pork and moldy bread became the ordinary fare. A thrice-daily ration of beer was the only relief for the fortunate.

Hardship was normal on an Atlantic crossing and tragedy not unexpected. Crowded conditions on board the ships were common, and the voyagers, especially if their numbers included soldiers, prisoners, or the poor, often carried lice or other vermin. Typhus, dysentery, and typhoid, which could rapidly decimate the crew and passengers, spread easily in such circumstances; their toll was especially great among the children. Scurvy and starvation were added to the hazards when adverse weather protracted the time required for the passage.[1]

The experiences of Jasper Dankers and Peter Sluyter, who made the ocean journey to New York in 1679, were probably typical. Labadist ministers, they left their native Holland to search for a place of refuge in America for the members of their sect. Nominally aligned with the Dutch Reformed Church, the Labadists stressed the direct working of God on the hearts of men and the desirability of establishing a visible community of the elect. Dankers and Sluyter paid seventy-five guilders apiece to make the crossing in the flute-ship *Charles*. Manned by a crew of ten, the *Charles* was small but seaworthy; at least, its owner, Margaret Philipse, the wife of New York's wealthiest citizen, Frederick Philipse, was willing to entrust to it her life and that of her daughter Annetje.

Departing from Amsterdam on June 8, 1679, the *Charles* sailed to England, where it remained in port for several weeks. The vessel raised anchor at Falmouth on Friday, July 21, 1679, but contrary winds forced it to return to shore, where rumors of pirates operating off the coast added to the passengers' worries. Fortunately, the news proved to be false, and the ship finally got underway.

Most of the voyage was uneventful, but even ordinary days at sea were filled with delays and danger. The ship had to change course constantly in order to catch the shifting winds, and when clouds covered the sky, estimating latitude became impossible. Storms were the gravest threat, and the *Charles* encountered a severe one off the Bermudas on September 2. The wind blew so strongly that the crew members and the passengers could not hear each other's shouts. Dark grey waves of majestic heights burst over the ship and drenched all on board. Not even the combined efforts of three men could hold the vessel's tiller in position in the rough seas.

Human frailty added to the problems caused by nature's fickleness. Life at sea was attractive only to the daring, the desperate, and the profit-minded. Sailors had a reputation for coarseness, which gives credence to Dankers's description of the crew as "wretched." But Dankers was equally harsh in his evaluation of the owner of the *Charles.* Margaret Philipse, one of the grand dames of early New York, comes down through history as an avaricious woman too cheap to repair the ship's pumps and contemptuous enough of her employees to risk their lives in a vain attempt to retrieve a mop which fell overboard.

Anticipation of arrival replaced memories of difficulties when the ship drew near the American continent. The wonders of nature became increasingly obvious as the vessel entered New York bay. As remarkable as the report may appear today, early commentators were consistent in their descriptions of the wildlife of the vicinity. Whales and porpoises cavorted in the offshore waters, and fish in varieties both familiar and unknown to Europeans swarmed in the bay. Birds drifted across the sky, and only the occasional plunge of an eagle or other predator to snatch a fish swimming near the surface broke the peace.

With the approach of the vessel, the shoreline came alive. As the ship passed through the Narrows, Indians came out in their canoes to meet it. The natives climbed aboard, inspected both passengers and equipment, and departed after receiving gifts of biscuits and brandy. When the ship came into view of the fort, which was located at the tip of Manhattan Island at the division of the East and Hudson rivers, the soldiers inside hoisted the English colors in greeting. Concluding its journey, the *Charles* passed the fort and moved into the East River. Even before it reached the municipal dock at the lower end of the eastern shore of Manhattan, a number of persons came out to the ship in small boats looking for friends or for an opportunity to do business.[2]

The East River was the focal point for commerce; it was a watery highway connecting the city and the independent towns and villages found on

Long Island in present-day Brooklyn and Queens. The Hudson River, flowing along the city's western shore, was an important artery connecting New York with the fur-trading station at Albany, but it did not afford as sheltered or as centrally situated a harbor as the East River.

Visitors agreed that New York was a lovely city to approach. The land was high and most of the buildings were made of brick and stone. Particularly striking to the newcomer's eyes were the red and black tile roofs which added muted color to the town's appearance. The tiles were a mark of the Dutch influence which continued to affect the city even after the English seized the colony in 1664. Dutch-style houses, built with the gable ends facing the street, dominated the city's skyline. The sides of each gable rose to meet one another by a series of indentations, which produced the appearance of two opposing stairways joined at the top. Large iron letters affixed to the structures indicated the initials of the owners and the dates the buildings were erected.[3]

As a vessel drew near the shore in 1676, the persons on board probably heard the sounds of carpenters and other workmen building the new municipal dock. In January of that year the Common Council, the governing body of the city, ordered the construction of a new wharf to foster commerce. The project, which required an estimated 18,000 cartloads of stone, was completed by 1679. It consisted of two curved piers stretching out from the land to form a large semicircle. An open space at the outermost point on the arc allowed vessels to enter and seek a berth.[4]

When the ship finally dropped anchor and the passengers disembarked, the new arrival found himself on the shores of a compact city. The jurisdiction of New York included only the two areas of settlement on Manhattan. The more important, which was the heart and soul of the port, was hardly more than a handful of streets and houses at the southern end of the island. Relatively few people lived north of Wall Street, and most of them resided along the shore of the East River in an area known as the Smith's Vly or Valley. The other inhabited section, New Harlem, which was named after Haarlem in the Netherlands, was an unincorporated village located north of a line drawn on today's map between 74th Street at the East River and 125th Street at the Hudson River. During the period of Dutch rule, when the city had been known as New Amsterdam, Harlem was beyond its jurisdiction. The first English governor ended Harlem's political independence, but it remained physically isolated from the main center of population and constituted a separate social and economic unit.[5]

The traveler, if fortunate, was greeted by acquaintances and taken home. But, if he knew no one, the visitor had to seek lodging. He probably obtained temporary quarters at an inn or sought long-term accommodations in a rented room. A goodly portion of New York's householders, it seems, took in boarders; the practice provided them with money and was a necessary service in a community which seafarers were constantly entering and leaving.

After resting and eating his first satisfactory meal in some time, the visitor was likely to take a walk around the town. He might have begun his tour at the fort, the largest structure in the city. In terms of today's map, it would have been bordered by Bowling Green, Whitehall Street, and Bridge Street; State Street would have run through its western side.

Wouter Van Twiller, the director-general of the province of New Netherland of which New Amsterdam was the capital, had the fort erected between 1633 and 1635. It was approximately 300 feet long and 250 feet broad. The sides were, for the most part, earthen; the four corners, which formed arrowhead-shaped projections, were stone. Guns and mortars were emplaced along the parapets, and a variety of buildings were housed inside the walls. The director-general's or governor's home lay along the east wall, the quarters of the garrison's officers along the north, and the soldiers' barracks along the west. A large stone church, built in 1642 by the Connecticut contractors John and Richard Ogden, stood near the governor's residence. The church, which measured 72 feet in length, 52 feet in breadth, and 16 feet above the ground, appears clearly in a famous sketch of the city made by Jasper Dankers in 1679.[6]

Outside the sally port, on the northern side of the fort, was the Great Plain or Bowling Green. The field served many purposes; it was a village green, a parade ground, and a playground. In 1659 the municipal authorities designated Bowling Green as the site for the sale of fat and lean cattle which was to be held for forty days each autumn. The market included a substantial tile-roofed "shambles," or slaughterhouse, which was locked and watched at night.[7]

Standing on the plain, the visitor was afforded a panorama of the city. Looking south he could see the bay on the other side of the fort, and north he could see the city's protective wall at the end of Broadway. The Hudson River lay but a few yards to the west, and by peeking around the houses to the east, the sightseer probably could catch a glimpse of the ships along the waterfront. Lower Manhattan was narrower in 1676 than it is today; in the past three centuries the city has recovered a considerable amount of land from the surrounding waters. In 1676 the East River shore lay along the range of present-day Pearl Street, east and north of Whitehall Street; the southern strand lay along today's State Street, west of Whitehall Street; and the waterline of the Hudson lay generally along contemporary Greenwich Street.[8]

Cities of the colonial era and, for that matter, of all the period before the invention of the streetcar were "walking cities." Pedestrians had to be able to reach any point in the community in a modest amount of time, and the inconveniences of travel placed limits on the expansion of the towns. People had to live near their work, and the line between home and office was not sharply drawn for the self-employed. The commercial area of a city, including the waterfront which was the heart of a port's economic life, was likely to be its most luxurious residential section. New York's most fashionable streets were within the shadow of the fort. So many of the city's wealthiest citizens lived in this area that the residents, on the average, paid the highest taxes in a levy collected in 1677. The inhabitants of the section of the Water Side south of the fort, of Stone Street, and of the portion of the Marketfield adjacent to these blocks were especially affluent. Two of New York's most prominent citizens, the Dutch-born merchants Olof Stevensen Van Cortlandt and Frederick Philipse, made their homes on Stone Street. Van Cortlandt also had a malthouse on the block, which had originally been called Brouwer Straat or Brewers Street. The later name for the street appears to have been adopted after the government in 1657 ordered stones placed in the street to make it the first paved thoroughfare in the city.[9]

Peter Jacobs Marius, a merchant, lived on nearby Pearl Street. Although not one of the wealthiest men in 1676, he was well-to-do and eventually became one of the most substantial residents of the city and the holder of several important offices. At his death in the year 1704, the administrators of his estate made a detailed inventory of his household goods. This remarkable document provides a rare opportunity to learn something about the quality of life in early New York.

Marius's house was divided into six major areas: a lower back room, an upper chamber which was above the great kitchen, a little chamber on the left of the upper one, a writing closet, and a foreroom and shop. The house had a loft and a cockloft. A kitchen in the yard, a great storehouse and a small one, and a cellar were also on the property. Beds were everywhere in the crowded house. Two feather beds, one bolster, six pillows, and two blankets were found in the lower back room. One bedstead with iron rods, six blue curtains, head cloth, bolster, and quilt were in the upper chamber. Three more bedsteads were in the little chamber, the writing closet, and the loft.

The lower back room was the repository for the family's linens and valuables. Marius had eight calico and twenty-three linen sheets, two linen tablecloths, and sixteen small cupboard cloths; he also had seven tablecloths and sixty-one napkins made of diaper, a fine-figured silken or linen cloth which was often decorated with geometric or flower patterns. His collection of gold and silver was impressive, especially in an age in which possession of any precious metal marked the owner as a person of secure social position. Marius had 218 ounces of silver serving pieces or plate, three gold chains, six gold rings, two gold diamond rings, and a variety of other such items.

The lower room served as a living room as well as a bedroom. Marius kept there a small Dutch bible, a black-framed looking glass, sixteen small pictures, a black walnut table, a carpet, six turkey leather chairs, one blue elbow chair, a matted elbow chair, and thirteen old matted chairs. He also had a red cedar chest and an old fashioned clock.

The upper chamber apparently was the dining room and storage area for kitchen utensils. Among the items in the room were a black walnut table and eight black walnut chairs covered with blue material. Marius also had a red cedar cupboard, twenty-four pewter dishes, six plates, and a baby's dish. His kitchen utensils included five brass and three copper kettles, three brass stewpans and covers, a skillet, a saucepan, and two chafing dishes.

Marius's store contained the varied holdings of a typical merchant. Cloth, the most important of New York's imports, was the dominant product in his stock. Along with other materials, Marius had 24 pieces of blue tape and 38 yards of white holland, which was a type of cotton cloth. He also had 17½ ells of painted calico and 157 ells of blue linen. (An ell was a measurement which in England amounted to 45 inches.) But like most colonial shopkeepers, Marius kept an assortment of other goods, including fifteen old children's bodices. Seamstresses could choose from Marius's 33¼ pounds of hooks and eyes; householders could select among 29 scrubbing brushes and could pick up nails of all types for their carpentry chores; and a doting mother or father might dip into the more than 22 pounds of sugar candy that the merchant kept in a tin box.[10]

The items mentioned above constituted only a portion of the worldly goods in the inventory of Peter Jacobs Marius's estate. But attempting to make generalizations from this single case about the standard of living in early New York would not be possible or prudent. Marius was a member of the city's economic elite, and the ordinary resident of Manhattan in the late seventeenth century possessed much less wealth.

The visitor to New York did not have to walk far from the downtown area to find less affluent sections. Rich and poor had to live in proximity in these walking cities, but some economic differentiation of residential areas existed. Persons who had houses on the major roads leading away from the tip of the island, such as the Water Side north of Broad Street, on Broad Street itself, or on Broadway, were substantial citizens; some of them, like Gabriel Minvielle, were even wealthy. Minvielle, though born in France, spent his early years in Amsterdam, established himself as a merchant in New York in 1669, and became the city's mayor in 1684. But the typical inhabitant of these streets could not be counted among New York's most well-to-do citizens.

The smaller streets of the downtown areas and sites at the fringe of town were the least attractive. Distance from the center of the community was a disadvantage in colonial days. In 1676 the New Yorkers with the least money had addresses such as Smith Street, Mill Street, Wall Street, and Broadway north of Wall Street.[11]

Proceeding from Bowling Green, the new arrival might have walked north along Broadway, the city's largest thoroughfare. Known also as the Great Highway, the road would have led the sightseer to its intersection with Wall Street. That site gave no hint of the excitement which the address Broadway and Wall Street would convey in later centuries. Trinity Church did not exist in 1676; a score of years would pass before New York's Anglican communicants would build their house of worship at Broadway and Wall. The ground on which the present Trinity stands was agricultural land. Owned by James Stuart, Duke of York, the proprietor or owner of the colony, and reserved for the use of the governor, it was known as the "Duke's Farm." As for Wall Street, perhaps no single block in New York has changed as much in the past three hundred years. In 1676 the name was descriptive; the street lay alongside the barricade which enclosed the city.

Peter Stuyvesant, the last Dutch governor of New Netherland, was responsible for the erection of the Singel (Circuit) or city wall. He recognized that New Amsterdam required defenses against its two enemies—the English, whose colonies in New England and settlements on eastern Long Island were dangerously near, and the Indians, who were being displaced by the incursions of the Europeans. The fort provided protection against the English who were likely to come by sea, and he hoped that a wall along the city's northern flank would discourage the Indians from attacking over land.

Stuyvesant's wall, which was completed by May 1, 1653, was in its early years a formidable obstacle. Rounded timbers twelve feet tall and pointed at the top formed the outer barricade; most of the logs were eighteen inches in circumference, but some were twenty-one. Split rails ran along the length of the wall two feet below the top; they were nailed to the larger timbers which were placed at one-rod intervals. A sloping dirt breastwork, three feet wide at the top and four at the bottom reinforced the palisade. The great wall ran a short distance along the East River and then traversed the island to a steep bluff which provided a natural barrier along the Hudson River. The palisade had two gates, both of which were built in 1656. The Water Gate was located on the strand at present-day

Pearl Street, and the Land Gate was situated at Broadway. By 1676 the wall was past its prime. It never had to serve its military purpose, and that was fortunate. The structure, primarily composed of wood and dirt, was liable to quick decay. Despite repeated efforts by the government, the palisade was collapsing before the end of the seventeenth century. Moreover, the city was outgrowing its confines, and the population outside of the wall was increasing rapidly. In 1698 the Common Council requested Governor Richard Coote, the Earl of Bellomont, to raze the remaining sections of the barricade.[12]

Passing east on Wall Street, the walker would have come to the strand of the East River. He might have proceeded north out the Water Gate to inspect the new areas into which the city was expanding, but eventually he would turn back and make his way toward the dock. As the sightseer continued to stroll, he would have arrived at the final significant landmark of his tour, the City Hall. In terms of present addresses, it would have been at 71-73 Pearl Street, facing Coenties Slip. The building, which was fifty feet square and had stone walls that were three stories high below the base of the roof and two more above it, dwarfed its neighbors. Director-General Willem Kieft built the structure as a tavern in 1642, but it soon became the seat of the city government. The Dutch called it the Stadt Huys, and many continued to use the name even after the English conquerors began referring to it as the City Hall. The building was by no means ancient in 1676, but it was showing signs of disrepair. The authorities spent considerable sums of money on the Stadt Huys during the next two decades, but by 1697 they decided that the government needed another home. The new City Hall, built in part with materials salvaged from the old palisade, was erected at Broad and Wall streets and served New York through the rest of the colonial period. After the adoption of the Constitution of 1787 it became the original home of the United States Congress and the site of the first inauguration of George Washington as president.[13]

Having completed his circuit of the town, the traveler would have returned to his lodgings and might have spent the rest of the day in contemplation of what he had seen. To the European eye, New York must have appeared raw. Though its setting was striking and several of its buildings noteworthy, the city was just an outpost in the wilderness. It lay open to attack, and the authorities were able to provide only the most elementary services.

By a January 1676 directive of the Common Council, the town gates were closed each night between 9 p.m. and dawn. With the city secured against attack from the outside, a constable's watch spent the intervening hours preventing domestic disturbances. Armed with their own guns and swords, they made frequent rounds to insure the maintenance of order and to prevent the drinking of intoxicants in the public houses after 10 p.m. Unfortunately the guardians of the peace occasionally contributed to its disruption, and the Council found it necessary to provide a fine for those who absented themselves from duty or who became very drunk.[14]

Fire was an even greater hazard than invaders or felons, and putting out those which occurred involved the whole community in a "bucket brigade." The city provided a number of ladders at public expense but directed each inhabitant who had two chimneys on his house to own one bucket for emergencies. Individuals who had more than two hearths had to acquire an additional bucket, and brewers and bakers, perhaps because their activities generated serious fire hazards, had to keep six and three apiece, respectively. In 1691 the Council made the city's tenants responsible for the procurement of buckets. In return for a rent rebate, each tenant was directed to obtain a bucket and to mark it with his landlord's initials.

Preventing fires was a major concern of the Common Council. The lawmakers directed the inhabitants to keep their chimneys in working order and appointed a sweeper to clean them periodically for a fixed fee. The municipality also forbade the storage of hay or straw in or near dwellings and the dumping of smouldering ashes in the streets. Regular inspections supplemented the fire prevention laws. In 1683 the city appointed overseers of chimneys and hearths who were to check for violations at least every two weeks. The authorities usually chose masons like Tobias Stoutenburgh, Olphert Suerts, and Dirck Vanderburgh as overseers. Their expertise made them especially capable of performing this task. In 1697 the Council made the aldermen and assistants, the chief elected officials in each ward, responsible for the maintenance of safe chimneys and hearths, and they in turn appointed a pair of inspectors to make weekly rounds.[15]

By 1676 the authorities had just begun to introduce amenities to urban life in New York. In June, the Common Council rid the city's residential areas of a malodorous nuisance by banishing slaughterhouses and tanneries to locations outside the gates. And the government organized the inhabitants to keep the area within the walls livable.[16]

Cleaning the streets required the cooperation of every resident. Under both the Dutch and English governments, every householder was responsible for sweeping into heaps the dirt in front of his or her home. According to an ordinance of November 1675, the licensed cartmen who were the city's truckers (with a primary duty to the docks) were to remove the accumulated rubbish each Saturday and deposit it at an appropriate dumping ground along the water front. The cartmen were not fond of this assignment, and in November 1676 the government threatened them with dismissal for neglect of this duty. Continued nonfeasance probably was the cause for the city's discharge of twelve carters in October 1677, but the government allowed the offenders to resume their posts after they promised to be more diligent.[17]

During the last quarter of the seventeenth century, the Common Council supplemented its efforts to keep the city clean with orders to pave all the roads south of Wall Street. Each householder was required to take care of the section of street in front of his or her home. In May 1684 the Common Council directed that Beaver Gracht be "paved on each side eight foot in breadth from the houses by the person owning the lot therein each person before his own lot." By specifying the number of feet to be covered, the Council allowed for the creation of a small ditch down the center of each road. Rain falling on the city followed the course of these channels to the water side. The run-offs were useful, but they could not prevent the deterioration of the pebblestone pavements. As a result, the roadways needed frequent replacement; Beaver Street, for example, was repaved in 1693, 1696, and 1701.[18]

Fresh water was just as important as paved and cleaned streets for the health of the community. In order to provide a dependable supply, the Common Council ordered the emplacement of wells at various spots in the city. The government chose the sites for each well and gave one person responsibility for its construction. The city paid one-half the expense of digging and enclosing the wells, and the residents of those neighborhoods supplied with water shared the remaining costs.[19]

A frontier town in 1676, New York, as might be expected, did not have a vibrant intellectual life. Indeed, it did not even have a newspaper until 1725. The Dutch founders of the city were exclusively men of business, nor did their English successors possess the spiritual outlook which made the leaders of New England so distinctive. In its early years, New York lacked the leaven of introspective men and women capable of producing profound literature and anxious to foster learning.

Although literature had only a marginal existence on the banks of the Hudson, New Amsterdam was able to boast of three minor poets—Jacob Steendam, Nicasius de Sille, and Henricus Selijns. The first was a merchant, who arrived in the city around 1653; the second, a lawyer and public official who came in 1654; and the third, a clergyman who reached New Amsterdam in 1660. The three worked in the tradition of the "rederijkers" or "speech-enrichers" of the Netherlands, to whom poetry was a metered, rhymed verse imparting an edifying lesson.

Selijns favored poems about love and marriage and was the author of a number of eulogies. De Sille and Steendam made New Netherlands the topic of their most important works. De Sille wrote of the pleasures of tilling the soil, and Steendam's *'T Lof van Nuw-Nederland (The Praise of New*

Netherland), published in 1661, encouraged emigration from Europe to the bounteous province. Steendam's most important piece, the allegorical poem *Klacht van Nieuw-Amsterdam* (*Complaint of New Amsterdam*), which he sent to Amsterdam as a manuscript in 1659, had political overtones. It suggested that the Netherlands govern the colony directly rather than through the West India Company.[20]

Education in New York also was rudimentary and, as elsewhere in the colonies, closely associated with the preparation of children for church membership. Under the Dutch the schoolmaster served also as the reader, song leader, and sexton of the church. Unfortunately, ecclesiastical office was not a guarantee of good character. The first schoolmaster, Adam Roelantsz, who held the post between 1638 and 1642, was later accused of street fighting, selling bad pork, drinking while on duty as provost, and forcing his attentions on a young woman. Roelantsz's successors were more worthy, and the last of the Dutch schoolmasters, Evert Pietersz, who served between 1661 and 1686, was an outstanding teacher and person.[21]

Public education received little mention in the municipal records of the late seventeenth century. The only reference to it in the *Minutes of the Common Council* concerns a dispute over the selection of a schoolmaster in 1676. On July 24, Ebenezer Kirtland offered to teach the youth of the city reading, writing, arithmetic, and Latin or Greek. The incumbent schoolmaster, Matthew Hilliard, complained of the endeavors of Kirtland, a late arrival, to take away his post. Hilliard admitted that some parents had found his work unsatisfactory but argued that his frequent changes of residence caused by the lack of a sufficient house was the root of his problem. The Common Council continued Hilliard in his position but extracted from him the promise of better behavior and changed his remuneration from £12 per annum to the provision of a suitable room.[22]

Business was the mental activity that most excited New Yorkers. The city did everything possible to foster its commerce. The Common Council in 1697 even ordered all householders to place lights in their streetfront windows on moonless nights of the winter so that the activities of the port could continue into the evening.[23]

New York's leaders had the responsibility for maintaining the efficiency of the port. After the completion of the new dock in 1679, they established regulations to facilitate the arrival and departure of vessels and to insure the safety of the anchorage. And they had to make provisions for the rapid loading, unloading, and delivery of all cargoes, but especially of perishable commodities. Erecting the dock was a sizable undertaking for the small city; the stone alone cost £1800. To pay for the work, the Common Council levied a tax on the city's inhabitants. Frederick Philipse, the wealthiest man in the community, paid £81.5s. Of course, Philipse and almost all the other wealthy citizens were merchants who benefited directly from the docks. Indeed, the well-to-do paid less than their fair share, because the tax rate of one penny and a half per pound of assessed valuation remained constant for all citizens.

Taxes are never popular and some New Yorkers of the 1670s tried to avoid payment by resorting to tactics which would remain familiar three centuries afterwards. Late in 1676, the Common Council heard rumors that twenty-five residents were planning to move outside the city's jurisdiction before the tax collectors made their rounds. The authorities were angered that these persons, some of whom were engaged in trade and were liable for taxes of more than £20, were trying to reap the benefits of the city without sharing in its burdens. Accordingly, they ordered the city treasurer, Peter Stoutenburgh, to obtain payment from these men immediately and to distrain their property if they attempted to leave suddenly.

The need to control use of the new dock soon became obvious, and the Common Council issued a comprehensive set of regulations in March 1684. The lawmakers established two schedules of rents, which varied according to the size and home port of the vessel using dock space; bottoms based in New York paid fees annually and those from other towns, monthly. Most of the rules dealt with safety and sanitation. No vessel could block the entrance to the dock, nor, except for a brief period of time in fair weather, could it be moored on the outside of the anchorage. Crews were forbidden to keep fires burning on their craft at night. And at no time could sailors cast an anchor or grappling hook near the dock lest it endanger other bottoms, nor could they heave overboard "dung draught dirt or anything" which would pollute the dock area.[24]

In order to insure the rapid handling of cargo and the careful distribution of merchandise, the Common Council licensed carmen or cartmen who served as the city's truckers. In 1683 they numbered twenty. The authorities granted the carters a number of privileges, including protection against competition from slave labor, and in return they demanded a variety of services. The cartmen's most important function was to support the port. The rules required that they unload vessels immediately upon arrival and that they give priority to the removal and storage of corn and meal. The cartmen were to behave civilly to all persons, avoid riding their vehicles through city streets, and make restitution for any goods which they damaged.

The Common Council set the rates to be charged by the cartmen. For most loads carried to any point within the city gates, the cartmen received three pence; but for wines, lime, pantiles, bricks, and large cables they were paid twice as much. Firewood fit in a special category. The carters received one shilling six pence for each cord of wood which they took from the delivering boat to the place of cording and then to the purchaser's house, and one shilling for each load of uncorded wood brought directly from the dock to the buyer. In all cases, the rates doubled when the cartmen had to go beyond the city gates.[25]

Having the responsibility of fostering the city's commerce, the authorities jealously guarded New York's prerogatives as the port of the province. They looked with disfavor at any practices which threatened to discredit the goods produced there. And they were especially protective of Manhattan's role in the processing and distribution of flour.

During the first half-century of European settlement along the Hudson, Manhattan had become the center of the flour trade. When communities outside the island began their own milling operations in the 1670s and engaged in direct trade rather than shipping their produce by way of New York, the city fathers were outraged. They protested to Governor Edmund Andros about the deviation from customary procedure, and in 1680 he confirmed the monopoly over the bolting and export of flour which the legislature had officially granted to the city two years earlier. When the abuses continued, Deputy Mayor William Beekman and the aldermen, in April 1683, ordered the sheriff to seize all flour bolted outside the city which was brought to the port for sale or transportation.

The crisis came early in the tenure of Governor Thomas Dongan. On March 17, 1684, the mayor and aldermen asked him to reconfirm the port's unique position in the flour trade, but the new executive delayed his response until the city prepared arguments justifying its request. The Common Council directed four aldermen, Nicholas Bayard, John Inian, John Lawrence, and William Pinhorne, all of whom were merchants, to draft a statement of the city's case.

The committee attempted, by arguments which across the span of three centuries seem disingenuous, to argue that the prohibition was beneficial to all parts of the province. The members contended that New York needed the monopoly in order to survive. The other settlements in the colony enjoyed natural advantages which provided them with economic security. Long Islanders engaged in whaling and husbandry, residents of Esopus or Kingston in tillage of the soil, and the people of Albany in the Indian trade or husbandry. New York City as the metropolis of the province brought wealth to the entire colony, but its commerce was in large measure based on the manufacture of flour and bread. To deprive the port of its privileges would hurt the colony as well as the city. Decentralization of production would undermine the city's system of quality controls for the manufacture of flour and bread, and these safeguards were the source of the fame and reputation of the colony's grain products. Moreover, the end of the flour monopoly would lead to the decline of the port and the termination of the services it provided.

Dongan was receptive to New York's plea and on May 22, 1684 confirmed the city's control over the bolting of flour and the production of bread for export. The port enjoyed the monopoly for another decade, until the counties of Long Island and of the upper Hudson River succeeded in 1694 in having the Bolting Act of 1678 repealed. The defeat temporarily shocked New York's merchants but the trade continued to remain important to the port's development.[26]

Two beavers join the windmill and two flour barrels on the official seal which the proprietor granted to New York City in 1670. They represent the other major export of colonial New York—the skins of fur-bearing animals. The Hudson River connected the city with the center of the fur trade at Albany,150 miles to the north. Furs were becoming less important in the New York economy in the late seventeenth century, but the surviving port records indicate that the trade still had vitality.[27]

The city was concerned with maintaining its reputation for high quality skins and hides. On August 12, 1676, the Common Council appointed Coenraet Ten Eyck and William Boyle as searchers and sealers of leather, with responsibility for inspecting and marking with an official seal all leather and hides before shoemakers and tanners were allowed to sell or process them. Less than two weeks later, on August 25, the Council named John Harperding and Jacob Abrahamson to be tanners and Peter Pangborne to be currier for the city, and it forbade all others to exercise these trades.[28]

As a port, New York had special problems. Maintaining an adequate food supply in the city was a continuous challenge. Exporting New York's processed grain to other colonies, especially to the West Indies, was so profitable a venture that residents of the city and visitors claimed they were sometimes unable to find bread for purchase. Responding to these complaints, the Common Council in June 1676 ordered Manhattan bakers to be ready to sell both biscuit and household bread and threatened to bar the uncooperative from practicing their trade and from engaging in the export business. The warning apparently was not successful, and the Common Council repeated it in November.

The city and the bakers eventually reached a compromise on the means of insuring an adequate supply of bread for the inhabitants. In January 1686, the Common Council established a schedule according to which twenty-four bakers were assigned on different days of the week to produce at least one batch of white and of coarse bread. The authorities ordered four bakers to produce for the public on Mondays, Wednesdays, and Fridays, three to work on Tuesdays and Thursdays, and six to sell on Saturdays. Five of the appointees were women, Geesie Lewis, Catrina Hooghlant, Marritie, the widow of Nicholas the baker, Anna Van Vleck, and Anna Poppelaers.

Regulating the production and sale of bread was a constant activity. Many times the Common Council set guidelines for the size and price of loaves. In May 1684, for example, the Council established that a thirteen-ounce loaf of white bread would sell for one-and-a-half pence, that an eight-pound loaf of ranged wheat bread from which the coarsest bran had been removed would cost nine pence, and that a seven and one-half pound loaf of rye or coarse wheat bread would retail for six pence.[29]

New Yorkers needed more than bread to sustain themselves however, and the authorities sought to guarantee that an adequate supply of provisions reached the city. Most residents of the municipality did not farm, and therefore depended on crops raised by the people living north of the town and on Long Island. In 1677, Governor Edmund Andros called for an annual three-day market for cattle, grain, and other country produce to be held on the plain in front of the fort in early November. Andros also established a weekly market to be held Saturdays at a market house on the East River strand near the bridge and weighhouse. In 1680 the Common Council added another market to be held on Wednesdays at the same place.

The Common Council proclaimed a new set of market regulations in 1684. Meat could be sold only on Tuesdays, Thursdays, and Saturdays at the bridge market. Butter, cheese, eggs, fish, fruit, herbs, poultry, and roots might be sold on any day at the market or at other convenient places, including boats along the waterfront. The mayor and aldermen promised to appoint a clerk who would lease stalls in the market place and enforce the regulations, one of which provided for a heavy forty-shilling fine for vendors who offered tainted meat or produce.[30]

Regulation of the traffic in liquor in New York City had aspects of both "consumer protection" and of social control. The city licensed retailers, limited the number of establishments selling alcohol, and set the price of liquor. The mayor and aldermen suggested to the governor in 1676 that there be six houses selling wine, brandy, and rum and eight more dispensing beer, cider, rum, and mum, which was an ale. Two of the wine houses and four of those retailing beer were to be inns or ordinaries. Wines from France retailed at 1 shilling 3 pence per quart, from the isle of Fyall at 1 shilling 6 pence, and from Madeira at 2 shillings; brandy sold for 6 pence per gill or quarter pint and rum for 3; cider brought 4 pence per quart, double beer 3, and mum 6. A meal at a wine ordinary cost one shilling and lodging 4 shillings per night; at beer houses the same services bore charges of 8 and 3 pence respectively. The governor apparently agreed to more lax standards, because there were twenty-three licensed retail establishments in 1680.[31]

To the newcomer, the people of New York were probably its most fascinating aspect. The commercial potential of the port drew to it men and women from many nations, and the materialistic attitude of the city's leadership led to a broad, though less than perfect, tolerance of this diversity. By 1676 New York had become the prototype of the polyglot American metropolis of which the city later became the archetype.

Indians never failed to capture the imaginations of visitors, but the curious had to leave the city in order to find sizable numbers of the natives. The Indians appeared frequently in New Amsterdam during the early years of settlement, but relations between the Europeans and the natives had turned bad by 1640. The whites initially prized friendship with the Indians as a means of obtaining the valuable skins of the forest animals, but they lost the urge for association when the natives learned to bargain shrewdly. The Europeans allowed their contempt for Indian culture to show, and Director-General Willem Kieft aggravated the situation by attempting to tax the natives. Bitter warfare marred the early years of the 1640s, and the residents of New Amsterdam killed many Indians during raids on Staten Island and present-day New Jersey and Westchester. When the hostilities came to an end in 1644, the line of demarcation between the European and Indian communities became clearly defined.

Seventeenth-century visitors devoted many pages of their travel accounts to the native Americans. They willingly journeyed to Long Island and into the Hudson Valley to observe Indian communities. Writers such as Daniel Denton, an early settler of Jamaica, Long Island whose *Brief Description of New York* appeared in 1670, Charles Wooley, an Anglican minister, whose *Two Years Journal in New York* covered the period between 1678 and 1680, and the Labadist Jasper Dankers gave detailed, though sometimes fanciful descriptions of the Indians. The Europeans were especially impressed by the natives' use of paint and animal grease on their dark skins and black hair and by their practice of dressing in loin cloths and animal skins. The authors discussed the Indians' sea-shell money, which was called "wampum" or "sewant," and their marriage and burial customs. And they analyzed the Indians' religious beliefs, which they found primitive and inferior to Christianity.[32]

Touring New York City, the visitor saw many more whites than Indians, but the sight nevertheless was unlike anything the traveler had ever encountered. New York, even in 1676, was home to many nations and races. In modern times residents of the city have found this facet of its character both attractive and repellent. They have simultaneously praised the virtues of the melting pot and gloried in the variety of a cosmopolis. But the heterogeneity of the populace has also been a source of uneasiness and fear. Commentators in the seventeenth century felt a similar ambivalence. To the European observer of early New York, the city's mixture of peoples was interesting but not especially encouraging. The attitude of Father Isaac Jogues, a French Jesuit missionary who visited New Amsterdam in 1643 after escaping from his Mohawk Indian captors, was typical. Jogues marveled at meeting not only Dutch Calvinists, whose presence he expected in an outpost of the Netherlands, but also a Polish Lutheran, an Irish Catholic, and even a Portuguese Catholic woman who displayed an image of the Jesuit martyr Aloysius Gonzaga in her home. He estimated that 500 persons speaking a total of eighteen languages inhabited the town, but he was not pleased. "The arrogance of Babel," Jogues commented, "has done much harm to all men; the confusion of tongues has deprived them of great benefits."[33]

In 1676, more than a decade after the English conquest of the city and colony, the Dutch were still the preponderant element in the population. Examination of the assessment lists of 1677 suggests that they accounted for approximately 81 percent of the taxable citizens. The numerical importance of the Dutch was not surprising; they had been present on Manhattan since the 1620s and thus enjoyed what a researcher in demography might judge a considerable "initial advantage."

The Dutch came to Manhattan under the auspices of the West India Company. Chartered in 1621 by the States General, the governing body of the Netherlands, the Dutch West India Company was an association of merchants to which the government granted a trading monopoly in order to encourage the establishment of colonies in the New World. In its form and purpose, the West India Company resembled the Virginia Company which established Jamestown in 1607 and the Massachusetts Bay Company which settled Boston and its environs in 1630.

Manhattan received its first major influx of Europeans in 1625. That year the Dutch West India Company sent about 200 people and approximately 100 head of cattle along with some farm animals to the settlement which it called New Amsterdam. In the following year Peter Minuit, the first director-general, arrived and made his famous acquisition of the island for the price of 60 guilders.[34]

If the Dutch were the first sizable non-Indian group in the population, Africans were the second. The Dutch were active in the slave trade, and in 1619 they brought the first blacks to Virginia. In 1626 the West India Company imported eleven male slaves to New Netherland to work on projects which could not attract free men. Two years later the company brought over three black women. Throughout the history of New Netherland, the Dutch resorted to the importation of blacks to meet the labor needs of the province. In 1648 the States General removed the West India Company's monopoly of the slave trade and authorized the people of New Netherland to send grain, cattle, and other basic commodities to Dutch settlers in Brazil in return for blacks, whose labor would increase the agricultural output of the Hudson River settlement. In 1652, the government allowed the New Netherlanders to obtain slaves directly from the Dutch colony of Angola, but the African outpost never became a popular source. Like other residents of the North American mainland, the New Netherlanders preferred slaves who had been "seasoned" to their unfortunate lot over freshly captured ones. After the Portuguese captured Brazil in 1654, Curaçao, the Dutch island colony off the coast of South America, became the major supplier of Africans for New Amsterdam.

Lack of accurate statistics makes it impossible to estimate the exact number of slaves present in New York in 1676, but it was large. In 1664, the final year of Dutch control, a single ship, the *Gideon*, brought three hundred blacks to the province. Slavery spread even more rapidly after the English conquest, because the proprietor of the colony, the Duke of York, enjoyed a direct interest in the Royal African Company, a powerful slave-trading corporation. By the end of the seventeenth century blacks accounted for perhaps 15 to 20 percent of New York City's population.[35]

Ownership of slaves was widespread in New York City. According to a census taken in 1703, more than 40 percent of the white heads of families held bondsmen. But the average number of blacks in each household, just over two, was low, and 147 of the 318 owners had only one. Most slaves in the American colonies were agricultural laborers, but those on Manhattan were primarily artisans and domestic workers. The census and the records of land transfers suggest that they lived in the houses of their masters. Females were as numerous as males, and a majority of the families owning only one slave held women. And many owners, such as merchants, "gentlemen," and widows, would have had little use for slaves other than as household help.[36]

Life in the city made control of the slave population difficult. The presence of a number of free blacks in the population must have been a constant reminder to the bondsmen that their lot could be different. Moreover, some whites were willing to associate and do business with slaves. The practice disturbed the Common Council, whose members were convinced that the slaves were being encouraged to pilfer their masters' goods. In August 1680 it forbade residents to entertain blacks or to give them liquor in their homes and to accept goods or money from them. But enforcement of such laws was lax, and New York's slaves gained a reputation for boldness. In August 1696, Mayor William Merritt reported that a slave struck him in the face when he ordered a group of them to cease their noisy behavior near his home.[37]

New Yorkers were willing to tolerate the peccadilloes of their slaves, and, compared to owners in the South, were mild in their handling of blacks. Descriptions of runaway New York slaves, for example, make no references to brands or mutilations as distinguishing marks. But New Yorkers responded brutally to any serious threat by slaves against the social order. In 1712 a group of slave conspirators set fire to some buildings and from ambush killed five of the whites who came to douse the flames. Within two weeks the authorities jailed seventy slaves, and a special court ordered eighteen of them put to death. The executions, which included the eight to ten hour roasting of one of the condemned, were grisly sights.[38]

Jews, who now constitute the largest single ethnic group in the New York population, first came to the city in the 1650s. Like so many of their successors, these immigrants were refugees from persecution to whom Manhattan represented the end of a long journey. At the end of the sixteenth century a number of Marranos, Jews who outwardly accepted Christianity while practicing their old beliefs in secret, fled the Iberian peninsula to seek religious liberty in the Netherlands. Some later migrated to Dutch Brazil, but the Portuguese conquest of that colony forced them to take flight again. They went to the Dutch settlement at New Amsterdam but received no welcome. Director-General Stuyvesant thought that Jews were usurers and wanted to deport them. Only the intervention of the West India Company, which was well aware of the investments the Jews of Amsterdam had made in the company, made it possible for the exiles to remain in the New World. Similarly, pressure from the company forced Stuyvesant and the leaders of New Amsterdam to allow the Jews to own real estate and to engage in commerce.

The integration of the Jews into the life of New York continued under English rule. In 1685 they requested permission to practice their religion freely. Governor Thomas Dongan referred the petition to the city's Common Council which declared that only adherents of Christian religions were eligible for toleration. But the government must have reversed its decision within the following decade, because the Jews had a synagogue in Manhattan no later than 1695—Shearith Israel.[39]

In 1676 the English formed the only numerically significant nationality other than the Dutch in the European population of New York. During the existence of New Netherland, Englishmen from the New England colonies established a number of settlements, including Southampton, East Hampton and Southold on the eastern end of Long Island and were also present in towns such as Hempstead, Newtown, and Jamaica in the western half. But few Englishmen made their homes on Manhattan before the Dutch surrender of the colony.

England conquered New Netherland in 1664. The English had always claimed authority over the region, and in 1650, by the Treaty of Hartford, Stuyvesant had reluctantly recognized their control of an area of Long Island lying east of a perpendicular line drawn from Oyster Bay to the Atlantic Ocean. King Charles II, who ascended the English throne in 1660, determined to eliminate the Dutch presence entirely. He granted the disputed territory to his brother James and dispatched a fleet of three vessels with a complement of about 600 men to enforce his decision. The expedition arrived in the waters off New Amsterdam in August 1664, and when the inhabitants of the city proved unwilling to fight, Stuyvesant on September 5 bowed to the English demands for surrender.

The Dutch were a group with whom the English had to deal carefully. In order to assure their surrender, Colonel Richard Nicholls, commander of the invading force, had to offer generous terms. The Articles of Capitulation guaranteed the people of New Amsterdam uninterrupted possession of their houses, lands, goods and inheritances, and allowed them to follow the practices of the Netherlands regarding estates and inheritances. The conquerors wisely decided not to impose the Church of England on the colony and permitted the Dutch to continue allegiance to the Calvinist Reformed Church.

Despite the concessions by the English, the Dutch were not completely satisfied subjects of the Crown. They had not found the West India Company an attractive master, but when war erupted between England and the Netherlands in 1672, at least some of them had hopes of coming under the direct control of the Dutch government. When two Dutch men-of-war appeared in the harbor in July 1673, Dutch citizens declined to assist the English in defending the city and instead busied themselves spiking the guns of the battery in front of the city hall.

The appearance of the Dutch caught the English off guard. Colonel Richard Lovelace, the governor, was away in Connecticut, and Captain John Manning had command of approximately fifty troops. The Dutch naval commanders, Cornelis Evertsen and Jacob Benckes, demanded surrender of the fort, but Manning asked for a day to make his decision. The Dutch refused to allow more than half an hour, and when the allotted time expired, they opened fire on the fort with ten guns. Captain Anthony Colve landed about 600 Dutch soldiers and advanced toward the fort. Faced with inevitable defeat, Manning offered to surrender if his troops were allowed to leave with their arms and baggage. Colve agreed, and the city again was in Dutch hands.

New Orange, as the Dutch renamed the city, had a brief history. The war between England and the Netherlands was soon terminated, and the Treaty of Westminster of February 1674 restored to their previous possessors all the territories taken during the conflict. The Dutch officially vacated Manhattan on November 10, 1674, and the English once more controlled the Hudson.

England's reconquest of Manhattan did not completely pacify the city. The English accounted for just slightly more than 16 percent of the population, and the Dutch were an easy match for them in wealth and social prestige. The Dutch complained that the oath of allegiance to the crown demanded by the new governor, Edmund Andros, was more stringent than the one required after the 1664 takeover and failed to guarantee their immunity from bearing arms against the Netherlands in time of war. The English, for their part, were wary of the Dutch majority. The Duke of York ordered Andros to act impartially toward all the inhabitants but to watch carefully the residents who cooperated in the capture of the fort in 1673. Occasionally mutual animosity between the English and Dutch became evident. In January 1676 the Common Council warned the members of the civilian guard, which protected the city at night, against making quarrels with each other over their differences in nationalities. And in 1679 William Merritt, a prominent English citizen, reported to the Mayor's Court that he saw the night watch beating Englishmen and heard them yelling "Slay the English dogs."[40]

Dutch practices and observances were ingrained in the culture of New York City and were to become part of the national heritage. The name "Bowling Green" testifies to the role of the Dutch in introducing a form of that popular sport to New York, and they also brought over skating, coasting, and sleighing. The Dutch Santa Claus, who as Saint Nicholas had been the patron saint of New Amsterdam, continued to bring the children of the town gifts at Christmas, and the residents kept up the Dutch use of eggs in the celebration of Easter. And, of course, many Dutch words such as boss, cookie, cruller, and stoop became part of the English language.[41]

Despite the wishes of the Dutch and the influence of their numbers, New York in 1676 was becoming an English city. The changing street names were the most obvious indication of the transformation to a visitor. Some residents still referred to De Heer Wegh, Het Marckvelt Steegie, and De Singel but others used the English terms Broadway, Marketfield Street, and Wall Street. The alterations involved more than the translation of titles. Slowly the city was losing geographic features which had recreated the ambiance of old Amsterdam. In 1676 the Common Council authorized the filling-in of De Heere Gracht, a canal which wended its way from the waterside through the center of the city to Wall Street. The mayor and aldermen made the householders living along the Gracht responsible for doing the work and for paving the street upon its completion. Thus was Broad Street born.[42]

The observant newcomer to New York would soon have recognized that street name changes were symptoms of more fundamental shifts. Important developments were occurring in the realm of government, where English forms and practices were becoming the standard. At the request of the citizens of New Amsterdam, the Dutch West India Company had conferred municipal status upon the city in 1653. The Director-General of New Netherland appointed a schout or sheriff-procurator, two burgomasters, and five schepens. These officers, whose positions were familiar to the city governments of the Netherlands, had judicial jurisdiction over civil and criminal cases and the legislative authority to make regulations useful to the improvement and orderly life of the settlement. After the system was in operation for a few years, the magistrates even gained the right to nominate their own successors, who could take office after being confirmed by the director-general.

English governmental arrangements replaced the Dutch after 1664. Governor Richard Nicolls in June 1665 abolished the offices of schout, burgomasters, and schepens and established the traditional English municipal posts of mayor, aldermen, and sheriff. Appointed annually by the governor, these officers had full power to rule and administer the city. In 1670 the Duke of York sent the municipal officeholders gowns for ceremonial functions, a mace to be borne before them in processions, and an official seal for the city. During the interval of Dutch rule in 1673 and 1674, government again took the form of schout, burgomasters, and schepens, but the return of the English brought the reappearance of the mayor, aldermen, and sheriff.

In appointing the city officers for the year 1676, Andros gave a simple description of the functions of the municipal government. The mayor and aldermen had the authority to rule the inhabitants of the city, to keep a court for the administration of justice, and to name lower ranking officials necessary for the execution of the law. Four of them, of whom (except in extraordinary circumstances) the mayor or deputy mayor was supposed to be one, constituted a quorum; in cases of tie votes, the presiding officer had the deciding voice.[43]

New York's leaders in the following years sought a better definition and an extension of their powers. In 1683 they petitioned Governor Dongan for a charter which would confirm all of the city's customs, privileges, and liberties. They also sought permission to establish six wards in the city and to replace the gubernatorial appointment of the Common Council members with popular election by the residents of those districts. On April 27, 1686, Dongan granted the charter to New York City on behalf of the proprietor, who had ascended the English throne in 1685 as King James II. The city awarded the governor £300 for obtaining the patent.

Dongan's charter was New York's first official frame of government. It guaranteed the city's "privileges, liberties, franchises, rights, royalties, free customs, jurisdictions, and immunities" insofar as they did not conflict with the laws of England. The document confirmed the city's possession of all public facilities, including the City Hall, two market houses, the bridge to the dock, the dock itself, the burial grounds, and the ferry to Long Island. New York also received full control over the streets, highways and unappropriated lands on Manhattan Island. In return, the king demanded a symbolic quitrent of a single beaver skin, or its value in money, to be delivered annually on March 25 which, according to the Old Style or Julian calendar then in use in England, was the first day of the year.

Dongan's charter identified the municipal government as the Mayor, Aldermen, and Commonality of the City of New York. The governor retained the right to appoint the mayor, the sheriff, and the recorder, who served as a legal adviser. The charter established six wards on Manhattan and gave the inhabitants of each the right to choose one alderman and one assistant. The election was to take place each year on September 29, which was Michaelmas Day or the feast of Saint Michael the Archangel; all officials took their posts on October 14.

The mayor and recorder, in combination with three or more aldermen and three or more assistants, constituted the Common Council. That body was empowered to make laws and ordinances, sell land, tax, and levy fines. The government also enjoyed judicial powers. The mayor, recorder, and between three and five aldermen were to be justices of the peace, with jurisdiction over "all manner of petty larcenies, riots, routs, oppressions, extortions, and other trespasses and offenses." The mayor, recorder, and aldermen, or any three of them, of whom the mayor or recorder had to be one, formed a Court of Common Pleas which was to meet on Tuesday each week. The court had jurisdiction over civil matters such as debt, ejectment, and trespass and had the authority to grant the freemanships which allowed residents to practice their trades and businesses in the city. The same officials also held a court of sessions four times a year to try criminal cases.[44]

More basic than the change in governmental forms was the alteration in the relationships among the city's major white nationality groups. Englishmen naturally provided much of the leadership in New York after the conquest ended Dutch control. The first mayor, Thomas Willett, had come to America in 1629 and settled in Plymouth. One of the earliest to engage in trade on Long Island Sound, he established a residence in New York about 1645. Matthias Nicoll, who became mayor in 1672, was a lawyer who served as the first secretary of New York province. Thomas Dervall, who served as mayor in 1675, was originally a Boston merchant. But successful Dutch residents could also aspire to political power. Stephanus Van Cortlandt, for example, held the office of mayor in 1677, 1686, and 1687. The first mayor of the city to be born in America, Van Cortlandt was a prominent merchant and was married to Geertruyd Schuyler, a member of a leading Dutch family from Albany.[45]

English influence increased in New York in the last quarter of the seventeenth century. Englishmen gravitated to the city as it was absorbed in the English economic orbit. The businessmen among them used their connections with the mother country to move ahead in commerce, and even ordinary Englishmen had the advantage of native fluency in the official language of the city and colony. After the revocation of the Edict of Nantes in 1685, French Protestants took refuge in New York and became closely associated with the English residents. By the end of the seventeenth century, the English and the French accounted for between 41.5 and 45 percent of the city's white population, and they had ended the economic and social dominance of the Dutch.

The Dongan charter had the potential of minimizing the resentment caused by the changes occurring in New York in the late seventeenth century. Its grants of limited local autonomy and of election privileges guaranteed that the Dutch majority could retain an important role in the city founded by their forbears. Unfortunately, the decision of the London authorities in 1688 to incorporate New York and New Jersey with the New England colonies in a single government, known as the Dominion of New England, destroyed the possibility. The Dutch might have been able to hold their own in New York, but the city and colony were now made only minor parts of a larger English confederation.

The creation of the Dominion of New England alienated a group of New York City leaders. Most of them were Dutch, and their leader was Jacob Leisler, a German immigrant and rich merchant, whose influence in the city had declined precipitously since the final English takeover in 1674. When rumors reached New York in 1689 that a revolution had deposed James II in favor of his daughter Mary and her Dutch husband, Prince William of Orange, Leisler demanded the immediate proclamation of the news. The incumbent leaders, composed of English appointees and some Dutch inhabitants who had prospered under the new regime, were reluctant to comply, and their hesitance undid them when the news of the Glorious Revolution proved true. Leisler and his followers seized power, and he assumed the title of lieutenant governor.

Leisler held power only until 1691 when Henry Sloughter, a new governor appointed by the Crown, arrived in the colony. Sloughter agreed with those citizens who accused Leisler of treason for overthrowing the old government, and the erstwhile lieutenant governor and his son-in-law, Jacob Milborne, were executed. But the divisions fomented by the rebellion affected politics for at least the next generation.

Leisler's Rebellion was only one of several uprisings which took place in the American colonies in the closing years of the seventeenth century, but the genuine popular involvement associated with it makes it perhaps the most important. Colonial politics was normally the affair of the social elite. In an age unburdened by a democratic ethos, the rich and well-born were sure that they were able and that they knew more than ordinary citizens about the public weal. And the typical citizen, lacking education and tied to an occupation which afforded him neither the money nor the time to seek the unpaid political offices, tended to agree.

The struggle within New York's elite between those who had lost and those who had gained wealth and power after the English conquest had an analogue within the general population, where the Dutch were falling behind the English socially and economically. The division among New York's leaders appeared to many of the city's inhabitants as a competition among the dominant ethnic groups in the population. This perception, in turn, activated the interest of the common folk and united them with the politicians in a novel way. The consequence was the birth of a set of rudimentary political parties, a phenomenon unknown in the homogeneous communities which were typical of much of the rest of colonial America. Most Dutch residents supported the Leislerians, and the English and French combined in the anti-Leislerian coalition.[45]

New York in the seventeenth century was thus the least English and at the same time the most American of the colonial cities. It was a forecast of the mixing of peoples and races that would become the essence of the American experience. And its experience provided insight into the painful clashes inherent in the formation of heterogeneous society and into the crucial role that nationality, religion, and race would play in the pluralistic political system that underlies the American version of democracy.

NOTES

1.   John Duffy, "The Passage to the Colonies," *Mississippi Valley Historical Review,* XXXVIII (1951), 21–38.

2.   Jasper Dankers and Peter Sluyter, *Journal of a Voyage to New York and a Tour in Several of the American Colonies in 1679–1680,* ed. Henry C. Murphy (Brooklyn, 1867), especially pp. 40–42, 53, 78–80, 98–100.

3.   Daniel Denton, *A Brief Description of New York, Formerly Called New Netherlands,* ed. Gabriel Furman; reprinted in *Historic Chronicles of New Amsterdam, Colonial New York, and Early Long Island,* ed. Cornell Jaray, 2 Ser. (Port Washington, N. Y., 1968), pp. 2–3, 27–29. See also Dankers and Sluyter, p. 99.

4.   New York City, *Minutes of the Common Council of the City of New York, 1675–1776,* ed. Herbert L. Osgood, 8 vols., (New York, 1905), I, 10. Hereafter cited as *MCC.* The "Labadist View," a sketch of New York City by Jasper Dankers, shows the dock. The Long Island Historical Society owns the original.

5.   James Riker, *Revised History of Harlem* (New York, 1904).

6.   David T. Valentine, *History of the City of New York* (New York, 1853), pp. 27–29.

7.   Spenser Trask, "Bowling Green" in the *Half Moon Series: Papers on Historic New York,* ed. Maud W. Goodwin et al., 2 vols. (New York, 1897–1898), II, 167–68, 174–75.

8.   See the map of the Dutch grants in Isaac N. P. Stokes, ed., *The Iconography of Manhattan Island, 1498–1909,* 6 vols. (New York, 1915–1928), II, 359, Plates 87 and 87a.

9.   *MCC,* I, 50–62 (1677 tax lists); Valentine, *History,* pp. 319–30.

10.   Inventory of the estate of Peter Jacobs Marius, December 29, 1704, Historical Documents Collection, Paul Klapper Library, Queens College, City University of New York.

11.   *MCC,* I, 50–62; Valentine, *History,* pp. 238–39, 319–30.

12.   Ruth Putnam, "Annetje Jans' Farm," in the *Half Moon Series,* I, 89–95; Oswald Garrison Villard, "The Early History of Wall Street, 1653–1789," ibid., I, 102–115.

13.   Alice Morse Earle, "The Stadt Huys of New Amsterdam," ibid., I, 1–8; Valentine, *History,* p. 213.

14.   *MCC,* I, 8.

15.   Arthur E. Peterson, *New York as an Eighteenth Century Municipality: Prior to 1731* (New York, 1917), pp. 177–81; *MCC,* I, 28–29, 73, 187.

16.   *MCC,* I, 20, 85–86.

17.   Ibid., 28, 64–65.

18.   Ibid., 151, 314–15, 402; II, 144.

19.   Ibid., I, 181.

20.   Ellis L. Raesly, *Portrait of New Netherland* (New York, 1945), chap. 10.

21.   Ibid., chap. 11.

22.   *MCC,* I, 22–24.

23.   Ibid., II, 21.

24.   Ibid., I, 9, 17, 26, 29–37, 143–44.

25.   Ibid., 111, 136.

26.   Ibid., 80, 142–43, 148–50; II, 7.

27.   Julius M. Bloch, et al., eds., *An Account of Her Majesty's Revenue in the Province of New York, 1701–1709: The Customs Records of Early Colonial New York* (Ridgewood, N. J., 1966); Thomas E. Norton, *The Fur Trade in Colonial New York, 1686–1776* (Madison, 1974), chap. 7.

28.   *MCC,* I, 23–24.

29.   Ibid., 20, 29, 150, 176.

30.   Ibid., 4, 111, 139–40, 291.

31.   Ibid., 11, 80–81.

32. Valentine, *History*, chaps. 1, 4; Denton, *Brief Description*, pp. 6-13; Charles Wooley, *A Two Years Journal in New York*, ed. Edmund B. O'Callaghan, in *Historic Chronicles*, ed. Jaray, 1 Ser., pp. 26-63; Dankers and Sluyter, *Journal*, passim.

33. "Letter and Narrative of Father Isaac Jogues, 1643, 1645," in "Novum Belgium, by Father Isaac Jogues, 1646;" J. Franklin Jameson, ed., *Narratives of New Netherland, 1609-1664* (New York, 1909), pp. 253, 259.

34. Thomas J. Condon, *New York Beginnings: The Commercial Origins of New Netherland* (New York, 1968), and George L. Smith, *Religion and Trade in New Netherland: Dutch Origins and American Development* (Ithaca, N. Y., 1973).

35. Edmund B. O'Callaghan, ed., *Voyages of the Slavers "St. John" and "Arms of Amsterdam," 1659 and 1663* (Albany, N. Y., 1867), introduction; Edgar J. McManus, *A History of Negro Slavery in New York* (Syracuse, 1966), pp. 1-25.

36. "Census of the City of New York [About the Year 1703]," in Edmund B. O'Callaghan, ed., *Documentary History of the State of New York*, 4 vols. (Albany, 1849-1851), I, 611-624.

37. *MCC*, I, 85-86; New York County, Minutes of the Court of Quarter Sessions, Aug. 28, 1696, Criminal Court Building, New York, pp. 15-16.

38. Kenneth Scott, "The Slave Insurrection in New York in 1712," *New York Historical Society Quarterly*, XLV (1961), 43-74.

39. Jacob R. Marcus, *The Colonial American Jew, 1492-1776*, 3 vols. (Detroit, 1970), I, 215-43, 306-308, 401-402; Hyman Grinstein, *The Rise of the Jewish Community of New York, 1645-1860* (Philadelphia, 1945), chap. 1; David de Sola Pool, *Portraits Etched in Stone: Early Jewish Settlers, 1682-1831* (New York, 1952), chap. 1.

40. Valentine, *History*, chaps. 12-13; *MCC*, I, 8; Peterson, *Eighteenth Century Municipality*, p. 162.

41. Herbert I. Priestley, *The Coming of the White Man, 1492-1898* (New York, 1929), chap. 12.

42. *MCC*, I, 19.

43. Ibid., 1.

44. Ibid., 290-305.

45. Valentine, *History*, pp. 233, 239, 243, 246-47.

46. For a more detailed discussion of the social and economic changes in New York City and of Leisler's Rebellion and its aftermath, see Thomas J. Archdeacon, *New York City, 1664-1710: Conquest and Change* (Ithaca, N. Y., 1976).

SUGGESTIONS FOR FURTHER READING

SOURCES

Readers can gain an intimate sense of everyday life in early New York from published official documents. The *Records of New Amsterdam from 1653 to 1674*, edited by Berthold Fernow (7 vols., New York, 1897), cover the years of Dutch rule, and the *Minutes of the Common Council of the City of New York, 1675-1776*, edited by Herbert L. Osgood (8 vols., New York, 1905), those of English suzerainty. *Select Cases of the Mayor's Court of New York City, 1674-1874*, edited by Richard B. Morris (Washington, D. C., 1935), brings the reader close to the affairs of the common man with its analysis of the business transacted before the local civil bench. Isaac N. P. Stokes, ed., *The Iconography of Manhattan Island, 1498-1909* (6 vols., New York, 1915-1928) contains a marvelous assortment of maps, deeds, prints, and other materials pertinent to the development of the city. Edmund B. O'Callaghan, ed., *Documents Relative to the Colonial History of the State of New York* (15 vols.,

Albany, 1856-1887) and *Documentary History of the State of New York* (4 vols., Albany, 1849-1851) place the city's experience in the context of the province and the empire.

TRAVEL ACCOUNTS

Accounts by travelers and others who spent time in the city supply much of the available information about its appearance and inhabitants. J. Franklin Jameson brought together a number of these in his edition, *Narratives of New Netherland, 1609-1664* (New York, 1909). *Historical Chronicles of New Amsterdam, Colonial New York and Early Long Island,* edited by Cornell Jaray (First and Second Series, Port Washington, N. Y., 1968), includes a number of essays previously available only in old and sometimes rare editions. Among them is Daniel Denton's *A Brief Description of New York, Formerly Called New Netherland* (London, 1670). *The Journal of a Voyage to New York and a Tour in Several of the American Colonies in 1679-1680,* written by the Labadist ministers Jasper Dankers and Peter Sluyter and translated by Henry C. Murphy, Vol. I of the *Long Island Historical Society Collections* (Brooklyn, N. Y. 1867) contains one of the longest descriptions.

GENERAL HISTORIES

James G. Wilson, ed., *The Memorial History of the City of New York* (4 vols., New York, 1892-1893), is a starting point among the secondary sources dealing with the early history of the community, but Maria Griswold [Mrs. Schuyler] Van Rensselaer, *History of the City of New York in the Seventeenth Century* (2 vols., New York, 1909) is much more detailed. David T. Valentine, *History of the City of New York* (New York, 1853), and J. H. Innes, *New Amsterdam and Its People* (New York, 1902), contain informative biographical sketches of many citizens as well as information about politics, commerce, and the expansion of the municipality.

Edmund B. O'Callaghan, *History of New Netherland* (2 vols., New York, 1855), remains a standard treatment of the Dutch colony. Thomas J. Condon, *New York Beginnings: The Commercial Origins of New Netherland* (New York, 1968) and George L. Smith, *Religion and Trade in New Netherland: Dutch Origins and American Development* (Ithaca, 1973) discuss the ideas and goals of the founders. Henry Kessler and Peter Rachlis, *Peter Stuyvesant and His New York* (New York, 1959), focuses on the last and most famous Dutch governor. Ellis Lawrence Raesly, *Portrait of New Netherland* (New York, 1945), examines cultural and literary as well as political history.

SPECIALIZED STUDIES

Arthur E. Peterson, *New York as an Eighteenth Century Municipality: Prior to 1731* (New York, 1917) is an examination of the city's response to problems of government, commerce, fire, police, health, and sanitation. James Riker, *Revised History of Harlem* (New York, 1904), is the standard history of that community. The *Half Moon Series: Papers on Historic New York,* edited by Maud W. Goodwin, Alice C. Royce, and Ruth Putnam (2 vols., New York, 1897-1898), contains essays on a variety of topics related to the city, and Alice Morse Earle, *Colonial Days in Old New York* (New York, 1896), offers insights into its social history.

The articles in the *New York Genealogical and Biographical Record* provide a great deal of information about New York's Dutch and English citizenry. Edgar J. McManus, *A History of Negro Slavery in New York* (Syracuse, N. Y., 1966), examines the black experience in the colonial city. Charles W. Baird, *History of the*

Huguenot Emigration to America (2 vols., New York, 1885; reprinted Baltimore, 1966), discusses the coming of the French Protestants to the city. Hyman Grinstein, *The Rise of the Jewish Community of New York, 1654-1860* (Philadelphia, 1945), and David de Sola Pool, *Portraits Etched in Stone: Early Jewish Settlers, 1682-1831* (New York, 1952), recount the story of the city's original Jewish community. Thomas J. Archdeacon, *New York City, 1664-1710: Conquest and Change* (Ithaca, 1976) analyzes the social, economic, and political relationships among these elements in the populations.

Information about the city is also available in books concerned primarily with broader subjects. Herbert A. Johnson, *The Law Merchant and Negotiable Instruments in Colonial New York* (Chicago, 1963), and "The Advent of Common Law in Colonial New York," published in George A. Billias, ed., *Law and Authority in Colonial America* (Barré, Mass., 1965), treat legal and economic matters. Lawrence Leder, *Robert Livingston, 1654-1728, and the Politics of Colonial New York* (Chapel Hill, 1961), views the history of the province from the perspective of a leading merchant and politician. Jerome R. Reich, *Leisler's Rebellion: A Study of Democracy in New York, 1664-1720* (Chicago, 1953), focuses on the upheaval which took place between 1689 and 1691, and David S. Lovejoy, *The Glorious Revolution in America, 1660-1692* (New York, 1972), places New York's rebellion in context with the other colonial revolts occurring in the late seventeenth century.

View of New York from the northwest, ca. 1773. From the *Atlantic Neptune* (courtesy of the New-York Historical Society)

Bruce M. Wilkenfeld

REVOLUTIONARY
NEW YORK, 1776

A view of New York, Governor's Island from Long Island.
Engraving from *Town and Country Magazine,* October, 1776.
(courtesy of the New-York Historical Society)

The decision taken by the Continental Congress in July 1776 to sever all political ties with Great Britain marked the end of over a century of uninterrupted English rule in the city of New York. These years, from 1674 to 1776, were a relatively peaceful and unexciting period in the community's history. There were, to be sure, occasional high (or low) points: the Leislerian revolt of 1689-1691; particularly vicious political campaigns in 1701 and again in 1734; the acquisition of the new "Montgomery" charter in 1731; slave revolts in 1712 and 1741. All of these events were, however, merely isolated incidents, and none resulted in overwhelming changes in the character of life in the city. Yet, during these decades—a period that has been labeled the "forgotten century" of New York's history—slowly, and at times imperceptibly, changes took place. The changes cumulated and multiplied, and by 1776 the city that greeted the Revolution was one whose way of life was radically different from the city of the 1670s. But more, many of the changes that had taken place by 1776 were developments that would continue to shape the patterns of the city's life for decades to come.

To visitors in the decades before the Revolution, it was immediately clear that New York City was a large community, although exactly how large (both in absolute and in relative terms) was somewhat open to question. Lieutenant Isaac Bangs, a physician serving with the Continental Army, recorded after his arrival in New York City in the spring of 1776 that "the City is nearly as populous as the Town of Boston."[1] A decade earlier, Lord Adam Gordon's description of the community had been somewhat different, at least in detail. In his 1765 travel diary, the Scottish nobleman reported that "the City of New York has long been held at home the first in America, though it neither comes up to Philadelphia in Beauty . . . or in the number of its inhabitants. . . ."[2] Gordon's estimate of the city's population was 20,000 at the time.

It is impossible to say with precision how many people lived on Manhattan Island (and therefore within the eighteenth-century borders of New York City) in 1776. The colonial government had, however, sponsored a census of population in 1771, and the sheriff's reports indicated that in that year New Yorkers numbered 21,863—including 18,726 whites, and 3,138 blacks—mostly slaves.

What makes this census record particularly useful is that it was the latest of a series of ten such tabulations which had been made during the previous 75 years—tabulations which make possible a few general remarks about the direction of the city's population growth during the eighteenth century.[3]

Population of the City of New York, 1698–1771			
Year	White Population	Black Population	Black Percent	Total Population
1698	4,237	700	16.5	4,937
1723	5,886	1,362	23.1	7,248
1731	7,045	1,577	22.4	8,622
1756	10,768	2,272	21.1	13,040
1771	18,726	3,137	16.8	21,863

As the above table indicates, New York City's population growth during this period was continuous. It is also clear, however, that the rate of growth—whether by race or for the city as a whole—was not constant. Two trends in particular had major consequences in the shaping of the pattern of life in the metropolis of the 1770s. First, a significant percentage of the total growth of the white population for the entire century took place in the period after 1750. The growth rate of this segment of the population accelerated from 1.49 percent a year in the 1698–1723 period to 4.62 percent between 1756 and 1771. This unprecedented expansion quickly resulted in a variety of social and economic consequences.

The striking fact about the racial composition of the city's population is that while the slave population continued to grow, its growth rate did not match the accelerating pace of the free population. New York City in 1776 was still, as it had been since the 1690s, the largest center of slave population in the northern colonies. Nonetheless, the demographic and economic significance of the non-free population was becoming increasingly less as the total population expanded.[4]

To be sure, even the total population of 21,863 seems rather small to modern New Yorkers. Based upon the 1970 Federal Census, such a total would rank a town among such New York State communities as Mineola Village (21,744), Massapequa Park Village (22,112), and Depew Village (22,158). In contrast, New York City's population in 1970 was 7,895,563, and even the total on Manhattan Island alone was in excess of 1.5 million.

In the context of the late eighteenth century, however, New York City's population in 1776 ranked it as a leading urban area not only in the New World but in the entire Atlantic community. Of all the cities in Britain's empire in the western hemisphere, only Philadelphia, with a population of between 30,000 and 40,000, exceeded New York's total. Boston, which had been the population leader for a century, had by the 1770s fallen considerably behind the city on Manhattan Island. While none of these communities could rival the central capitals of Western European nations—London's 800,000, for example, or the 650,000 in Paris—those cities were the only ones with such a magnitude of population. Compared to the leading regional centers of England—Bristol, Liverpool, Birmingham, Manchester—towns whose populations were between 27,000 and 35,000—New York City's numbers hardly ranked it as less than a first-class urban center.[5]

After noting the sheer size of the population, travelers to New York frequently commented upon the physical characteristics of the built-up area of Manhattan Island. Once again, little evidence is available for the city precisely as it existed in 1776. However, there is considerable data regarding the city during the decade beginning in 1765, and there is no indication that any significant change occurred in the final years before the Revolution. Of primary importance in this investigation is a map of the city drawn in 1767—"the Ratzer plan." Prepared by Bernard Ratzer, a lieutenant in the 60th Regiment, the map provides the best picture of the built-up area of settlement on the eve of the Revolution.

The map indicates, first, that by the 1760s, New York's "urban" area stretched northward approximately one mile from the southern tip of the island. The most highly developed portion of this urban core—where most of the major docks were concentrated and much of the population was to be found—was the section along the East River stretching northward from the Battery. (Currently the area would extend to approximately the site of the Brooklyn Bridge). A traveler continuing north along the shoreline would soon pass a number of scattered homes and "rope walks" but would then find himself at the edge of the vast area of the island that was still devoted to agricultural production.

Along the Hudson River, too, the "urban" area was strikingly limited—reaching only to the modern Reade Street. Beyond these rows of houses only a famous "pleasure garden"—the Ranelagh—separated the central core of the city from the farmlands of Nicholas Bayard and others. Only in the center of the island—between Division Street and the Bowery Lane—did settlement extend farther north. Even if this area is included, settlement north of modern Grand Street was only minimal.

Wherever they lived, almost all New Yorkers shared at least one characteristic: their homes were on remarkably narrow and convoluted streets. Accurate as Ratzer's plan is, it can give only a partial suggestion of the reality—and of its inevitable social consequences. Even at the time, in a period when narrow streets were customary in cities, travelers found the crowding in Gotham to be noteworthy. Lord Gordon, for example, remarked that the streets were "neither regular nor wide."[6] Robert Honeyman, a Scottish-born doctor who set out in 1775 to tour the colonies to the north of his home in Virginia, commented in that year that "the streets are by no means regular, and the ground is very uneven."[7] Concurring in this view was Patrick M'Robert, a Scot of some means, who in his travel diary of 1775 complained that "the streets are in general ill paved, irregular, and too narrow."[8] In the entire city, only Broadway and Broad streets (whose names are the best reflection of their most notable aspects) were more than sixty feet wide. Even more important for the kind of communication and transportation possible within the city, few of the "thoroughfares" could in fact be followed for more than a very few blocks before a traveler found himself faced with a sharp turn or an actual cul-de-sac. New York in 1776 was a city for pedestrians or, at most, for small vehicles traveling slowly and cautiously.

If more of the city dwellers' experiences were similar in the kinds of streets on which they lived, they were not equally so in the homes they inhabited. Of the material used, Robert Honeyman commented in 1775 that "the houses are built indifferently of stone or wood or brick, or some partly of all the three."[9] The buildings varied as well in size, ranging from multiple-storied townhouses to single-level home-shop combinations. They differed most strikingly, however, in architectural style. Many of the houses in the city gave evidence of the community's early colonial history—and were accordingly of the "Dutch style." In the eighteenth century, this meant above all the presence of a gabled roof—whether steeply pitched or "crow stepped" facing the street. Ornamental iron reinforcements and iron figures showing the date the building was erected, solid wood shutters, and "Dutch doors" (divided horizontally) were additional evidence that the inhabitants (or at least the builders) were adherents to the old ways.

By 1776, however, many of the city's houses and perhaps a majority of the homes of the wealthy and powerful were "English" in character, which in this period meant "Georgian" architecture. The style was reflected, for example, in the Kennedy mansion at Number One Broadway. A low-pitched roof, the absence of ornamental "dates," the abandonment of yellow tiles on the exterior—all of these were symbols of adherence to the new and rejection of the city's early heritage.

Many of the characteristics of physical New York, however, still represented a basic continuity with the past. As early as the Dutch period, the East River—with its relatively slow current, its easy ties to Long Island, and its potential for shelter during winter storms—had been the center of the city's shipping and, as such, the center of its property and population. Too, reflecting a heritage that went back to medieval towns, New York City even in the seventeenth century had been a community of small, winding streets.

Yet not even in its physical configuration had the city remained unchanged during the eighteenth century or even during the final twenty-five years of the colonial period. Housing—one of the more striking, though ultimately less significant, reflections of this change—witnessed by 1776 a clear shift away from the Dutch heritage. In 1716, for example, a full four decades after the final English conquest of the city, the Reverend John Fontaine, on a visit to the colonies in search of land for the other members of his Irish Huguenot family, observed that "the houses for the most part [are] built after the Dutch manner. . . ."[10] By 1750, however, the shift from the physical heritage and supremacy of the Dutch past was well underway. James Birket, an Antiguan merchant, writing of his voyage to New York in 1750–1751, recalled that "not any of the modern houses are built with the Gable end to the street as was formerly the fashion amongst all the old Dutch settlers."[11] Moreover, the change in architectural style was, as will be noted later, only the physical reflection of a broader shift in the power balance between the various ethnic groups in the city.

The appearance of the houses was changing, but even more significantly, the city itself was changing. Compared either to the modern city or to the vastness of Manhattan Island, the built-up regions in 1776 were still extraordinarily small. They were however, considerably larger and more complex than their counterparts of a century earlier. The most dramatic change in the settlement of the island had been a shifting of part of the population away from the East River side and toward the Hudson River. Through the first quarter of the eighteenth century, population remained almost entirely east of Broadway. The settlement of the area to the west had been hindered by two separate factors. The region north of Warren Street was deemed unusable because of the presence of a swampy region at the base of the "Chalkie Hook" (a small hill near the current intersection of Canal and Church streets). Not only was it particularly damp, but the whole west side was a breeding ground for mosquitoes, "fevers," and disease. To this problem was added a man-made one. Much of the area west of Broadway was owned by Trinity Church. By requiring that prospective settlers accept the land in leasehold (instead of permitting

outright purchase in "fee simple") Trinity inevitably slowed the development of this area.[12]

Only from the 1730s on, when increasing population began to suggest
that the region could be developed profitably, was action taken to make
the area acceptable for settlement. The draining of the swamps (done by
private landowners with the approval of the city government) turned the
area into potentially fertile—and dry—land. The result, the gradual migration of some of the city's population away from the eastern wards, would
be traceable on every map or plan produced during the remaining years
to the Revolution.

The patterns of 1776 reflected, moreover, not only the spread of settlement over existing land but also an increase in the amount of land area
itself. Comparison of the Ratzer plan with any modern map of Manhattan
island quickly indicates that the southern tip of the island was still considerably smaller in the Revolutionary era than it is today. On the East
Side, most of modern Front and South streets were still entirely under the
waters of the East River. To the west, the Hudson River flowed unimpeded
where today Washington and West streets stand. Yet, at the same time, the
city was not only more populous and spread out further but actually larger
in area than the city of a century before.

One of the powers which the city government held—and indeed, one of
its major sources of revenues—was the right to grant "water lots."[13] These
rights permitted individual citizens to take possession of underwater land
extending out from the current borders of dry land into the rivers. Even
during 1775–1776, when it was clear that the Revolution was imminent,
this process, by which New Yorkers were literally building their own city,
continued. At the meeting of the city's Common Council on March 21,
1775, for example, the minutes record that

> the clerk produced to this Board the several engrossed Grants for Water
> Lots on Hunter's Key, to wit, to William Brownjohn, Jacobus Van Zandt,
> Henry Carmer . . . and also one other engrossed Grant to Henry H. Kip for
> a Water Lot on Burnet's Key . . . all of which several grants being read
> and approved of were by order of this Board signed by Mr. Mayor and
> Alderman Blagge; and Ordered to be delivered to the several Grantees
> therein named on the Executing counterparts thereof.[14]

Through this process, first utilized in 1686 when the city had sold lots
in order to pay the costs incurred in securing the city's new "Dongan"
charter, New York City had added land and ultimately streets. It was this
process that during the eighteenth century, had created Water Street and
Burnet's Key, and increased the city's width substantially from the five
blocks which comprised the distance between the rivers in 1700.

The city might spread its very land area, but as the Revolution approached, the race between the pressure of population and the availability of usable land was rapidly being won by the former. To be sure, New York City had always been noticeably crowded. In 1697, for example, the New England physician Benjamin Bullivant had observed that "the houses of N[ew] Y[ork] stand closer than in Boston, and so Contiguous generally that theyr yards, and Backsides are very small ... theyr fronts are mostly narrow, seldome above 25 foote, excepting some few principall buildings."[15] His remarks were echoed in the lament of a royal official who complained in 1701 that "I have eight in family and know not yet where to fix them, houses are so scarce and dear, and lodgings worst in this place."[16]

The problem was becoming increasingly severe, particularly in the period after the 1740s. The critical factor was the nature of the transportation system available to the eighteenth century community. Geographically limited by the need to be within easy walking distance of the major docks and shipping centers, the majority of New York's traders and artisans remained within the perimeter of the old central core. Population concentration, while still far less than in the modern city, rose; real estate values went up and, eventually, rents as well. For the rich, this meant an increase in the kinds of investments they could make. Those of William Bayard, a merchant, are illustrative. According to an affidavit filed by him in 1778, Bayard, before the Revolution, had acquired real estate holdings that included three three-story houses renting for £360 a year, five smaller houses, two storehouses, and a pier—in all, property valued at £17,000.[17] For the larger numbers of New Yorkers who rented rather than purchased for speculation, the result was disastrous. According to at least one student of the period, heads of families desperately looked for smaller houses at a yearly rent of £10 or £15, and to make ends meet, two or more families often occupied one dwelling.[18] The possibilities for great wealth and the potential for increased hardship were growing simultaneously. An exacerbation of social tensions was the consequence of the increasing economic inequality.

Sizable in population and geographic extent, New York City in 1776 was also a community with a large number and variety of both public and private institutions. In 1774, M'Robert found that "the public buildings and places of worship are generally very neat, and well finished if not elegant."[19] Lieutenant Bangs, in 1776, added a comparative note when he remarked that alongside of Boston, New York possessed "public edifices greater in number."[20]

The institutions most crucial for the city's prosperity were those related to transportation and communication—docks and piers, roads, and ferries. As the Ratzer plan clearly discloses, the Revolutionary-era city was quite adequately provided (in numbers at least) with waterfront facilities. Virtually the entire East River shore between the Battery and Cherry streets and the banks of the Hudson River between Stone and Partition streets were extended into the rivers by wharfs, slips, and docks. Some of these had been built by private individuals, using rights granted by the government. Others, notably the "Great Dock" at the foot of Broad Street, the Albany Pier adjoining it, and the Corporation Dock, on the North River, were the city's direct contributions to the international transportation network.

While most of the city's economic preeminence came from its role in intercolonial and international trade—and hence centered upon its docks and piers—much of the daily round of existence for New Yorkers arose from ties to other parts of the New York Bay area. To facilitate these communications, New York City's government in 1776 regulated five different ferry operations. When traveling to "Nassau Island" (modern Brooklyn), New Yorkers could choose between Elisah DeGrushe's ferry at Coenties Slip, Samuel Baldwin's operation from Peck's Slip, or Thomas Ivory's vessel, which departed from the Fly Slip. For travel across the Hudson River, New Yorkers could board vessels at the end of Thomas Street and at the site of the Bear Market that would take them to destinations in New Jersey and Staten Island.[21]

Of the public institutions not devoted to transportation, the one which attracted the most attention from visitors was the fort at the southwest tip of the island. Built originally by Peter Minuit in 1626, the fort, which had been known at various periods as Fort Amsterdam, Fort James, Fort William, Fort William Henry, Fort Anne, and Fort George, had theoretically been strengthened by the creation of a formal gun battery and platform during the 1730s. Whatever its name, and whether built of wood or stone, its purpose was always the same: to protect the city against a possible invasion by hostile European powers coming by sea. To some visitors, the institution seemed fully capable of its assigned task and fully worthy of considerable attention by the populace. Lieutenant Bangs, for example, remarked that

on the SouthWest part of the town . . . is a very strong and costly fort built by the Kings Troops and many masons men for the protection of the city. . . . On the outside of the Fort at the edge of the wall was a Battery, erected at a vast expense to the King, built of hewn stone, the outside about ten feet high, the inside filled up to form a plane that the Wall was not more than a foot and a half high. Over this Cannon were to play.[22]

The reality though, as the city's population knew, and as trained observers quickly realized, was sadly different. The fort—stone walls, battery, and all—was, in spite of all the care and expense that had been lavished upon it, actually the source of only minimal protection for the city and played only a limited role in the lives of its inhabitants.

It was, instead, the institutions which met the daily needs of the local population that loomed largest in the minds of New Yorkers; and in 1776, a number of such institutions existed to deal with a variety of urban problems. Scattered throughout the city were a City Hall to serve as the center of municipal government; a prison to house light offenders and debtors—designated the "Bridewell"; a "New Gaol" (built in 1759) to deal with more violent or dangerous criminals; an Almshouse for the indigent; and five different markets—the Fish, Fly, Old Slip, Peck, and Oswego markets—in which retailers could rent stalls and from which the city's inhabitants could secure fresh produce.

Oddly, though, in 1776 itself, it was none of these vital institutions that were the subject of the greatest interest on the part of the population. Uppermost in the public mind—perhaps even more so than the news from the Boston area—was the water works project that was taking shape at approximately Broadway and White Street.

The background to this effort was simple: New York City had always suffered from a shortage of usable water. Although numerous wells had been dug in the built-up areas of the city, the water available from them was uncertain in amount and, above all, horrendous to the taste. It had been traditional for New Yorkers of all classes to purchase potable water from vendors who carried water through the streets from the "Tea Water Pump," a relatively deep well just north of the city.[23] To remedy this situation and to ease the problem of fire fighting in the city's central core, the city government in 1774 accepted the plan of a Dutchman, Christopher Colles, who proposed building a steam pump which would draw up pure water to a reservoir to be constructed at Broadway and White Street. From here the water would be channeled throughout the city by wooden pipes placed under the city's streets.[24]

The project itself was never brought to fruition; the Revolution intervened, preventing the laying of the pipes. However, in 1776 the first, and really more exciting stage, the building of the engine, was finished. To prove his theories (and presumably to insure continued public pressure for support from the city for his project), Colles began to give exhibitions of the operation of his brainchild. In March 1776, when most other Americans were busy looking for signs of the British, New Yorkers were watching for Colles' flag—visible as far south as the Battery—which was flown to indicate that the pump was in operation at the moment.

If New York's supply of public institutions and facilities was remarkably varied in 1776, so were its private and quasi-private agencies. Most numerous of these, entirely profit-oriented in conception, yet fulfilling a multiplicity of nearly-public functions, were the city's taverns. By the 1770s, nearly 400 taverns (about one for every twelve adult males in the city) were licensed as purveyors of liquors on a retail basis. These ranged in size and trappings from the three-story high Queen's Head Tavern (later Fraunces Tavern), which was described in 1775 as having "fourteen fireplaces, a most excellent large kitchen, [and] five dry cellars,"[25] to the numerous small groggeries scattered throughout the city but concentrated especially near the docks.

The clienteles differed sharply, but all the taverns met the same kind of need. Hotels, restaurants, places for transacting business (whether legal or not), places of entertainment—all these were rare or nonexistent in New York City in 1776. As in other cities, it was the tavern which served these multiple purposes. It was here that mail could be collected, goods auctioned, insurance coverage secured, and sailors found to man outgoing vessels; and Mrs. Patience Wright could exhibit her collection of "waxworks."

Many activities could, however, be pursued in far more specialized institutions and settings. For those New Yorkers who sought reading matter but could not or would not purchase the volumes themselves, the New York Society Library, organized in 1754 and now housed in a room in the City Hall, had a large collection of volumes on most subjects for the use of its subscribers.

While some sought self-improvement through reading, others hoped to accomplish the same goal through further education. In this area, public institutions were of little help. However, private agencies effectively filled the vacuum. For primary education, New Yorkers could choose between church-affiliated schools (such as those supported by Trinity Church and by the Society for the Propagation of the Gospel) and other, entirely private, institutions. Those seeking an education while employed could select from a variety of night schools and academies created just for the working population. Music, fencing, surveying, and foreign languages were only a few of the numerous subjects taught in the evening hours.

Higher education and advancement into the learned professions could also be secured locally. Situated on lands donated by Trinity Church, King's College (now Columbia University)—chartered in 1754—was by 1776 entering its third decade. A multiplicity of problems—small size, precarious financial position, hostilities engendered by the manner of its creation and by the strong role played by the Anglicans in its governance, the recent flight of its president, Myles Cooper, because of his pro-English leanings—all posed threats to the institution. Yet, in spite of all its uncertainties and problems, the college had advanced sufficiently so that by 1769 it had come to grant baccalaureates in medicine as well as in the liberal arts, and by 1774 its first published "catalogue" had made its appearance.

Finally, New Yorkers seeking entertainment rather than erudition could find in the city a variety of institutions to suit particular tastes. In 1776, the John Street Theatre, a gaudy, red-painted wood building set sixty feet back from the sidewalk (to which it was connected by a wooden, covered walkway), was silent—the victim of orders from the Continental Congress decrying public entertainments at a time of national crisis. As recently as 1774, however, this edifice had been the scene of much activity. It was here that the "Old American Company" had performed a repertory of plays ranging from Shakespearian histories to outright farces. To these performances came not only the very wealthy—who appeared in the evening to claim the choice seats that their servants had been occupying since the early afternoon—but also hundreds from the city's middle classes.

Those inclined more towards active participation were offered a variety of clubs which held periodic gatherings and parties. Devotees of Terpsichore, for example, welcomed announcements such as one in October 1772, indicating that "the dancing assembly begins Thursday the 22nd inst. John Reade, John Jay, Robert S. Livingston, Junr., Managers."[26]

Finally, lest the impression be given that New York City's recreations were entirely pristine, it should be noted that in 1775, according to M'Robert, "above 500 ladies of pleasure keep lodgings contiguous within the consecrated liberties of St. Paul's (Chapel)."[27] Because of this latter association, the area was known with some accuracy, but also presumably with a special joyous irony, as "the Holy Ground." In the eighteenth century, as in the twentieth, New York City possessed the reputation of being able to fulfill virtually any desire.

Thus, a multiplicity of institutions of all kinds has always been a feature of life in the city. As early as 1700, New York possessed ferries and docks to facilitate travel; a room in the jail for the housing of malefactors; numerous taverns in which to relax from business (or in which to conduct it); and a market from which to buy goods. Private schools were available as early as the period of Dutch rule; theatrical performances were always part of the range of entertainments available at the taverns. Finally, while not yet virtually organized and recognized as a special district of the city, New York's prostitutes were already by no means inconsiderable in number in 1700.

Yet, there was a difference—a difference of degree that had become, during the Revolutionary era, a difference of kind. To a remarkable extent, the specific institutions—both public and private—which existed in

1776 had been created during the preceding quarter century. Until 1755, malefactors condemned to incarceration were all confined in a room in the basement of the City Hall. In the two decades following, however, both the New Gaol—a four-storied structure with barred windows—and the Bridewell, had been erected. The construction of a more secure prison did not, however, reduce the level of crime in Gotham. An editorial remark published in the *New York Mercury* on February 18, 1774, for example, complained, in connection with a report of an attempted burglary, that "from so many recent attempts of this sort in different parts of the city we must conclude that there are amongst us a number of gentry who have no other Employment...."[28] At least when they were captured, however, there was now some chance that the thieves could be kept separate from simple debtors.

It was during the period after 1750, too, that such varied institutions as the Royal Exchange (1752), King's College (1754), the New York Society Library (1754), the Albany Pier (1751), and the New York Chamber of Commerce (1768) were created. Indeed, during the decade of the 1770s itself—in the very shadow of the forthcoming conflict with Britain—the ferry routes between the city and Long Island were increased from one to three, the Bridewell was built (1774), and the very ill were moved into the newly-chartered New York Hospital (founded in 1771).

Both individually and as a group, these institutions had considerable significance. In the decades just prior to the Revolution, New York City was in the midst of a transformation. Increasing wealth and population were making possible the fulfillment of long-sought goals, at the same time that they evidenced the existence of new or exacerbated problems. The result was a shift from general-purpose to more specialized institutions. Points of contact between differing groups and classes were thereby reduced, as their activities were organized through institutions with finer (but therefore narrower) focus. The impact upon the overall relationships between groups was a development that would have to be dealt with by the city as a whole.

Fueling the progress of the city, but also reflecting it, was the town's growing economy. In 1776, as throughout the entire colonial period, this meant, above all, the upsurge of New York as a center of trade. The city's advantages as a commercial center were as evident in the eighteenth century as in the twentieth. Almost every visitor to the city commented upon the fine harbor, the access to the interior provided by the East and "North" rivers, and the relative freedom from ice. The city was also perfectly centrally positioned with respect to the other islands scattered in New York bay. To these advantages were added the expertise and ingenuity of the city's traders—whether merchant-princes who owned numerous vessels and large warehouses filled with trading goods or ship's captains who operated vessels in which they owned only a small share.

Based upon these advantages, New York's trade, like its population, increased virtually continuously during the eighteenth century. In 1772, for example, approximately 700 vessels passed through New York's harbor on intercolonial or international voyages. The total recorded value of the goods involved in these shipments was in excess of £420,000. In each case, the figures reflected increases of more than 600 percent as compared with similar data from a quarter-century before.[29] Even in 1776, when growing conflict had cut the current influx of shipping, the newspapers were filled with advertisements that reflected the extraordinarily wide range of contacts that New York traders had developed during the colonial period. Rum from the West Indies, wine from the Madeira Islands, tobacco from the South, "dry goods" from Philadelphia and Boston, manufactured goods and luxury items from London and the "outports"—all of these flooded into the shops of New York City. In return, acting as both middleman and ultimate shippers, New York's merchants organized a continuous flow of exports, including both native New York products (flour, wheat, meat) and re-exported goods from the southern colonies or from the other northern seaports.

Trade was not the only source of employment for New Yorkers in the Revolutionary era, however, No census exists to permit a precise analysis of the population by occupation. A variety of other evidence suggests strongly, however, that while those associated directly with trade—merchants, seamen, ship's captains—formed the largest single group in the community, there were large numbers who found work in the eighteenth century version of manufacturing.

Largest in any such tabulation were those in trades which had close, but still indirect, ties to the sea. Shipping required casks, and a large, locally-owned fleet provided employment for numerous coopers. Repairs had to be made to ships and sails, and groups of sailmakers and ship's carpenters developed to fill this need. Flour was a major product of the colony. Ever since political muscle had won for the city a brief-lived monopoly on flour production within the colony, a thriving bolting industry had been part of the community's economic life.

All of these occupational groups had arisen in New York by the early eighteenth century, but none had changed the overwhelmingly mercantile character of its economy. In the decades after 1750, however, change piled upon change, and by 1776, the prevailing pattern showed marked discontinuity with the past. Within the last pre-Revolutionary decade alone, local advertisements told of the creation of linen factories, whalebone processing plants, and sugar houses. Given the crucial nature of iron and other metals in the further advancement of industry, it was perhaps especially notable that in August 1767, an advertisement in the *New York Journal* announced that an air furnace erected by Peter Curtenius, Gilbert Forbes, Richard Sharpe, and Thomas Randall had just begun full operation.[30] Indeed, the prospects for local manufacturing had advanced so far by the Revolutionary era that when this furnace was accidentally destroyed by fire in November 1772, it was less than three months before an advertisement in the *New York Mercury* (February 22, 1773) announced that "Sharpe Curtenius and Lyle have rebuilt at a considerable expence the New York Air Furnace . . . and as they have provided themselves with a sufficient stock of pig metal etc. they propose to carry on the foundry business in all its Branches. . . ."

New York's shippers were not declining by 1776, in absolute terms. Indeed, in the period between 1716 and 1764, the city's merchants had gained an increasing share of even the trans-Atlantic shipping that had formerly been the preserve of their English-based counterparts. It was rather the appearance of a new industrial sector of ever-growing importance that created the structural change which characterized the New York City economy in the decades just prior to the Revolution.

New York's geographic and economic pattern in 1776 was also reflected in its social structure. At the apex of society was a relatively small elite, identifiable by distinctive clothing styles, entertainments, furnishings, and, to some extent, geographic location within the city. For the very rich males of the city in 1776, for example, to be properly attired required clothing that adhered to the style known as "the macaroni." Introduced in London in 1770, this fashion, which was quickly imitated in New York City, called for short waistcoats, enormous wigs, small cocked hats, and sticks with long tassels. Some within the wealthiest classes might reject the demands of current fashion—but not many. A letter to the *New York Mercury* (January 31, 1757), for example, complained of the widespread attitude that "one might be as well out of the world as out of the mode." To be sure, New Yorkers were by no means unique in this tendency towards emphasis upon fashion. The journal of a Miss Sarah Eves of Philadelphia records (January, 1773), that "the good Doctor thought his clothes were not good enough to wait upon us in, therefore he delays his visit until he gets fitted up in the Macaroni taste. . . ."[31]

If dressing "a la mode" was one sign of elite status, the possession of a coach was another. During the eighteenth century, the extension of roads northward made longer drives possible, and the habits of arriving royal appointees set a fashionable example by the importation of luxurious coaches. By 1750, the first local coachmaker, James Hallett, was advertising in the New York City press, and by the 1770s at least eighty-five vehicles were to be found within the city limits.[32]

Distinctive on the road by their clothes or their means of conveyance, the city's elite citizens were equally identifiable through their home furnishings—elaborate sideboards and cabinets, carved chairs, imported carpets, complex and expensive wall hangings. Moreover, not only a home's interior, but its very location, tended to establish it as the residence of a member of the city's upper class. New York City was simply too small for the creation of entirely separate class or ethnic districts. Settlement patterns of various economic strata did, however, reflect clear elements of concentration. By the 1770s, the population as a whole had begun to shift not only north along the East River shore, but also toward the western and northwestern fringes of the build-up area of settlement. The vast majority of those in the city's uppermost economic ranks, however, while perhaps purchasing country estates on the western side of the island, usually retained town homes and stores in the East River wards.

The contrast between the elite's lifestyle and that of those in the lower ranks of New York City's society could hardly have been greater. At the very bottom were those who required actual assistance, either short- or long-term. For these unfortunates—victims especially of old age, accident, or illness (mental or physical)—the city provided two kinds of relief. Some, particularly those who were totally incapacitated and likely to be long-term charges, were consigned to the Almshouse. Even before the outbreak of actual conflict began to swell the ranks of the destitute, approximately 300–400 inmates were confined there each year during the 1770s.[33] In the Almshouse, strict regulation of food, clothing, and activity guaranteed that the city's maintenance services would be accomplished as expeditiously and as cheaply as possible.

Not all of those who required aid in 1776 were, however, to be found in the Almshouse. Many of the city's destitute had friends or relatives (or strangers) who were willing to keep them—at least as long as the city helped foot the bill. Others in society, for the most part families or individuals who were usually able to support themselves, found that short-term increases in the price of food or fuel threatened economic disaster. For these groups, the city's solution was to provide "outdoor relief," in the form of either money or commodities.

These groups were the most obvious of the poor. In absolute numbers, however, even in 1776, the problem of total destitution just was not an issue that affected a substantial proportion of the population. Nevertheless, the problem of poverty was real—and far from invisible. No more than 1½ to 2 percent of the city's population might require assistance, yet there was a large community, numbering in the thousands, of residents whose incomes provided little beyond subsistence and whose life-styles were patterned accordingly. Settled in disproportionate numbers in the newly built-up areas in the west and northwest, composed to a large extent of citizens from a number of specific occupational lines—seamen, day laborers, cartmen—these citizens would have been readily identifiable to even the most casual visitor. Inventories of personal estates especially point to the striking kinds of differences that poverty could make in the eighteenth century: wooden knives, spoons (frequently no forks at all), and plates instead of pewter or silver, an old chest and bed instead of carved, mahogany furnishings, a one stroy shop-home in lieu of a multi-leveled mansion, and above all—clothing. Problems of being "a la mode" were not for this group. The era of imitative ready-to-wear clothing was not yet born, and the lower class of New York City accordingly carried in its outer clothing an unmistakeable emblem of its economic status and of the vast gulf between the poor, on the one hand, and the merchants, lawyers, and large landowners, on the other.

A lower class of poor and very poor; an elite of the wealthy and very wealthy. Neither of these two classes were of a kind to set New York apart from any other city in the English empire, or even from the social patterns of the white communities of the West Indian sugar islands. But New York City (like other large cities in the mainland colonies) did stand out. What distinguished these communities, especially when contrasted with the colonies and islands to the south, was the existence of a large, powerful, self-assertive middle range of property holders—the urban middle class.[34] That such a group existed, distinctive at the same time from the extremes of both poverty and wealth, was widely recognized by contemporaries. Thomas Pownall, later royal governor of Massachusetts, writing of his impressions of New York City in the 1750s, noted

> To give some idea of the manner in which their houses were furnished I here insert a speculative estimate made for me by the Vendue—master extracts of the averages of the value of the Plate and furniture of the First, Middling and lower Class of Householders. He averaged the first at £700, the second at £200, The third he subdivided into two Classes and averaged the value of the first of these at £40 and the second £20.[35]

This middle class drew its strength and numbers from a variety of craftsmen and small shopkeepers.[36] These were individuals who prospered from the relatively higher wages that their skills attracted in the New World. Possessing in their large numbers the ability to make their demands heard in the political sphere, these groups also served to turn the city's social structure into an unbroken continuum. Patrons of the press and of the theatre, these middle-class citizens were perhaps the single most dynamic group in the city and were instrumental in creating the vitality and vibrancy of New York's life. In an era when newspapers, for example, survived through paid subscribers, and when a minimum of 600 such orders generally were necessary to make a paper self-sufficient,[37] it was this substantial middle range—aware, concerned, able to pay—that permitted the city to support four different newspapers—John Anderson's *Constitutional Gazette,* Hugh Gaine's *New York Gazette and Weekly Mercury,* John Holt's *New York Journal,* and Samuel Loudon's *New York Packet*—during 1776 alone.

In many ways, these social characteristics of the Revolutionary city reflected basic continuity with the past. In 1701, for example, an assessment was made of all New York's "citizens, strangers, and sojourners." This tabulation reveals that in that year, the top 20 percent of the city's population—a group of about 200—held some three-fifths of the total assessed wealth in the community. In contrast, the 505 lowest-ranking citizens—the bottom 50 percent of the assessed population—together held less than one-fifth. That left, however, a middle range—a group of about 300 New Yorkers—with holdings well below those of the elite, but still sufficient to maintain life styles considerably above the pure subsistence level.[38]

Yet, once more, while continuity with the past was part of the social pattern in New York City's Revolutionary era, change and its effects were also evident. While the number of the very poor was, even in the year of the Revolution, still far from really alarming, it was considerably larger, in both absolute numbers and as a percentage of the population, than during the earlier decades of the century. As late as 1738, for example, when New York's population included about 8,000 free citizens, the records of the church wardens indicate that relief was given to less than 50 persons in the poorhouse.[39] Too, as was indicated earlier, the problems of those who were poor but not destitute may well have been becoming increasingly severe as a byproduct of the overcrowding and higher rents that came with the increasing rate of population growth.

There was, moreover, another change which was less dramatic but perhaps ultimately more significant. Social tensions in the city had traditionally been kept within manageable levels through a variety of factors. On the one hand, the presence of a full range of classes—i.e. the existence of a strong middle class—meant that the gap between social groups was never so large and so unbridgeable as to breed total contempt, on the one hand, or total hatred, on the other. A second factor, perhaps of even greater importance, was the potential for personal and intergenerational mobility that existed in colonial New York City. Of the leading property holders in 1701, for example, nearly three-fifths had fathers who ranked within the middle or lower economic strata of their generation, when the 1676 tax assessment had been levied. Moreover, to reach the top in 1701 was not a guarantee of permanency at that level. Of those in the top 10 percent of the population in 1701 who were still in the city in 1708, over one-fifth had fallen out of the upper rank of property-holders by that year.[40] If the "elite" is defined in occupational rather than property terms, similar conclusions may be reached. Analyses of lists of leading commodity shippers (1701) and owners of shipping (1716) indicate that individual mobility and intergenerational mobility were truly part of the city's social structure in the early years of the eighteenth century.[41]

By the Revolutionary era, however, the extent of such mobility—the opportunity to enter the uppermost ranks of society and the economy—appears to have declined. Of the leading shipowners of 1764, nearly three-quarters were the children of the topmost elite of the generation of the 1720s and 1730s. Opportunity, the possibility of movement, and hence general willingness to accept the system without tension and hostility, was in the process of change as the Revolution approached.

A similar combination of continuity and change may be observed in the political life of the city. The charter granted by Governor Thomas Dongan in 1686 gave the city a government which included an appointive mayor and recorder and a large number of local officials who were selected by the city's voters. The latter were organized into seven geographic wards, and elections were held annually "on ye feast day of St. Michael the Arch Angell." These elected officials included the constables, charged with major responsibility for the enforcement of the city's laws; assessors, required to apportion the tax burden; and collectors, charged with collecting the apportioned taxes. Above all, the voters of the city selected the members of the Common Council, the ruling legislative body in the city. Although limited in some ways by the authority of the colonial government, on the one hand, and by the influence of the appointed mayor, on the other, this elected body still had enormous power over the economic life and administration of the city.[42]

Although voting statistics do not exist for the 1775 elections, and even though the right to vote during this era did not automatically follow as a prerogative of residence, it is clear that the right to vote for members of the local government was quite widely distributed. As the estimate recorded by Pownall suggests (an estimate confirmed by rent records and by probated wills and inventories of estate), New Yorkers of the "middling" range and above could in most instances meet the basic property requirements for voting in all elections. Even those below this economic level were not necessarily disenfranchised in local contests. Every inhabitant of the city who had acquired the status of "freeman"—whether by purchase from the city government or by gift therefrom—possessed the right to vote and hold office locally. Throughout the colonial period, but especially after the middle of the eighteenth century, this method of enfranchisement permitted large numbers of local citizens—particularly laborers—who might otherwise not have been able to meet the voting requirements, to participate in local elections.[43] As in the rest of colonial America, apathy frequently held down the numbers of those New Yorkers who actually voted, but eligibility to vote was in fact quite widespread.

New Yorkers constituted, moreover, both an active and informed electorate. Long before Martin Van Buren and the Albany Regency had worked to perfect the techniques and rationale of party politics during the Jacksonian Era, New York's voters had come to accept—and even to expect—almost all the classical political accoutrements. Escalating rhetoric (both in terms of quantity and virulence), public nominating meetings, mass rallies—all were part of the repertoire of eighteenth-century politics in New York City.[44]

New Yorkers, moreover, had a local source of continuing political tension. Although the structure of the government remained relatively constant during the eighteenth century, the composition of the Common Council's membership was not equally static. Not surprisingly, given the awareness and the wide eligibility for participation that were features of local politics, the Council was at all times far from becoming a totally "closed" institution. Throughout the century, citizens from the crafts and from the ranks of small shopkeepers could be found serving on the Council alongside of large landholders and leading merchants. Yet, a number of changes were taking place. During the period after 1735, tenures in office grew longer—from an average of 4.4 years to 4.8 years; and increasing percentages of the Common Council members—and, especially, of the aldermen, who were the more prestigious half of the total membership—came from the upper occupational groups. Most portentously, the members of the Council were drawn more frequently from a very select group of families and were becoming just as frequently restricted in fact (though not, it should be stressed, in law) to the offspring of the previous generation's economic and political leaders.[45] In the local political arena, an element of rigidity, of illiberality, was setting in. In New York City, where, as John Honeyman observed in wonderment (1775), "contrary to what I found at Philadelphia, where people only minded their business, but here nothing is heard but politics,"[46] such a situation would not be permitted to continue unchecked for very long.

The final determinative factor in New York City life in 1776 was the extraordinary heterogenity of the population. Ethnically, while Dutch and English elements were strongest, substantial communities of Frenchmen, Scotch-Irish, and Germans were all to be found in the city. If the situation was complicated in ethnicity, it was virtually chaotic in the related, but not identical, area of religious affiliation. In 1776, at least twenty-two houses of worship—a minimum of one for every 800–900 individuals in the city—competed for loyalty and support. There was no question as to the identity of the single most impressive church edifice in the city. Built originally in 1696 and rebuilt in 1737, Trinity Church, the center of Anglican worship in New York City, reigned supreme. Supported from the beginning by contributions from the crown, this edifice impressed virtually every visitor to the city by the richness of both its architecture and its interior trappings.

However, in spite of this physical prominence and a status in some ways approximating legal establishment, the Anglican Church in New York held a far from unchallenged position either in numbers or power. Both the Presbyterian Church and its community, based in three different congregations in 1776, and the Reformed Dutch Church, also encompassing three separate groups, existed to contest for local religious leadership. Conflict between religious groups had never been entirely absent during New York City's history. Since the 1750s, however, when propositions relating to the establishment of a college in the city had suggested, especially to members of the Presbyterian community, that the Anglicans were seeking to advance their special interests at the expense of the broader goal of local higher education, this hostility had become somewhat more open and virulent.[42]

The presence of three major competing denominations would by itself have set New York City apart from many other communities in the British Empire. It was, however, the proliferation of additional groups that contemporaries found to be most striking—or alarming, depending upon ideological position. In 1776, English-speaking Protestants in New York City could choose from, among others, services at a Quaker meeting house, an Anabaptist congregation, or a Lutheran Church. French Huguenots could gather at L'Eglise du St. Esprit; Jews could band together at Shearith Israel, on Mill Street. Even Roman Catholics, perhaps the most hated and feared religious group within the Empire, could find some outlet for their religious sentiments. Though the climate of public opinion made the establishment of a formal church impossible, even in New York City, Ferdinand Steinmeyer, a Jesuit Father, came north from Maryland regularly to celebrate mass within the private homes of his coreligionists.[48] Indeed, in 1776, when at least twelve separate religious denominations were represented within the city, New York was perhaps as far from religious homogeneity as any community in the entire British Empire.

As with almost every facet of the city's life, the religious pattern of 1776 reflected both continuity and change when compared with the

previous century. As the heir to Dutch policies of relatively wide toleration of religious and ethnic differences, New York City had always been
known for the diversity of its population. In 1692, for example, Lt.
Colonel Charles Lodwicke noted that "our chiefest unhappiness here is
too great a mixture of nations, . . ."[49] Not surprisingly, the various groups
had thereafter sought to legitimize their existence by formal institutions
and New York City had thus acquired, even before 1700, a rather wide
array of churches and religious centers.

Nevertheless, changes came before 1776. Most obvious to contemporaries, but probably of least actual long-range importance, was an
efflorescence of church construction after 1750. Of the twenty-two edifices in existence in 1776, at least ten had been built or largely renovated
since that date. To an extent, this construction simply reflected the over-
all growth in the population and the consequent increase in the number of
congregants in each denomination. While Trinity Church had served the
needs of the local Episcopalians quite nicely for over fifty years, in the
period after 1750 two new chapels—St. George's and St. Paul's—were
opened to accommodate the increasing numbers and growing geographic
dispersion of the Anglican community. Intradenominational divisions—
perhaps exacerbated by increasing crowding—also played a role. The North
Dutch Church, for example, was built after a dispute regarding the use of
English (as opposed to Dutch) in the weekly services proved impossible
to compromise.[50]

Other changes which were reflected in the 1776 city were less obvious
in a physical sense but were more significant in their consequences. In
particular, the period after 1730 saw a realignment in the power of the
leading denominations. On the one hand, the Reformed Dutch Church—
emblem of the Dutch community—which had survived the English conquest and had remained strong during the first decades of the eighteenth
century, increasingly found its current position and its future hopes
eroded. Study of the leading owners of shipping in New York City between 1716 and the 1760s, for example, indicates clearly that decade by
decade, the political and especially the economic elites of the city were
being drawn from other groups within New York's polyglot population.[51]
A declining position had become, before 1776, not only a current problem
but a self-nurturing and self-fulfilling prophecy for the Reformed Dutch
Church. As elite members came increasingly from other groups, those
among the younger cadre of the Reformed Dutch community who had
expectations of entering those select circles found the pressure to shift
allegiance increasingly strong. In consequence, in 1776, as in the decades
immediately earlier, the position as the principal local dissenter group—
in energy, if not yet in numbers—had been taken by the Presbyterian

Church. Led especially by three lawyers—William Livingston, William Smith, Jr., and John Morin Scott—it was this community that would spearhead the struggle against what appeared to be an Anglican drive to secure religious conformity and uniformity.[52]

Yet, in an analysis of religious patterns, the emphasis should not be upon these areas of change or of interdenominational dispute. It should not even be upon the occasional appearance of relatively advanced notions regarding religious freedom. Rather, it is the ongoing reality of a complex and heterogeneous society forced by circumstances to work out a pattern of mutual acceptance on a day-to-day basis that was the most striking characteristic of New York City's ethnic and religious life in 1776.

Thus, New York City in 1776 was a city with clearly-defined social, economic, political and religious characteristics. Commercial-industrial, politically active, and heterogenous, it was a city that had experienced major alterations during the preceding century. To a certain extent, these features and this change paralleled developments in other communities of the American colonies in the Revolutionary era. The movement toward an increasingly "closed" local elite was only one example of the points of congruence between Gotham and the rest of the future American nation.[53] Yet, in many other respects, while the patterns that prevailed in New York City made it a virtual prototype for the later nation, in the context of the third quarter of the eighteenth century they made the town seem different and therefore suspect. Indeed, it was the "different" character of New York City and New Yorkers that seems to have most forcefully impressed visitors during the 1770s. John Adams, for example, who stopped in the city while on his way to a meeting of the Continental Congress, recorded in his diary (August 23, 1774) that "with all the Opulence and Splendor of this City, there is very little good Breeding to be found. . . . They talk loud, very fast, and all together. If they ask you a Question, before you can utter 3 Words of your Answer, they will break out upon you, again—and talk away."[54] Major Samuel Shaw, serving under Washington in the Revolutionary army, visited New York City in May 1776, and reported that "the honest sincerity . . . for which the inhabitants of our once happy town [Boston] were so remarkable, are not to be found here. . . . The people of this place are a motley collection of all the nations under heaven."[55]

More than just odd, perhaps even subversive. For a town which seemed to share so little of the characteristics of the rest of America could easily be suspected of somewhat less than total loyalty to the Revolutionary cause. From Maine to the Carolinas, there was a collective sense that New Yorkers had not, and would not, carry their share of the burden.

Actually, New York had a number of very specific and very good reasons to fear and to avoid the coming conflict. As we have seen, the fort, designed to protect the community from external attack, actually had little potential to fulfill this role. Surrounded by islands from which invasions could be launched, New York City was a doomed town if the British even decided to bring their naval superiority to bear. It stood in peril even if the British landed not a single soldier in the city. Crowded, heavily built up, containing numerous homes with wood shingle roofs, New York was a virtual prisoner, a hostage to the threat of fire started by a broadside of cannon fire.

The danger went far beyond the threat of purely physical destruction. There was a question of a way of life and its protection. By the Revolutionary era, it is clear, New Yorkers had carved out a reasonably satisfactory set of social and economic patterns. To give up the prosperity, to risk the disruption of a carefully arranged set of relationships both within the city and with the rest of the Empire—this was not a decision that could be taken or should be taken lightly.

Yet, with all their reasons to stay aloof, New Yorkers in spite of their reputation at the time—and during the two centuries since—actually exhibited every one of the appropriate "revolutionary" responses during the decade after the 1760s. If Boston enjoyed a Stamp Act riot, so too did Gotham. On November 1, 1765, a large mob paraded through the streets of New York City, ending up ultimately in front of the fort. Here they burned an effigy of Lieutenant Governor Cadwallader Colden. Too, before dispersing, the New York mob, like its Boston counterpart, moved against the property of those who were notable local supporters of the stamp duty. In New York City, this action involved the wrecking of the home of the British Major Thomas James, who seemed to threaten enforcement of the detested measure through the use of force.[56]

Nor was the Stamp Act crisis the only time when New Yorkers actually performed in an "approved" manner. Bostonians might boast of their "Massacre," but if the question of the first blood shed in the cause were to be raised, New Yorkers could point with equal justice to the "Battle of Golden Hill." To be sure, this had been a brief encounter with no lasting ideological or practical consequences. In January 1770, attempts by British soldiers to nail up broadsides attacking the Sons of Liberty quickly produced widespread popular hostility. The result was a brief skirmish on January 19 in which, according to one report, "a number of people were wounded. . . . one sailor having his head and finger cut, and a Quaker his cheeck slashed."[57] The incident was minor, to be sure, but except that later rhetoric kept the affair in Boston continually in the public mind, the two events were not really very dissimilar.

New Yorkers in 1775 and 1776 were, however, as charged, somewhat laggard about signing up for the common defense. As late as July 1775, even after the battles at Lexington and Concord, New York's elite especially was still extremely slow in participating in the enlistment process. On the other hand, in the first real American engagement, the campaign against Quebec in December 1775 led by Brigadier General Richard Montgomery, it was the much-maligned New York "sweepings"—John Lamb's Artillery Company—who proved to be the most tenacious. As such, they had the dubious distinction of suffering numerous casualties during the failure of that expedition.

Actually, it was not really surprising that New Yorkers ultimately came into the war of their own volition. Local political and religious conflicts had exposed New Yorkers on a number of occasions to the dangers of attacks on liberty. Issues as varied as the founding of King's College and the question of the tenure of judges had, well before 1776, sensitized the local population to both the issues for which the Revolution would be fought and the language in which it was to be articulated. Additionally, local characteristics also tended to spur the city into participation in the Revolution. The overall patterns of life, as we have seen, claimed the support and protection of New Yorkers. At the same time, there were in New York causes for local anxiety and internal tension: the nature of the city's society, its geographic configurations and its politics. To the extent that they played a role in New York City's decision to go to war, these developments represented another area in which the city's response to the issues of 1776 mirrored that of other parts of the new nation.[58]

Whatever the reasons for deciding to participate actively in the war, for its trouble, New York was subjected to the attack and occupation it had so much feared. In August 1776, General William Howe landed his forces at Gravesend, across the East River from the city. By September 15, British troops were on Manhattan Island; by the end of September, all of the built-up area of the city was in British hands; and by November 1776, Washington and the Continental Army had been driven north of the Harlem River, and all of Manhattan Island—legally, all of the city of New York—was under occupation.[59]

It was not until November 25, 1783—seven years later—that the occupation was finally lifted, the British army and its civilian allies evacuated, and the city restored in effective terms to its earlier status as an American city. Given the duration of the interlude, it seems appropriate to conclude by inquiring into the changes wrought by this occupation.

At first, they seemed enormous. When the Committee for the Southern District—set up by the State of New York to prepare for the final day of the British presence—moved into New York City in December 1783, the image was one of widespread ruin and upheaval. During the preceding years, the city had been ravaged by its status as a barracks town, by two disastrous fires (in 1776 and 1778), and by the need to secure food and, more, fuel from within the island itself (since the normal sources of supply on Staten Island and Long Island were all in American hands). As a result, large areas of the city were denuded of the shade trees that had been the community's pride; homes were destroyed or vastly altered; fences and farms were left in disarray. The city's commerce, obviously halted during the Revolution, seemed likely to remain stagnant. Long dependent for much of its prosperity upon trading links within the British Empire, New York City found (as it had always known) that independence did indeed have an economic price—in this instance exclusion from the very real benefits of the British mercantile system. Finally, upheaval was evident in the movements of thousands of persons. At the same time that perhaps 20,000 loyalists were departing, thousands of patriots were returning to take up their old lives. Many more were arriving with plans for vengeance.

Other significant changes had been wrought by the intervention of time and war. The upheavals which resulted brought to a halt—temporarily in any case—the gradual flow of power towards a small, multigenerational elite. During the period 1784–1800, the membership of the Common Council was much more like that of the early decades of the eighteenth century than of the period between 1734 and the Revolution.[60] Terms were once again shorter; the membership was more diverse in occupations; and family origins were somewhat more representative of at least the middle and upper class population. Too, the personnel which made up the city's economic elite underwent striking alteration. War-time and post-war confiscations of property, combined with the decline in some of the traditional trading networks, opened a large number of new positions in the upper ranks. Into these openings stepped numerous "new men"—new in many cases not only to the upper class but to the city itself.[61]

In general though, the changes which seemed so real in 1783 turn out on closer examination to be either extraordinarily short-lived or, in the end, the basis of only marginal variations over pre-existing patterns. In ethnicity and religious affiliation, the period between 1783 and 1800 saw a substantial increase in the local population of Frenchmen, Irishmen, and New Englanders. Too, in this period, the Anglican Church lost its earlier prerogatives and began to find it necessary to fight for status. These changes, however, were really peripheral. The long-range trends—the decline of the Dutch church and community, the rise of the Presbyterians—were not seriously affected. Even more important, the pattern that had been set in the Revolutionary city—of multiple sects and ethnic groups, of toleration and competition rather than enforced conformity—this pattern, New York's legacy to the rest of the nation, remained uncompromised.

In economic terms, to add simply one more example, the same incidental variation from the pre-Revolutionary pattern was observable. Trading routes changed, as commerce with the French and Dutch increased while business with English merchants declined, at least in relative terms. There were alterations, too, in the types of manufacturing for which New York City had been known. The production of rum and flour became relatively less important, as the fabrication of a whole range of goods multiplied at the local level. These changes, though, did not really affect the basic shape of economic life. During the eighteenth century New York City had developed an economy based upon a blend of commerce and industry and this mixture remained during the national period as the dominant economic characteristic of the community.

Even the physical destruction, the aspect which seemed to returning thousands to be the most terrible result of the war years—even that soon passed from memory. By 1789, when the French journalist Brissot de Warville visited the city, he remarked that "the activity which reigns everywhere announces a rising prosperity; they enlarge in every quarter."[62]

Despite the variety of its consequences, the War for Independence was not the revolutionary experience that contemporaries hoped for (or feared). New York City would face the nineteenth century in a form shaped largely by the patterns of the Revolutionary city. America itself would change, however, and by the nineteenth century, New York City would cease to be merely a precursor but would become a paradigm for much that had happened and was happening to the American nation and people.

NOTES

1.   Edward Bangs, ed., *Journal of Lieutenant Isaac Bangs, April 1, 1776–July 29, 1776* (Cambridge, Mass., 1891), p. 24.

2.   Lord Adam Gordon, "Journal of an officer's travels in America and the West Indies, 1764–1765," in Newton D. Mereness, ed., *Travels in the American Colonies* (New York, 1916), p. 414.

3.   The census tabulations are conveniently available in Edgar J. McManus, *A History of Negro Slavery in New York* (Syracuse, 1966), pp. 197–99.

4.   Ibid., pp. 141–89.

5.   See Lewis Mumford, *The City in History* (New York, 1961), pp. 355–59.

6.   Gordon, "Journal," p. 415.

7.   Philip Padelford, ed., *Colonial Panorama, 1775; Dr. Robert Honeyman's Journal for March and April* (San Marino, California, 1939), p. 26.

8. M'Robert, *A Tour through Part of the North Provinces of America*, ed. Carl Bridenbaugh (New York, 1935; reprinted 1968), p. 4.

9. Padelford, ed., *Colonial Panorama*, p. 27.

10. Ann Maury, ed., *Memoirs of a Huguenot Family* (New York, 1835), p. 297.

11. Birket, *Some Cursory Remarks made by James Birket on his voyage to North America, 1750-1751*, ed. Charles M. Andrews (New Haven, 1916), p. 43.

12. See Ruth Putnam, "Annetje Jans' Farm," and George Hill and George Waring, Jr., "Old Wells and Water-Courses on the Island of Manhattan," in *Historic New York: The Half Moon Series*, 2 vols., ed. Maud W. Goodwin et al. (New York, 1899), pp. 121-58, 193-262.

13. Arthur Peterson, *New York City as an Eighteenth Century Municipality: Prior to 1731* (New York, 1917), pp. 82-84.

14. Herbert L. Osgood, ed., *Minutes of the Common Council of the City of New York, 1675-1776*, 8 vols. (New York, 1905), VIII, 85.

15. Wayne Andrews, ed., "A Glance at New York in 1697: The Travel Diary of Dr. Benjamin Bullivant," *New York Historical Society Quarterly*, XL (1956), 66.

16. Quoted in Carl Bridenbaugh, *Cities in the Wilderness* (New York, 1938; reprinted, 1955), p. 148.

17. Virginia Harrington, *The New York Merchant on the Eve of the Revolution* (New York, 1935; reprinted Gloucester, Mass., 1964), p. 134.

18. Carl Bridenbaugh, *Cities in Revolt* (New York, 1955), p. 226.

19. M'Robert, *A Tour*, p. 3.

20. Bangs, *Journal*, p. 24.

21. George Edwards, *New York City as an Eighteenth Century Municipality: 1731-1776* (New York, 1917), pp. 72-75.

22. Bangs, *Journal*, p. 24.

23. See Charles Weidner, *Water for a City* (New Brunswick, 1974), chap. 2.

24. *Minutes of the Common Council*, VIII, pp. 40-41.

25. Quoted in Esther Singleton, *Social New York Under the Georges* (New York, 1902), p. 367.

26. Ibid., p. 304.

27. M' Robert, *A Tour*, p. 5.

28. Quoted in I. N. P. Stokes, *The Iconography of Manhattan Island*, 6 vols., (New York, 1915-1928), IV, p. 846.

29. Harrington, *New York Merchant*, pp. 202-204.

30. Stokes, *Iconography*, IV, p. 777.

31. Quoted in Elizabeth McClellan, *Historic Dress in America, 1607-1800* (Philadelphia, 1904), p. 241.

32. George W. Houghton, *The Coaches of Colonial New York* (New York, 1890), pp. 24-25.

33. Raymond Mohl, "Poverty in Early America: A Reappraisal," *New York History*, L (1969), 15.

34. Bruce M. Wilkenfeld, "The Social and Economic Structure of the City of New York, 1695-1796" (unpublished Ph.D. dissertation, Columbia University, 1973), chap. 2.

35. Pownall, *A Topographical Description of the Dominions of the United States of America*, ed. Lois Mulkearn (Pittsburgh, 1949), p. 45.

36. Wilkenfeld, "Structure of New York City," pp. 27-30.

37. See Arthur M. Schlesinger, *Prelude to Independence: The Newspaper War on Britain, 1764-1776* (New York, 1965), p. 304.

38. Wilkenfeld, "Structure of New York City," pp. 20-23.

39. Mohl, "Poverty in Early America," pp. 9-12.

40. Wilkenfeld, "Structure of New York City," pp. 65-70.

41. Ibid., pp. 51-72. See also Wilkenfeld, "The New York City Shipowning Community, 1715-1764," *American Neptune* (forthcoming).

42. Wilkenfeld, "The New York City Common Council, 1689-1800," *New York History*, LII (1971), pp. 252-55.

43. See Beverly McAnear, "The Place of the Freeman in Old New York," *New York History*, XXI (1940), pp. 418-30.

44. Milton M. Klein, *The Politics of Diversity: Essays in the History of Colonial New York* (Port Washington, 1974), pp. 11-34. See, too, Gary B. Nash, "The Transformation of Urban Politics, 1700-1765," *Journal of American History*, LX (1973), pp. 605-632.

45. Wilkenfeld, "Common Council," pp. 262-66.

46. Honeyman, *Journal*, p. 31.

47. Klein, *Politics of Diversity*, pp. 53-109.

48. Stokes, *Iconography*, IV, p. 909.

49. Lodwicke, "New York in 1692," New York Historical Society *Collections*, 2 ser., II (1848), p. 241.

50. Stokes, *Iconography*, IV, pp. 840-80.

51. Wilkenfeld, "Shipowning Community."

52. Klein, *Politics of Diversity*, pp. 97-109.

53. Wilkenfeld, "Social and Economic Structure," chap. 4. See also Klein, *Politics of Diversity*, pp. 183-204.

54. Adams, *The Diary and Autobiography, 1771-1781*, ed. Lyman Butterfield, et al., 4 vols. (Cambridge, Mass., 1961), II, p. 109.

55. Stokes, *Iconography*, VI, pp. 36-37.

56. Carl Becker, *History of Political Parties in the Province of New York, 1760-1776* (Madison, 1960), pp. 23-52.

57. Ibid., p. 82. See also Stokes, *Iconography*, IV, p. 803, and Lee R. Boyer, "Lobster Backs, Liberty Boys, and Laborers in the Streets," *New York Historical Society Quarterly*, LVII (1973), pp. 281-309.

58. Gordon Wood, "Rhetoric and Reality in the American Revolution," *William and Mary Quarterly*, XXIII (1966), pp. 3-32.

59. Bruce Bliven, *Under the Guns: New York, 1775-1776* (New York, 1972).

60. Wilkenfeld, "Common Council," pp. 266-71.

61. Wilkenfeld, "Social and Economic Structure," chap. 5.

62. Cited in Sidney Pomerantz, *New York as an American City, 1783-1803* (New York, 1938), p. 169.

SUGGESTIONS FOR FURTHER READING

GEOGRAPHIC AND DEMOGRAPHIC GROWTH

The starting point for any study of the city's growth during the eighteenth century is I. N. P. Stokes, *The Iconography of Manhattan Island, 1498-1909*, 6 vols. (New York, 1915-1928). The numerous maps and illustrations in these volumes provide a comprehensive view of the city's physical growth. The calendar of events provides an unmatched picture of the day-to-day pattern of life in the city, as well as an overview of the growth of the city's population. For those seeking a more traditional narrative, James G. Wilson, ed., *The Memorial History of the City of New York*, 4 vols. (New York, 1892-1893) provides a splendid, albeit primarily political, history. Finally, the changing dimensions, conditions, and importance of the city's slave population can be traced in Edgar J. McManus, *A History of Negro Slavery in New York* (Syracuse, 1966).

INSTITUTIONS: PUBLIC AND PRIVATE

Three general works are available for those interested in further discussions of the city's public institutions, religious communities, and cultural agencies. George W. Edwards, *New York City as an Eighteenth Century Municipality: 1731-1776* (New York, 1917) is based upon a meticulous study of the minutes of the New York City Common Council. This study is particularly strong in its discussions of the city's docks, piers, and markets. For discussions of the private institutions in the city, two volumes by Carl Bridenbaugh, *Cities in the Wilderness* (New York, 1928; reprinted, 1955), and *Cities in Revolt* (New York, 1955) should be consulted. These provide not only general discussions for the situation in New York City but place these findings in the context of developments in the other major American colonial cities. Further information regarding cultural developments in the city during the eighteenth century can be secured from Louis B. Wright, *The Cultural Life of the American Colonies, 1607-1763* (New York, 1962). Although somewhat encyclopedic in tone, this work provides considerable information regarding the development of both the "high arts" and the various crafts throughout the colonies. For an assessment of the cultural accomplishments of eighteenth century New Yorkers, and for some suggestions of the contributions to culture made by New Yorkers, see Milton M. Klein, "The Cultural Tyros of Colonial New York," in *The Politics of Diversity: Essays in the History of Colonial New York* (Port Washington, 1974), chap. 5.

ECONOMY

Unfortunately, no single work is available which adequately describes the development of the city's economy during the eighteenth century. Some data can be gleaned from Stokes's chronological listings, but attempts at analysis are generally lacking. Fortunately, discussions of the trade sector are more readily available. Virginia Harrington's *The New York Merchant on the Eve of the Revolution* (New York, 1935; reprinted, Gloucester, Mass., 1964) ably describes the business methods and opportunities of the city's merchants during the decade before the Revolution. Philip White's *The Beekmans of New York in Politics and Commerce, 1647-1877* (New York, 1956) while focusing entirely upon that one important family, provides numerous insights into the problems encountered by New York City merchants and into the solutions which they devised. Consideration of some of the characteristics of the labor system in New York City is available in Samuel McKee, *Labor in Colonial New York* (New York, 1934; reprinted, Port Washington, 1965).

SOCIAL PATTERNS

In this area, too, no published works exist which provide an adequate analysis of the changes and patterns which developed during the century. A number of specialized works do exist to facilitate the study of the extremes of society. Esther Singleton's *Social New York Under the Georges* (New York, 1902) provides both a detailed discussion of the life-style of those at the top of society and copious illustrations and photographs of period furnishings. Further insights into the varied production of local craftsmen can be secured from Rita Gottesman's *The Arts and Crafts in New York, 1726-1776* (New York, 1938). This work, a compilation of advertisements placed by artists and craftsmen in local newspapers, provides much information, particularly regarding the "luxury" crafts, such as jewelry making and goldsmithing. For those at the very bottom of society, Raymond Mohl, "Poverty in Early America: A Reappraisal," *New York History*, L (1969), 5-27, provides a detailed description of the public efforts to deal with the problem of destitution. For a study of one of the groups that made up the lower ranks of society, see Jesse Lemisch's "Jack Tar in the Streets: Merchant Seamen in the Politics of Revolutionary America," *William and Mary Quarterly*, XXI (1968), 371-407.

POLITICS

For the institutional arrangements, George W. Edwards's work, cited above, should be consulted. Bruce Wilkenfeld, "The New York City Common Council, 1689-1800," *New York History*, LII (1971), 249-76, analyzes changing patterns of political and social power and control through a study of the several hundred men who served in the city's Common Council during the eighteenth century. Patricia U. Bonomi, *A Factious People: Politics and Society in Colonial New York* (New York, 1971) is the most recent study of the development of politics and factions at the level of the colonial government. A superb study, it is of enormous use in establishing the background against which political disputes in the city itself developed. An early analysis of the meaning of that broader story can be found in Carl Becker's *The History of Political Parties in the Province of New York, 1760-1776* (Madison, 1909; reprinted, 1960). In particular, the first chapter of this monograph provides a broad interpretation of the colonial patterns and a suggestion of the relevance of that story to the coming of the Revolution in New York. For a more recent interpretation, which successfully challenges some of the broader implications drawn by Becker from the colonial patterns, see Milton M. Klein, "Democracy and Politics in Colonial New York," in *The Politics of Diversity*, chap. 1. Finally, for a reminder that low levels of participation are not equivalent to low levels of eligibility, see Patricia U. Bonomi, "Political Patterns in Colonial New York City: The General Assembly Election of 1768," *Political Science Quarterly*, LXXXI (1966), 432-47.

THE CITY IN THE REVOLUTION, AND AFTERWARDS

Bruce Bliven, *Under the Guns: New York, 1775-1776* (New York, 1972) provides a detailed and entertaining discussion of the military side of New York's preparations for war in 1775 and 1776. This volume also ably documents the extraordinary extent of distrust felt by other colonists regarding New York's reliability in the coming effort. A broader, but somewhat less detailed discussion can be found in Thomas J. Wertenbaker, *Father Knickerbocker Rebels: New York City During the Revolution* (New York, 1948), which covers the period 1763-1783. For the war years themselves, Oscar Barck, *New York City, 1776-1783* (New York, 1931) should be considered. The problems experienced by the city during the period of occupation— problems of fires, supplies of food and fuel, and overcrowding—are all given more than adequate coverage in this work. The lighter side of life in the besieged city— social life, entertainments, and the like—are also given full consideration.

For an assessment of the social impact of the Revolution, as reflected in changes in the city's political life, see Wilkenfeld, "The New York City Common Council," cited above. For a discussion of a variety of social, political, and economic trends during the two decades after the British evacuation, Sidney Pomerantz, *New York: An American City, 1783-1803* (New York, 1938) should be consulted.

New York, 1865. Lithograph by Don Bachmann. (courtesy of the New York Public Library Prints Division)

Albert Fein

CENTENNIAL
NEW YORK, 1876

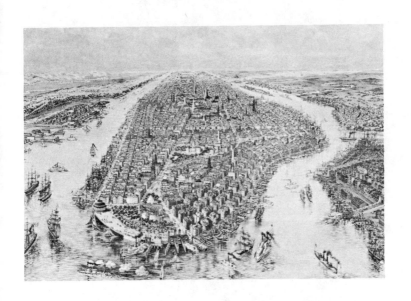

Panoramic view of New York City, 1876. (photo by
Joshua H. Beal, courtesy of the New-York Historical Society)

Centennial New York was, in many respects, the nation's true modern capital, reflecting both national strengths and weaknesses. The city represented the challenge of a democratic nation's capacity to plan for and maintain an urban environment to meet the needs of a uniquely heterogeneous population. As the nation had grown and prospered, owing to immense natural resources, virtually unlimited immigration, and the application of new technology, its principal city had been transformed as well. The national population more than doubled from 1850 to 1880,[1] and so had the city's, increasing from 500,000 to slightly more than 1,200,000. Even more significant was the diversity of national origin and religion of those who entered the country through the immigrant station at Castle Garden in the city's harbor. Many remained in New York, making the city distinctively representative of this nation of immigrants.[2]

The physical fabric of the city had altered, too. An Englishman, George T. Fox, visiting in 1868—having last seen New York in the 1840s, found the change startling. He likened his feelings to those of "poor Rip Van Winkle after his 20 years slumber on returning to his native village!" Fox noted that "the general features were the same—there was Governor's Island, the Battery, the North River and its wharves, Trinity Church, and some other well known features, but the rest was all changed." Among other things, Fox commented upon the disparity between the great wealth in the city and the equally great poverty reflected in a neglected public environment. The streets, for example, were badly maintained and filthy, and the open space at the Battery, once "one of the most delightful promenades," was in decay, "[for with] the population having fled uptown no one care[d] for it now." Fox might also have noted that in addition to abandoning the Battery, fronting New York's magnificent bay, the city had permitted the deterioration of two other precious natural resources, the two rivers that made it an island.[3]

Fox was correct, of course, in emphasizing the unplanned shift of population uptown—above 14th Street; but this was only for those who had a choice. In 1830, a year before Fox first came to New York, the vast majority of the city's 202,589 persons lived below 14th Street; fewer than 12,000 lived above it. By 1875, more than 50 percent—511,021 persons—resided above 14th Street, with the other half million crowded into the very limited space of the original city. Adding to the congestion, noise, and filth in that part of the city were most of the commercial and manufacturing establishments.[4]

Within the same forty-five years there had taken place a dramatic expansion of urban services in such matters as water supply, police and fire protection, education, and public parks. It was on the basis of those amenities that the city's centennial orator, the Reverend Richard Storrs, a Congregational minister, proclaimed New York a national example of democratic achievement for all the world: "This [is a] great city, whose lines have gone out into all the earth, and whose superb progress in wealth, in culture and in civic renown, is itself the most illustrious token of the power and beneficence of that frame of government under which it has been realized."[5]

But Dr. Storrs did not discuss the problems of disease, mortality, and crime associated with the living conditions of the poor. It was, even given the occasion, a curious omission, for the first group to recognize and attempt in some systematic way to remedy poverty and its related problems had been motivated by religious impulse. When Charles Loring Brace, a Congregational minister, called for the formation in New York City of the Children's Aid Society, he was drawing upon his own experience as an urban missionary as well as on hard data demonstrating that "the respectable and industrious moved out of certain quarters; and [that] such places as the Five Points began to be known. Streets once inhabited by the best people . . . were abandoned, and have since been held by lodging-houses of the poorest immigrants."[6]

By the time of the Centennial, the most significant efforts to plan for the city as a whole were being made by men and women who had found or invented secular outlets for their religiously-based humanitarian objectives. The issue was posed somewhat differently by the noted scientist Thomas Huxley, starting a three-week visit to the United States in 1876. Huxley was encouraged by the fact that New York's skyline was dominated by two buildings—the Tribune and the Western Union Telegraph—symbolizing the nation's capacity to utilize new building technologies. "Ah," said Huxley," that is interesting; this is America. In the Old World the first things you see as you approach a city are steeples; here you see, first, centers of intelligence."[7] But this, too, was a recent change. A generation before, the city's skyline had been dominated by steeples. The challenge, as Huxley and others understood it, was whether knowledge of science and industry could be channeled by social and ethical resolve into solving the nation's most serious problems—among them, the condition of its cities.

By the time Huxley had come to the end of his visit, he was less optimistic. Speaking at Johns Hopkins University, he cautioned Americans that size was not grandeur, nor could greatness be measured by the mere vastness of American space. What, Huxley asked, would Americans do with their material wealth? Had they contemplated the ends to which their industrial and physical might could be put? And Huxley focused on two issues particularly visible in the nation's most important city: corruption and pauperism. The country would have to decide "whether shifting corruption is better than a permanent bureaucracy; and as population thickens in your great cities, and the pressure of want is felt, the gaunt spectre of pauperism will stalk among you, and communism and socialism will claim to be heard."[8]

Huxley spoke less than two months before a presidential election in which the nation's commitment to honest government, as well as to the ethical principles that had motivated the Civil War, was being tested. The Democratic nominee was New York's governor, Samuel J. Tilden, whose political base was in the city and whose national reputation rested on his role in ousting New York City's corrupt political "boss," William Marcy Tweed. Tilden's reputation was well deserved insofar as he had played a prominent part in removing Tweed from political life. But Tilden's image also was one that had been carefully nurtured since the early 1870s. It concealed more than it revealed regarding his consummate role as a political leader who had formulated an urban ideology markedly inconsistent with the needs of a socially concerned democratic city. Tilden argued for greater home rule even as it became apparent that the city's functions were increasingly tied to state and national developments. Home rule served his particular needs as attorney for those economic interests which sought and achieved virtually unrestricted control over the use of the city's most valuable natural resources—its waterfront and public streets. At the same time, Tilden, who had opposed the Civil War, continued during Reconstruction to deny national responsibility for the newly emancipated Negroes.[9]

The parallel was exact. Just as the nation missed meeting its moral commitment to greater equality for Negroes, so was it failing in developing a rational system of urban government. New York, tied to national growth, was unable by itself adequately to minister to the emerging needs of its enlarged immigrant population. It was difficult to meet the costs of a water supply system, police and fire protection, education, and public park maintenance within a municipal budget that had risen from less than $1,500,000 in 1840 to almost $35,000,000 in 1876. In addition, the city's bonded debt had skyrocketed during the same period from almost $10,500,000 to nearly twelve times that amount—about $120,000,000. What made this all possible, of course, was an increased assessed valuation of property, an increase from roughly one-quarter billion dollars to about one billion by 1876.[10]

The end of Tweed's reign (1869-1871) did not halt the inflationary trend in municipal budgeting and borrowing based on assessed valuation of property. The economic system that had emerged was intricately related to a national and international economy over which the city had no power. Nor had it any control over the still virtually unlimited immigration passing through the federal station at Castle Garden and the inflated economy sparked by the Civil War and by intense post-war speculation.[11] A serious depression had been blanketing the nation since 1873, causing much suffering among the city's predominantly working-class population.

Even the most knowledgeable and socially responsible leaders were stymied. Charles Loring Brace, founder and director of the city's most prominent social-work agency for children, described 1876 as "a year of unusual hardship for the poor, and of narrow means for the well-off." The New York Ledger observed that "despair has seized upon many; and the columns of the daily papers abound with accounts of those, who—their reason having been overthrown by their embarrassments—have sought death at their own hands." The noted philanthropist, political figure, and landowner James W. Beekman lamented that all of the city's main commercial street, Broadway, was "to-let—and we live in painful uncertainty."[12]

The depression diminished enthusiasm for the Centennial. By the winter of 1873-1874, according to one estimate, nearly 25 percent of the city's laboring force—100,000 persons—was unemployed; from 1873 to 1874 the number of families receiving charity from the private New York Association for Improving the Condition of the Poor rose from 5,292 to 24,097. In 1875 the workers of the city were told by Mayor William Wickham, reflecting the national laissez-faire ideology, that "it is . . . no part of the business of Government, . . . to furnish work for any of its citizens." The depression affected immigration, too, which declined from more than 45,000 in 1875 to less than 11,000 in 1876.[13]

Although the Philadelphia Railroad provided special trains from New York to encourage visitors to view the Exhibition by day and return to New York at night, the city's residents did not quite flock to the Exhibition. There was a feeling that the centennial site had not been adequately drained, creating an environment conducive to disease, and that the exposition was not sufficiently representative of the city's resources. "As a New-Yorker," wrote one reader of the New-York Daily Tribune, "I must confess that several visits to the Centennial Exhibition have not added to my local pride."[14]

Still, New Yorkers did support the exhibition. The noted industrialist Abram S. Hewitt endorsed the idea of a state board to "look after the interests of New York at the Centennial"; the landscape artist Jervis McEntee served as a member of the art selection committee; Frederick

Law Olmsted, co-designer of Central Park and the nation's most widely recognized environmental planner, was for a time on a "Committee on Planting and Decorating the Grounds." And during the Centennial year, the *New York Times* was printed daily on the Walter Press in Machinery Hall at the exposition.[15]

The exhibition was, after all, a celebration of the founding of a democratic republic, and New Yorkers, like others, took pride in the fact that the nation had weathered its most serious internal challenge—the Civil War—and that this had led to "a stronger confidence at home and abroad in the peaceful endurance of our free institutions." It was particularly important that New York commemorate this event, for, as Reverend Storrs reminded his audience, the antebellum city, "linked by unnumbered ties with the vast communities [of the South]," held strong Southern sympathies, and in 1860 had voted "by immense majorities" against the election of Abraham Lincoln. Nevertheless, once war came, the city had "poured its wealth and life" into the battle to preserve the Union.[16]

Conspicuously absent from the Reverend Storrs's speech, as from every other commemoration of the event, was any mention of black people, either in the nation or in the city, where they numbered slightly more than 15,000, many clustered south of Houston Street. The black population was beginning to shift to locations farther north, and their homes in Greenwich Village were being occupied by new Italian immigrants. The trend for Negroes was toward less densely settled areas, so that by 1870, 17.3 percent lived between Houston and 14th streets and 36 percent between 14th and 86th streets. The greatest growth occurred in the upper teens and lower thirties on the west side of Manhattan. By 1890 the vast majority of Negroes—four-fifths—lived above 14th Street, with a substantial increase north of 86th Street.[17]

Storrs's silence was understandable in the light of national opinion—the country expressed little interest in or hope for the social condition of black people south or north; but his reticence was conspicuous because he—like the city's poet of the Centennial, William Cullen Bryant, and its songwriter, Bayard Taylor—represented an urban social consciousness that had made New York a center for all types of social reform before, during, and after the War.[18] Clearly, some reform activities had become decidedly muted.

The loss of commitment to social equality paralleled a decline in the power of New York City's reformers to preserve through planning the unique physical character of Manhattan Island and its principal suburbs, which were increasingly important to the city's growth and development. For example, at precisely the time in 1866 that the *Evening Post* was championing the planned development of streets, parkways, parks, and other amenities, editor Bryant was urging that newly emancipated black persons also be guaranteed the right to vote, opportunity for special education, and the chance to buy inexpensive agricultural land.[19] Planning the nation's major metropolis was linked with remedying the country's most challenging social ailment, and both required enlightened governmental leadership.

Despite considerable pressure, Bryant refused to endorse Tilden in the election of 1876.[20] He was personally and professionally acquainted with Tilden and while he respected the eccentric bachelor's commitment to literary patronage, he was also aware that Tilden had consistently and successfully championed the point of view of powerful private interests which opposed comprehensive public planning, and that he was one of the authors of the Democratic Party's national policy rejecting the extension of social equality to Negroes. For example, two of the most obvious environmental blights on the city in 1876 were the decay of the waterfront, one of its most precious resources, and the developing elevated railroad, which was reshaping the social topography of Manhattan Island by permanently separating the poor and the wealthy.

The deterioration of New York's waterfront was, like its economic depression, related to national conditions. Until the Civil War, the city had housed the nation's chief shipbuilding firms. The shrinkage in ship construction paralleled the startling national decline of naval strength, both public and private. The now almost-stilled Brooklyn Navy Yard once had led the nation in ship construction. By 1870 only one-third of the country's import-export trade was carried on in American vessels.[21] Supremacy had passed to England where steam-energy technology had been integrated into ship design and governmental policy had created the structure and physical facilities needed for such a national industry. By 1882 it was estimated that of the 46,000,000 bushels of grain exported from New York City's port, not a single vessel sailed under the American flag; 60 percent of the grain was carried in British ships. There was no longer a place in the life of the city or the nation for New Yorkers like William H. Webb, whose name was virtually synonymous with shipbuilding until his retirement in 1868 at the age of fifty-six. In 1866 Webb had built the coast steam vessels *Bristol* and *Providence* which plied between New York and Newport.[22]

The forces that brought about the deterioration of New York's port did not appear overnight. Private intrusions on the waterfront were obvious by the 1850s, as was the need for comprehensive planning and for assumption by the Federal government of responsibility in this area. In 1855 a state governmental commission pointed out that private interests had encroached upon the East River more than one thousand feet on the New

York side and similarly on the Brooklyn side, narrowing the river "to a strait one-half of its original width." Egbert L. Viele, a prominent geologist and civil engineer acting as a consultant to the commission—and one of the centennial city's most astute environmental critics—warned that "the great national character of the harbor of New York [was being] threatened by private cupidity."[23]

One year later, Alexander Dallas Bache, grandson of Benjamin Franklin and probably the most important single person in the evolution of the government's policy toward science and technology in the nineteenth century, was invited to provide a comprehensive planning policy for New York City's waterfront. Given the failure of local authorities to regulate the activities of private interests, it was asserted to be "the right and duty of the federal government to protect the navigable waters of the United States." Bache argued for "public action . . . to restrain individual cupidity when it would interfere with the general welfare." But such a policy was not forthcoming locally or nationally. Consequently, not only did the viability of the port decline, but the piers and landfill, inadequately drained and receiving raw sewage, became, as Bryant's *Evening Post* noted in 1865, a vile environment and a breeding place for disease.[24]

In the 1870s two plans—one a failure, the other successful—underscored the need for governmental intervention. First, there was the proposal by General George B. McClellan to rebuild the entire waterfront area around lower Manhattan, making it available for pedestrian use by creating broad riverfront avenues and constructing a bulkhead and a system of uniform piers. This plan emerged out of McClellan's experience as an engineer and from his wartime role as the commanding general who had organized the Union Army. The plan represented a national approach born of a comprehensive view of the country's serious problems. It was not adopted.[25]

During the centennial year, after repeated efforts to eliminate the dangerous whirlpool caused by a complex of reefs at Hell Gate, a strait located at the entrance to the East River, the city was compelled to rely upon the efforts of General John Newton of the United States Corps of Engineers to explode the rocks, an activity that became one of the gala events of the year. McClellan's failure and Newton's success should have made clear the painful paradox of an international capital city attempting to function without the guidance and support of the national government. They did not. Instead, the neglect of the waterfront continued according to the pattern established in the 1850s. In 1871 the able journalist-historian James Parton wrote that "the Corporation [of New York City] own more than twenty miles of wharves and waterfront, the revenue from which does not keep the wharves in repair."[26]

Samuel Tilden played a prominent role in the exploitation of the waterfront. In 1857, as attorney for the Balance Dock Company, he contended that the docks, unlike public streets, could be made through legislation to serve private interests. He declared to the court:

The most extraordinary fallacy that I have ever heard of is this idea that because there is no power to parcel out public streets to particular uses, there is therefore no power to parcel out these basins, piers, and wharves to particular uses. It is an idea that runs off simply from the single analogy that both uses are public, without stopping to inquire into the real nature of those uses and the practical operation of the business under them.[27]

Ultimately, Tilden was successful. The issue was not only that of resisting private intrusions and monopolistic use of public resources, but, more important, that of determining what was best for the common good—public planning. Tilden's argument in the pre-Civil War period that private interests should determine the development of the waterfront was extended after the War—his earlier disclaimer notwithstanding—to the misappropriation of public streets for a new form of mass transportation, the elevated railroad.

Elevated railroads symbolized the victory of those interests, buttressed by a dominant Social Darwinism, that deemed profitmaking more important than environmental quality. Protection of the public environment depended to a large extent on the capacity of the state government to regulate the power of local interest-groups. For example, during the 1850s and 1860s urban reformers had looked to Albany to curtail the wholesale misappropriation of the public streets for private interests. Editors such as William Cullen Bryant and journalists such as James Parton had opposed the unplanned, often destructive development of horse-drawn street railways, the major form of urban transportation from 1850 until the coming of the elevated lines. "New York," wrote a visitor from abroad in 1866, "is full of Street Railways and the cars run in all directions." It was estimated that street railways carried almost 94,000,000 passengers annually while horse-drawn omnibuses—the principal means of transportation until 1850 and more carefully regulated—carried only 7,000,000 passengers.[28]

These street railways, while needed in an expanding city, without planning and supervision created congestion, noise, and accidents. What made the matter worse was the failure of the city to maintain the streets, which, even in the centennial year, below 42nd Street continued to be paved with stones, many of them "lying loose about, some almost as big as boulder stones ... imply[ing] a City in the last stage of financial decay and adversity." The cars themselves were as uncomfortable as the streets they navigated.

People were packed in as tightly as in today's subways—but those were less callous times, and such overcrowding was considered insupportable. Silks and broadcloths were ruined in attempts to enter or exit. Pocketbooks, watches, and breastpins vanished via pickpockets. The air was poisonous and it was said that a healthy person could not ride a dozen blocks without a headache. Ladies and gentlemen preferred the stages, whose fare was ten cents. The streetcars cost only six. The common people could not afford more.[29]

The state government failed to control the venality of local interests. Street-railway franchises were related to illegal street openings and intense real-estate speculation, all of which led to corruption in the city legislature. As the journalist-biographer James Parton analyzed it in 1866:

About the year 1850, when it began to be perceived that omnibuses could no longer convey the morning and evening multitudes of people, and when street railroads in many avenues were projected, the Corporation conceived the fancy that they had the right to grant the privilege of laying rails in the public streets to private companies. In fact, it was taken for granted on all hands that this was their right; and it was in connection with those railroad grants that the corruption, on a great scale, began.[30]

The *Evening Post* described how the city "was being robbed by the politicians in collusion with the twenty horse-railways." In 1860 Bryant appealed personally to Governor Edwin Morgan to veto "the franchises given away by the railroad bills ... [as] the most outrageous misappropriation of public property ... ever known in the annals of legislation on this continent."[31]

A similar battle was waged during Reconstruction over alternative uses of steam technology to create a more rapid system of urban transportation. Ever since the 1830s New York had ceased to be a walking city. In addition to movement northward on the island, rapid transit was required to serve those new areas of the city—the 23rd and 24th wards—gained when a portion of southern Westchester County—the towns of Morrisania, West Farms, and Kingsbridge—was annexed on January 1, 1874. It was popularly recognized, too, that the city of Brooklyn, with a population in 1875 of nearly a half million, could be considered a suburb of New York, as could other areas surrounding the port—Staten Island and parts of New Jersey. It was estimated in 1871, for example, that 90,000,000 persons annually used the twenty-three steam-driven ferries connecting Manhattan Island with its adjacent territories; they ran every five to ten minutes during the day and every fifteen to twenty minutes in the evening, with fares ranging from two to four cents per passenger.[32]

Commuters, like city residents, had to be transported as expeditiously as possible to their places of work. The issue, therefore, was not whether to adopt the most advanced form of technology, but, rather, how to integrate it into the existing urban fabric with minimum harm to the environment and maximum comfort for its users. There were at least five alternatives available during the centennial year: a subway, which had already proved itself in London, England; an arcade over Broadway, which would have created a vehicle-free street with rapid transit on a higher level; a concrete viaduct to contain the railway; elevated trains on the perimeters of the city; and elevated trains running above the streets.[33]

The selection of the worst environmental and social solution—the elevated train above city streets—was more a concession to private interests than a recognition of public need. Real estate investors on the west side of the island above 59th Street, an area which had not proved as attractive to developers as the east side of the city, supported the elevated. At late as 1880 squatters occupied sites on the vacant lots there. Typically, those who stood to gain from the advent of the elevated train utilized in their campaign a whole set of environmental and social arguments which publicized the elevated train as the panacea for all of the city's physical and social ills—that is, as the form of rapid transit that could be built most expeditiously, making it possible for more persons to live in healthy and attractive suburbs.[34] Of course, it did no such thing.

The elevated train did succeed in scattering population and diminishing somewhat the overcrowding in certain wards. New Yorkers who could afford it—notwithstanding the depression, there were many—could more easily move into the "suburbs" of the centennial city. But the "El's" ultimate achievement was to reward the economic interests, which, by 1877, under the leadership of Tilden and financier Cyrus W. Field, had gained judicial approval of state charters giving them exclusive use of public streets. Andrew Carnegie's expressed wish to Tilden in 1875—"I hope we shall yet bag this Elevated business"—had been realized. By 1883 there were four lines—the Second, Third, Sixth, and Ninth Avenue railways—owned by two companies—the New York Elevated and the Manhattan Company. Consolidation several years later produced the Manhattan Railroad Company, which in 1892-1893 carried almost 220,000,000 fares.[35]

The elevated train became the principal environmental symbol of the post-centennial city, reflecting its speed, noise, social divisions, and economic ruthlessness. This was to be seen in later paintings and photographs which depicted the elevated surrounded by its zones of urban poverty and hopelessness. It was the dark side of the metropolis. "They kill the streets and avenues," said one of William Dean Howells' characters, "but at least they partially hide them, and that is some comfort; and they do triumph over their prostrate forms with a savage exultation that is intoxicating.[36]

As for the argument that this use of technology would lead to a higher quality of urban life, even in the case of those who could afford to use the elevated railroad solely as a means of commutation, we have the judgment of Frederick Law Olmsted that it did no such thing. Olmsted wrote in 1879 that "the Elevated Roads and the 'uptown' movement leads as yet to nothing better. For even at Yorkville, Harlem, and Manhattanville, five or six miles away from the centre of population there are new houses of the same ridiculous jammed up pattern, as dark and noisome in their middle parts and as inconvenient throughout as if they were in parts of a besieged fortress."[37]

The success of Tilden's interest in rapid transit paralleled his political victory in 1874 as governor. Moreover, the Democratic Party's capture of the state legislature represented, among other things, the defeat of Reconstruction principles regarding Negroes. In 1868 Tilden urged the national Democratic Party not only to reject the principle of Negro suffrage, but to adopt a racist posture. He wrote:

On no other question can we be so unanimous among ourselves. On no other question can we draw so much from the other side. . . . It appeals peculiarly to the adopted citizens—whether Irish or Germans; to all the working men; to the young men just becoming voters. The Republican party contains large numbers who are naturally reached by its position on this issue; and large numbers of old Federal and old Whig adherents who do not think that any poor white or black ought to vote; and though they may go along with their party on the theory that the blacks are a counterpoise to the adopted citizens,—their hearts misgive them. The pride of a superior race and self-esteem well founded in this case—are a universal power.[38]

The position expressed by the reactionary, if urban-centered, Tilden became the majority view of the states's Democratic Party, and in 1869 the Democratic legislature overturned the preceding Republican majority's ratification of the Fifteenth Amendment. But national adoption of the amendment by three-fourths of the states in March 1870 gave New York Negroes the franchise. In 1873, a year before Tilden became governor, the state legislature passed a law prohibiting the exclusion on the basis of race or color of any person from "full and equal enjoyment of any accommodation, advantage, facility, or privilege furnished" by public conveyances, innkeepers, theaters, public schools, licensed public amusements, and other places of public amusement. The 1873 law also deleted the word "white" from prior legislation.[39]

Despite these advances in civil rights, it is evident that the execution of Reconstruction policy was not realized in New York City. The cartoons

roes carried in the *New York Ledger* during the centennial year
e caricature of black persons on theater stages were demeaning.
ce grew when in 1883 the highest court in the nation nullified the
reueral Civil Rights Act of 1875. And yet in the 1870s, probably because
conditions were worse in the South, Negroes migrated to New York City.
The 1880 census showed 20,000 Negroes living there, an increase of 50
percent for the decade. From indices such as mortality rates and from contemporary descriptions, it is clear that mainly black people occupied the
lowest economic and social positions and lived among the worst environmental conditions.[40]

While those facilities defined by the 1873 and 1881 laws of the state
remained desegregated, others were not. The Colored Home and Hospital,
located on First Avenue between 64th and 65th streets, continued to care
for "all the colored paupers of the city." The Association for the Benefit
of Colored Orphans, once housed on Fifth Avenue between 43rd and 44th
streets, had been sacked during the Civil War riots of 1863 and relocated
on 143rd Street and Tenth Avenue. The conclusion of a principal scholar
of New York City Negro history is that "despite the gains Negroes had
achieved in the schools, the courts, the transportation facilities, and the
public places of New York City, they suffered many violations of their
rights."[41]

Tilden's cold-blooded and racist appeal to prejudice was successful.
He understood race as a powerful divisive force and acted on this insight,
which allowed him to pursue his economic ends more effectively behind
its smokescreen. Race was a great focus of popular attitudes. In 1870,
a journalist in New York City, John Swinton, soon to be radicalized by the
depression into a principal spokesman for the Socialist Party, condemned
Chinese immigration on the grounds that "the deepest dividing line between men is that of *race*." Although Swinton was talking mainly about
the large Chinese immigration to California, there were, by 1876, a small
number—about 200, mostly male—of Chinese living in New York, noticeable because of native dress and language. They established homes and
businesses on Mott Street.[42]

One of the distinguishing characteristics of centennial New York was
that it was most "American" by virtue of its predominantly "foreign"
population. By 1870 about 83 percent—or 782,000 persons—were either
of foreign or mixed parentage; of this number 54 percent had been born
abroad, the vast majority having come from northern Europe. In 1875 the
three largest groups represented among the 446,043 foreign-born were the
Irish—199,084; the Germans—165,021; and those from Great Britain—
39,340. In addition, however, during the 1870s there was a numerically
small but proportionately large increase of immigrants from southern and

eastern Europe, previewing the massive "new immigration" beginning about 1882. Between 1870 and 1880, for example, the number of emigrants from Italy increased from about 2,700 to 12,220; the number from Russia grew from 1,100 to 4,500; those from Poland rose from almost 2,400 to 9,000. These groups settled primarily in the lower half of the city, occupying either converted houses or tenements erected to exploit them. Each group clustered itself, providing the nuclei for what became popularly known by the end of the century as "ghettos." Social organizations such as the Children's Aid Society early had formed branches according to ethnic concentrations. "We have all nations represented in them," Charles Loring Brace wrote to a friend, "one school for Germans, another for Italians, etc."[43]

East European Jews were one component of this new immigration. Jews numbered about 50,000 persons, including the more dominant and affluent German Jews. The Jewish community in 1852 established Mt. Sinai Hospital on 28th Street and Eighth Avenue, moving in 1872 to a new site on the corner of 66th Street and Lexington Avenue. The hospital was known for its nonsectarian and charitable service in the same way that the community was known for such self-help institutions as an orphan asylum and a home for the aged. In addition, German Jews contributed to many interdenominational charities, including the Children's Aid Society, to which a "committee of Jewish-American ladies . . . very kindly furnish[ed] warm dinners to several . . . schools."[44]

Despite an outward uniformity of language and religion, the Jewish community of New York in 1876 was segmented, with the most obvious separations occurring among German Jews who had arrived in the 1840s and 1850s, newer immigrants from Eastern Europe, and a small number of Sephardic Jews who traced their origins to the fifteenth-century expulsion from Spain and Portugal. Most Reformed Jews were of German origin. There was no single spokesman representing either the Orthodox or Reformed branches of Judaism. There were as many different communities as there were synagogues which numbered about twenty-five, including the architecturally distinctive Reformed Jewish Temple Emanu-el on the northeast corner of Fifth Avenue and 43rd Street, considered the finest example of Moorish-style architecture in America. Despite a substantial middle class—by 1870 there were an estimated 1714 Jewish firms with commercial rating—Jews were weak politically. They were Republican in a Democratic city. Tilden found it difficult even to identify a Jewish Democrat for "safe" appointment to the State Board of Charities.[45]

For some measure of security, Jewish immigrants such as labor leader Samuel Gompers, like members of other ethnic groups, belonged to mutual benefit societies for the purpose of assuring themselves and their families of medical and burial services. But Gompers, a pioneer labor leader, represented a more secular and radical Jewish tradition. Orthodox Jews, compelled to work isolated in their tenement homes in order to avoid desecrating the Sabbath, generally were not part of the union movement.[46]

Racial attitudes such as those expressed by Tilden were threatening to Eastern European immigrants. One of the reasons, presumably, why most Jews identified with the Republican party and adopted Abraham Lincoln as their hero was that they accepted the myth of Lincoln as the Great Emancipator. Prejudice, however, was so embedded in national attitudes that it appeared even in the sympathetic accounts of such late nineteenth-century reformers as Jacob Riis. And it spilled over into a discernible hostility toward immigrants that led inexorably to legislative restriction.[47]

New immigrants entered the labor force in a city that was overwhelmingly working-class. More than 70 percent of males employed in 1870 were wage-laborers and less than 10 percent could be regarded as white collar. For example, between 1870 and 1880 the number of persons from Bohemia rose from about 1,500 to slightly more than 8,000. Initially settling in lower Manhattan, they moved, by 1890, to the Upper East Side, an area embracing Yorkville. Like most ethnic groups, they were concentrated in a specific trade: cigar manufacturing.[48]

Management avoided dealing equitably with largely foreign workers, believing them to be categorically different as people. Additionally, employers insisted that workers had no legal basis for bargaining collectively; they were economic units in a presumably "free" marketplace. The result was that most workers in New York City, as elsewhere during the centennial year, were "worse off than the negroes under slavery, as depicted by Harriet Beecher Stowe."[49]

The irony was that one of the centennial themes emphasized by Reverend Storrs was the affirmation of the "ancient place of labor" and the *New York Tribune* stressed the fact that the Civil War had been fought in part over the issue of slavery versus free labor. But Storrs was also quick to add that the nation represented "industry unfettered." The growth of industry and commerce after the Civil War had paralleled a decline in organized labor. An effort on the part of workingmen to obtain the eight-hour day failed. During the Civil War, an eight-hour schedule had been allowed in the city for a short period, but in 1865 the ten-hour day was revived.[50]

The status of unions was significantly reduced as a result of the war and the economic crisis that followed. A mass march on the part of labor in 1871 failed to restore the shorter workday. The winter of 1872 was one of deteriorating economic conditions; the city was the winter headquarters of itinerant workers. There were no employment agencies or organizations to direct labor to job openings. By the winter of 1873 the economic situation was so bad that soup kitchens had to be established to feed the hungry. A mass meeting of the unemployed on December 11, 1873, at Cooper Union grew into a demonstration that "filled the city's streets and squares," a "folk-movement born of primitive need—so compelling that even politicians dared not ignore [it] ."[51]

But the politicians accessible to the marchers were city-elected—the aldermen and the mayor—and although they now listened, their power was limited; effective power rested with the state legislature. The continuing and deepening depression led to massive confrontation and repression. On January 13, 1874, the unemployed held a large outdoor meeting in Tompkins Square Park; it was broken up by the police amid large-scale violence. The employment situation worsened during the centennial year; about two-thirds of the shops manufacturing cigars closed, for example. A year later the entire city was placed under martial law when the unemployed joined in sympathy with striking railroad workers protesting a 10-percent cut in wages.[52]

Popular unrest was an obvious concern of the centennial city. In addition to the crisis of unemployment there were the deeply-etched memories of the bloody Civil War riots of 1863 and of the religious and ethnic-based battles between Protestants and Roman Catholics from Ireland in 1870 and 1871. The violence that was part of the history and experiential reality of New York was captured in publications by participants in the daily life of the metropolis—Charles Loring Brace, in *The Dangerous Classes of New York* (1872), and Joel Tyler Headley, in *The Great Riots of New York* (1873). In addition, there was the precedent of the Paris Commune of 1871, the bloodiest urban uprising since the French Revolution of 1789 and a serious effort to establish a socialist society in the capital of an industrialized nation.[53]

Centennial New York also had a radical tradition. A small group of New Yorkers, mostly German Socialists who since 1868 had been affiliated with the First European International led by Karl Marx, took a prominent part in all of the labor demonstrations of the 1870s—which included carrying the "Red" flag and a banner with the French slogan "Liberty, Equality, and Fraternity" and sympathizing with the Parisian communards who were tried and executed. If radical rhetoric was flamboyant, their program was quite rational. After a careful census of the unemployed in one section of the city, radicals recommended employment on public works, financial maintenance of the needy for one week, and elimination of eviction for nonpayment of rent. The fact that the International dissolved in 1876 owing to internal dissension—to be replaced by the Socialist Labor Party in 1877—did nothing to allay the fear of New York's Superintendent of Police, who continued to urge his men to spy on labor meetings, warning that German and French revolutionaries were "doing their utmost to inflame the workingman's mind."[54]

Labor's power in the city would be determined by political power, not by social ideology. Centennial New York had representatives of all of the competing elements within the national labor movement—including the Knights of Labor, who insisted on an oath of secrecy. As Samuel Gompers phrased it, "New York City was the cradle of the modern American labor movement." Gompers, as one of the principal organizers of the American Federation of Labor, understood clearly how best to employ labor's strength—by pressure on state legislatures in which bloc-voting counted.[55]

The tactics of the Workingmen's Assembly, organized in 1865 to oppose legislation that would have made strikes conspiracies, were even more direct. The Assembly managed to elect some twenty state legislators by 1880. And when a recipient of labor support forgot his obligations—as in 1876, when one of them failed to press for an eight-hour day—he was reminded bluntly that he had been elected "as a workingman and as a workingman's friend" and should he lose worker confidence, "your small majority of 1.60 percent will be easily reversed to the other side when the opportunity favors."[56]

One of the principal obstacles to labor organization was the large number of workers in tenement houses. When the effort to unionize them failed, the unions turned their attention to outlawing tenement sweatshops on the basis of maintaining environmental standards. In this they had the support of the city's socially powerful reformers, who saw the tenement-factory as an evil, particularly for children and women. Such noted reformers as Brace, Olmsted, Elisha Harris, and Dorman Eaton advocated "the compulsory education of every child" and the prohibition of child labor in factories. They opposed the tenement house as a place for work or dwelling. "Cheap labor," wrote an officer of the Children's Aid Society, "however desirable the manufacturers may think it—in order to compete with foreign pauper-labor—is too costly for this country."[57]

The growing power of unions within the city—100,000 in 100 unions by 1883—and the frequency of strikes and fear of violence, combined with the support of an articulate group of reformers, made for an effective force and brought forth an increasing number of bills to achieve some of labor's goals. A state law of 1883 forbidding the manufacture of cigars in tenements was declared unconstitutional in 1886. But that same year labor displayed considerable power in organizing a third political party supporting the popular, influential, and "radical" economist Henry George for the mayoralty. Partly as a response to this expression of discontent and power there was passed and enforced in 1886 the first successful bill limiting the labor of children and women in factories. A year later the law was expanded to include the protection of all workers from certain hazards found in all factories.[58]

The reformers' support of labor was substantial, but it was not uncritical. They endorsed measures like compulsory education, but not to strengthen the unions or limit the labor supply. Their concern was rather with the future of the city, and it was inspired by the same moral imperatives which had motivated their opposition to slavery and their support of Reconstruction. They believed that the strength of the Republic lay in the health, welfare, and good will of its citizenry. William E. Dodge, a noted philanthropist and contributor to the Young Men's Christian Association, founded in 1852, epitomized the reformers' conviction that "the real security, under God, is in the virtue and intelligence of the people."[59]

The large ethical purposes of the civic reformers often conflicted with the special interests of labor. Unions, for example, opposed such reformer-sponsored measures as employing prisoners in productive labor. The Children's Aid Society, an organ of the civic reformers, charged that the restrictive practices of the unions shut out many poor youths from the trades by limiting apprenticeships.[60] In part, the reformers' high-minded program concealed a moral hostility to the new urban and industrial character of the city, but it was nonetheless a genuine effort to meet serious urban needs and to set high standards of performance for public officials.[61]

Civic reform was pursued through private as well as governmental agencies. These included the Society for the Prevention of Cruelty to Children, founded in 1875 by Henry Bergh, a former shipbuilder and diplomat; the Society for the Prevention of Cruelty to Animals, organized in 1866 also under Bergh's sponsorship; and two eccentric brainchildren of Anthony Comstock: the Society for the Suppression of Vice, incorporated in 1873, and the Society for the Prevention of Crime, established in the centennial year. There is surely something odd about the delegation by the Federal government of power to Comstock to monitor the mails in search of obscene material, and more than a touch of the ridiculous in his fanatical crusade to suppress pornography, gambling, and contraceptive devices; but Comstock was also concerned with such matters as fraudulent medical advertising and the adulteration of foods. The city's consumers, and particularly its poor and uneducated, needed some protection from unscrupulous advertising and shoddy merchandise, both of which grew in scope with advances in technology and the impersonalization of marketing.[62] This could only have been done effectively by the federal government.

An important national reform precedent was the creation of the United States Sanitary Commission, an organization conceived in New York in 1861 by women like Louisa Lee Schuyler, a pioneer in social work, and

Dr. Elizabeth Blackwell, the country's first woman physician, to furnish medical supplies and services to the Union Army. Directed during its first two years by Frederick Law Olmsted, the commission demonstrated to those New Yorkers most actively involved in its work the need for private institutions to help solve national and municipal problems.[63] One outgrowth of this conviction was the formation of the Union League Clubs whose founding principles were set forth by Olmsted in 1862. The club's organizers included men who had been prominent in the work of the Sanitary Commission: Oliver Wolcott Gibbs, a distinguished chemist; Cornelius Rae Agnew, an eminent opthalmologist; Henry W. Bellows, the city's most prominent Unitarian minister; and George Templeton Strong, a leading attorney and Episcopalian.[64]

Despite its élitist character—and perhaps because of it—members of the league urged such measures as the extension of public education as a necessary device for assimilating the city's large immigrant population. By 1870 the city's public school system enrolled over 237,000 students and employed more than 2,400 teachers, approximately 2,000 of them women. In 1869 the city approved the establishment of the New York Normal College. It opened in 1873 and became an important national center for teacher training. Located between 68th and 69th streets, and bounded by Fourth and Lexington avenues, it was the predecessor of today's Hunter College.[65] The city's first public institution of higher education was the Free Academy. Founded in 1847 and little more than a high school at the time, it had been converted in 1866 into the College of the City of New York, where "every child *may* arrive at a reading of Xenophon in the original Greek, and at a comprehension of the calculus."[66]

Public higher education went to the heart of the reform ideology. Jeffersonian principles required the removal of all barriers to the training of talent that might be employed in the public interest. But the venture did not go uncriticized. The city already possessed competent private institutions—such as Columbia College, on 49th Street, and the University of the City of New York (New York University) on Washington Square—with programs that duplicated those offered at the public college. And the City College did not seem to be doing very well. Despite a competitive entrance examination, the graduating class of 1879 numbered only about 50 students of about 650 admitted.[67]

The Children's Aid Society, founded in 1853 by Charles Loring Brace, was concerned with those children who were too poor to afford the luxury of full-time education. Brace's solution was a variety of devices intended to improve the children's lot within the framework of the "Christian family." He proposed industrial and night schools—a scheme later adopted by the Board of Education; half-day school programs for children engaged in street trades such as selling newspapers, shining shoes, and sweeping crosswalks; an early form of day-care center to enable older children responsible for rearing siblings to attend school by leaving their "little ones temporarily under the charge of a trusted woman"; and the resettlement of poor homeless children to the western part of the country. Between 1853 and 1893, the relocation program involved almost 86,000 children.[68]

Principles of social work similar to those pioneered by Brace were adopted by the philanthropic institutions of the city's largest religious group, the Roman Catholics, and by the United Hebrew charities, formed in 1874. By the centennial year there were about fifty Roman Catholic churches in the city and several important charitable institutions, including the Orphan Asylum of St. Vincent De Paul, founded in 1858 on West 39th Street, and the Society for the Protection of Destitute Roman Catholic Children, established in 1863 at West Farms. Each of these institutions received public tax funds and in separate ways responded to urban problems with remedies resembling Brace's. The Orphan Asylum emphasized secular primary education and complemented study with training in a craft. The Society for the Protection of Destitute Roman Catholic Children stressed a family-like rural setting as well as a practical education. Although the Catholic Church had an established parochial school system, Brace believed that his proposal to develop half-time school laws "would secure . . . the co-operation of the Catholic priests . . . inasmuch as attendance at half-time Church Schools would be sufficient to show that the child was not a vagrant."[69]

New York City's reformers were environmentalists and therefore particularly critical of the city's miserable housing conditions, which they linked with disease and crime. In an annual report for 1876 the Children's Aid Society noted:

The evils our Society deals with are deep-seated. They spring especially from the way in which our working classes are compelled to live. There never can be a healthy and moral condition of the poor, while tenement house life continues as it is in New York. Families cannot be crowded by the scores into a single house, with the young exposed to every bad influence; health sapped by foul air and unventilated rooms; privacy and family life destroyed; delicacy almost made impossible, without the children growing up naturally as vagrants, beggars, and outcasts.[70]

Housing was a topic discussed at the Philadelphia Exhibition by one of New York's leading environmental reformers, Dr. Elisha Harris. A specialist in public health and a former member of the U. S. Sanitary Commission, Harris was convinced that physical and social problems were best cured by preventive measures. The Tenement House Law of 1867 was one result of his and fellow reformers' efforts.[71] But it was quite clear by the centennial year that more radical measures were required than a largely unenforced law.[72] "Apartment houses," built on the style of French "flats," were too expensive to meet the needs of the city's masses. Equipped with the latest technology—steam heat, elevators, and even internal telegraph—apartment houses like The Stuyvesant, on east 18th Street, and the Haight Building, at 15th Street and Fifth Avenue, were beyond the reach of the poor and even of the middle-class New Yorker.[73]

An attempt to attract philanthropists to build model tenements failed,[74] as did an imaginative proposal in 1876 of an architect, Edward Potter, to create a series of lanes between the city's streets on which small individual homes might be erected.[75] The Tenement House Law of 1879 limited the amount of land on any lot that could be used for a building and required a window for every bedroom; but this statute led only to the infamous "dumb-bell" apartments. They provided narrow air shafts to comply with the law but otherwise increased population density and produced worse living conditions than before. Frederick Law Olmsted described the tenement situation in 1879 as "a calamity more to be deplored than the yellow fever at New Orleans because [it is] more impregnable; more than fogs of London, the cold to St. Petersburg or the malaria of Rome because [it is] more constant in its tyranny."[76]

The most visible evidence of the evils of tenement living was the incidence of disease. By 1876, half the city's population lived in tenements, and 65 percent of New York's mortalities occurred in these dwellings. Children fared even worse: tenements were the scene of about 90 percent of childhood deaths.[77] Rebuffed in their attempts to improve housing, the reformers sought to relieve the distress of the sick poor in the hospitals. Noting the crowded wards and unhygienic conditions in Bellevue, the city's principal hospital for the poor, Louisa Schuyler proposed a new profession for women—nursing. Bellevue's nursing school opened in 1873 with six students. By the centennial year, it was "the headquarters in the United States of the modern and enlightened system of nursing, and not only trains nurses but acts as a normal school also." Bellevue was supplying nurses for other hospitals and even other cities, and its system was adopted by Boston, Philadelphia, Brooklyn, and New Haven.[78]

Dr. Elizabeth Blackwell, a friend of Louisa Schuyler, built her Infirmary for Women and Children on Second Avenue and 7th Street rather than uptown so that it would be accessible to the residents of "the most extensive poor district in town." A medical college for women, opened in 1868 in connection with the infirmary, addressed itself directly to the needs of the city's tenement dwellers. Blackwell's plan of medical education sought to utilize tenement houses . . . for a sort of hygienic hospital practice . . . [and to] divide the students into classes who would spend a certain time daily in visiting these houses, to observe, report and remedy their defective hygienic conditions—reporting to the Prof[essor] of Hygiene, who would organize and direct their work.[79]

This approach saw medical practice as originating in the home of the client and requiring an understanding of that environment as part of the cure. Dr. Blackwell hoped that in a city housing some of the worst slums of any Western nation it would be possible "to turn the young doctors out thorough practical hygienists; to convert the great army of the medical profession into active agents for diffusing hygienic knowledge; and to direct the impulses of pecuniary reward and scientific investigation into researches on the meaning and condition of Health" and not only into those dealing with disease and death.[80]

The defeat of environmental planning was one of the most conspicuous failures of New York City during the centennial years; it pointed up the power of economic interests to evade the law and to subvert even the best-designed legislation to suit their own purposes. Certainly the city had a model piece of legislation in the Metropolitan Health Bill of 1865, drafted by Dorman Eaton, a young public-minded attorney. The bill, defeated that year, was passed in 1866 in the face of a cholera epidemic. By the late 1850s there had developed a sufficient empirical understanding of epidemic disease to persuade most scientists and publicists of the need for a reorganization of the city's preventive health measures. It was believed that the principal source of epidemic disease was a filthy environment aggravated by population density. As the *New York Times* put it, "every street which is left with its seething, rotting mass of slime, gorging the carriage-way from curb to curb is a hot-bed of disease."[81]

The new centralized Board of Health created a Metropolitan Sanitary District with unusual police powers over a very large area, including the counties of New York, Kings, Richmond, and Westchester, and a portion of Queens. The bill became a model for many other American cities; contemporary observers believed that its implementation averted large-scale epidemics. One commentator wrote in 1882: "So efficient has been the Board of Health and so skillful in its management, that since the cholera in 1865, that disease or scarcely any other has appeared in the city as an epidemic."[82]

But the establishment of the Board did not lead to a lowering of mortality rates among inhabitants of tenement houses. In 1873 the death rate in poor districts was 37.72 per 1,000 while that in more affluent districts was 20.44 per 1,000. The incidence of illness and death varied, of course, among different age groups and seasonally, but disease was particularly hard on children during the summer.[83] The Board's power over sanitary conditions in tenement houses was usually circumvented. The incidence of socially-rooted diseases, such as tuberculosis, continued to rise, although the casualty rate was less visible than that wrought by epidemics such as cholera. The tenement house problem was sustained by an unregulated housing market. The amount of capital invested was so large and the interest paid to owners in the form of rent so high that, as one critic wrote, "it may be almost an impossibility to accomplish any reform." Charles Loring Brace bitterly denounced "the profits made under such a system . . . wrung from the misfortune of the poor."[84]

Perhaps the most famous—and most caricatured—aspect of the reform movement was its dedication to civil service reform.[85] The fruits of that movement were not realized in New York until 1884, when New York State passed a civil service law requiring cities to establish civil service commissions;[86] but the men who worked to achieve that legislation were articulate advocates of such a measure during the centennial years both on a national and local level. To them, the connection between the deteriorating public services of the nation and the city and an incompetent and patronage-ridden civil service was inextricable. George W. Curtis, editor of *Harper's Weekly*, used the columns of that publication to plead the cause. In 1877 he helped to organize the New York Civil Service Association and later served as its president. In 1881 he was to lead the National Civil Service Reform League, formed after the assassination of President James A. Garfield.[87]

In his efforts at political reform Curtis was joined by men like Edward L. Godkin, editor of *The Nation,* and Frederick Law Olmsted, the codesigner of Central Park. Olmsted's frustrations with politicians during the course of the park's construction made him a strenuous advocate of governmental reform. In one of his frequent confrontations with the appointed Board of Commissioners of Central Park he decried the fact that only one out of ten persons employed through patronage was qualified and that the cost to the city was "200,000 out of every million expended for labor on the park."[88] In the Presidential election of 1876 Olmsted refused to support Tilden because of the governor's opposition to civil service reform. Tilden held the same decentralized laissez-faire views that he had during the Civil War. "There is today," Olmsted wrote, "the same difference between Mr. Tilden and myself [as during the Civil War] —a difference which has justified the killing of a great many thousand men and the waste of a vast amount of honest industry."[89] At the Philadelphia Exhibition Olmsted displayed not his work on Central Park but a plan for Buffalo—a comprehensive scheme of parks, public squares, parkways, and insane asylum grounds.[90] By 1880—four years before the creation of the city's civil service commission—Olmsted had left New York for Boston, sick of the former's politics and disappointed with its failure to make long-range plans for the city's needs. In 1882 he published an exposé of sorts, *Spoils of the Park,* widely read by Civil Service reformers.[91]

But politicians—not reformers—governed the city. New York in 1876 was under the control of the Democratic Party, led by men like Tilden; the new leader of Tammany Hall, John Kelly; businessmen like William Havemeyer; and industrialists like Abram S. Hewitt and Cyrus Field.[92] The machinery of the party functioned efficiently to serve social as well as political purposes: it integrated new immigrants into the city's public life and it assisted working people to secure jobs. The party not only put the faithful on the city's payroll—some 10,000 persons were in the municipal employ by 1880—but it also had at its disposal numerous places dependent upon government contracts for paving of streets, cleaning of streets, and maintenance of gaslights.[93]

The party benefited, too, from the weakness of divided municipal authority. Despite an elective mayoralty—since 1834—executive authority resided in the legislature, the Common Council. Until 1849 the council, through joint committees of its two branches, the Aldermen and Assistant Aldermen, "dictated even the details of administration."[94] Municipal authority was further diffused by the creation, between 1849 and 1869, of a variety of state-appointed commissions to supervise such new urban services as water supply, police and fire protection, and park construction and maintenance. The state, in effect, was exercising indirect rule over the city, a role upheld in the courts and incorporated in a municipal charter that had been revised at least six times between 1830 and 1873.[95]

Critics, however, generally directed their fire neither at the weak governmental structure nor at the economic basis of politics, but at the system of universal white male suffrage—instituted in 1826—which, they insisted, was the cause of the city's political ills. "The great City of New York," one hostile visitor observed in 1868, "is ruled by sans culottes and those who cater to them; ignorant and depraved men have the control of the municipal affairs of the City."[96] Ironically, it was not until the Democratic machine reached its peak in power and corruption that Boss Tweed forced through a new charter in 1870 which gave greater authority to the mayor but not enough to permit him to manage the city's government. The city's chief executive could remove department heads for malfeasance only by a court proceeding.[97] When the Republicans, who controlled the state government, imposed the charter of 1873—by which the city was governed in its centennial year—they gave the governor the power to approve the removal of city officials for inefficiency or wrongdoing.

At least one wholesome reform was contained in the new charter: official business was brought under public scrutiny by a requirement that all laws, votes, and public contracts be published in the *City Record,* New York's official journal.[98] If the Republican-controlled state government did no more to improve municipal politics, it may well have been because the leaders of both parties had reached an accommodation permitting them to share the spoils of New York City's corrupt administration.[99]

Under Tammany Hall's continued control, New York remained notoriously corrupt and inefficient. Abetting Tammany's rule was the system of gerrymandered wards, the boundaries of which had not been changed since the 1850s despite massive shifts in population. The kind of corruption the ward system made possible was evidenced in 1868, when the number of ballots cast in an election was 8 percent larger than the total number of eligible voters. In 1886 all but two members of the city's Board of Aldermen were indicted for bribery in connection with the granting of a street-railway franchise for lower Broadway.[100] Whether as cause or consequence of such municipal misgovernment, the city failed to attract into its administration the kind of talented individuals who were busily at work making New York "a great commercial, imperial city," whose growth was an "exponent of the rise and progress of the republic."[101]

While America's share of the world's carrying trade declined, foreign commerce as a whole continued to rise; and half of the nation's total—some $850,000,000's worth—was handled through New York City. In 1876 the Collector of the Port was Chester A. Arthur, and his salary—which was based on volume—was twice that of any other collector and $4,000 more than that of his superior, the Secretary of the Treasury.[102] The most noticeable evidences of commercial wealth were the buildings housing the retail establishments of Alexander T. Stewart. An immigrant from Ireland in 1818, Stewart by the mid-century had organized the largest retail store in the world. Extending from Chambers Street to Reade Street, the magnificent white marble Stewart emporium resembled a royal palace. In 1861 Stewart commissioned the architect John Kellum to design a new store on Broadway and 10th Street. The eight-story building, of innovative prefabricated cast iron, occupied an area equal to fifteen acres. By 1870 it was serving from 15,000 to 50,000 customers and averaging daily sales of $80,000. [103]

Stewart's success resulted from new retailing techniques: uniform and clearly marked prices, low pressure salesmanship, and high quality merchandise—all of which assured customer good will.[104] Rivaling Stewart's establishment was Rowland Hussey Macy's store, located at the corner of Sixth Avenue and 14th Street. Its distinction stemmed from the variety of products offered, the selection of merchandise growing with each enlargement of the store. When a second building was added in 1869, toys were introduced, and then house furnishings, soda water, stationery, and a ladies' restaurant.[105]

The large department stores came increasingly to depend on advertising; both grew together, and by 1876 New York was the nation's advertising capital. Ads appeared not only in newspapers and magazines but in unusual forms: signs-on-the-back, decorated gas illuminations, on blotting paper and on curb stones. Commerce bred a new dynamic partner, the advertising agency, of which there were no less than forty-two in existence by 1869. A leading figure was J. Walter Thompson, who in 1878 took control of Carlton and Smith, a firm specializing in publicizing religious periodicals, and converted it into an agency for general magazine advertising. By 1880 New York's merchants were spending at least $10,000,000 annually on advertising.[106]

The growth of the advertising industry was linked with the city's development as the nation's publishing center. By 1871 New Yorkers had available 13 daily newspapers, 240 weekly papers, and 110 monthly magazines. The leading dailies were the *Herald, Times, Tribune, World, Sun, Evening Post, Ledger,* and *Journal of Commerce,* all concentrated around Printing-House Square, just east of City Hall. The newspapers sought to appeal to readers beyond the city's confines—the *Tribune* published frequently on gardening and farming; so did the city's book and magazine publishers. Four of the nation's principal book publishers were located in the city: Harper's, Putnam's, Appleton's, and Scribner's; and so was the leading publisher of technical books on architecture, astronomy, chemistry, and photography—David Van Nostrand.[107]

For those New Yorkers who could not purchase the output of the book publishers, there were available the city's unique reference libraries: the Astor Library, grown from its original 70,000 volumes in 1853 to 200,000 in 1881, and the Lenox Library, opened in 1877 in a brand-new million-dollar building. Smaller than the Astor, the Lenox collection specialized in "rare and precious . . . memorials of the typographic art." The existence of these two private libraries spurred interest in a public circulating library system, leading to the establishment in 1880 of the New York Free Circulating Library. In 1888 there were two branches, one on Bond Street, the other, a German-language branch, on Second Avenue.[108]

Libraries were attractive adornments, but the substance of the city's national reputation lay in its productive capacities. In 1860 New York passed Philadelphia as the country's leading manufacturing center, and by 1880 it contained 11,162 factories employing 218,000 persons and producing goods valued at $448,209,248. The eight largest industries were clothing; meatpacking; printing and publishing; tobacco and cigars; the refining of lard, sugar, and molasses; furniture; baking; and machinery.[109]

Measured by value, however, smaller industries made a larger contribution to the city's prosperity: the fabrication of pianos, the production of lead pencils, and the manufacture of mail envelopes—to mention only some of the most innovative. By 1876 Steinway & Sons had achieved such distinction for its pianos that it received a special award at the Philadelphia Exhibition for "the highest degree of excellence in all their styles."[110] The pencil industry had been introduced from Germany in 1855 by Eberhard Farber, and by 1877 the company—located at 718-720 Broadway—manufactured a variety of stationery supplies and had its own cedar yard and sawmill in Florida. The leader in the mail envelope business was Samuel Raynor. His automated machines enabled one girl to turn out 25,000 envelopes a day, and by 1882 the firm was producing 700 different styles of envelopes at the rate of 200,000 a year.[111]

The availability of envelopes gave impetus to the mails; by 1870, over 100 tons of mail were being processed in the city daily. The single post office, long housed in the Middle Dutch Church on Nassau Street, had become outdated; and in 1875 it was replaced by a new main post office at the southern tip of City Hall Park. By 1883 there were 19 substations and 1,000 lamp post boxes, collections being made from twelve to twenty times throughout the day and night in all parts of the city below 59th Street.[112]

The improved mail service facilitated the city's extensive banking business and the operations of the two national financial exchanges that were headquartered in New York. The city was the nation's banking capital, a role it had begun to exercise during the Civil War. By 1870 its 56 national banks and its 32 savings banks—usually located at street corners—gave it preeminence over its pre-Civil War rivals, Philadelphia and Boston. A Clearing House Association facilitated exchanges between banks and the settlement of balances. By 1868, an average of $100,000,000 daily was being cleared through the Association. The Stock Exchange, founded in 1817, was the major center of the nation's security transactions. The volume of its business increased appreciably as the opening of the Atlantic Cable in 1866 and the introduction of the ticker machine extended and speeded up the transmission of financial information; Western Union operated the exchange's telegraph service, thus providing a national network of news. The Panic of 1873 and the subsequent depression ruined some of the Exchange's most important members, but the revival of the 1880s stimulated transactions of between 300,000 and 400,000 shares daily and made the market-value of a seat on the Board over $25,000.[113]

Fortunes were made on the city's exchanges and from its factories and commerce, but millionaires were produced also by real estate speculation. It was estimated that in 1868 about one-tenth of Manhattan's real property—assessed at over a half billion dollars—was owned by just ten men. In a few more generations, it was felt, the heirs of these ten might own the whole island. So huge was the concentration of wealth in the city that sixty-seven persons could among them purchase all of New York's exports and imports for any single year. Foreign critics could point to New York City, the national center where "every day the rich are growing richer and the poor poorer," as exemplifying the failure of democracy.[114]

What irked reformers was not so much the acquisition of wealth but its ostentatious display, evidenced by the opulent mansions of men like Stewart and the heirs of Commodore Cornelius Vanderbilt—the railroad tycoon whose estate was valued at over $100,000,000 upon his death in 1877.[115] These homes reflected a concern with private status often gained at the expense of the public interest. Matching the extravagance of the exterior of the mansions that lined Central Park along Fifth Avenue from 46th Street to 72nd Street were the luxurious interiors—elaborate stone and wood carvings, paintings, sculpture, tapestries, and upholstery, as well as stained glass, silverware, and jewelry probably purchased from the city's prime emporium of elegance, Tiffany's on Union Square.[116]

The technology that made possible the fortunes and the mansions of the wealthy were at times employed to provide the city with distinctive public structures as well: Grand Central Depot, a joint terminus of three railway lines, opened in 1875;[117] Cooper Union, the workingman's college, with a free reading-room and a public lecture-hall large enough to accommodate 3,000 persons;[118] and—most dramatic—the Brooklyn Bridge, begun in 1869 and completed in 1883. In the centennial year its magnificent twin towers were already rising on the horizon; a section of its suspension cables was considered novel enough to warrant display at the Philadelphia Exhibition. The bridge's designer, John A. Roebling, hoped that the great towers would "be ranked as national monuments." More practically, the bridge linked Manhattan and Brooklyn by three forms of separated transportation: trains, horse-drawn vehicles, and pedestrian traffic via an "elevated promenade."[119]

To some, the bridge was a symbol of civic hope as well as a monument to the nation's technological genius. When Abram S. Hewitt, the socially-conscious steel manufacturer, spoke at the bridge's opening, he used the occasion to urge his fellow New Yorkers to elect to office "good men" who would oversee the city's political welfare as the bridge's engineers promoted its technological progress.[120] Hewitt's hope was unrealistic, however. The kind of social planning he called for was initiated—if at all— by private men of wealth, not public officials. Between 1871 and 1881 the Steinway piano firm built in Astoria, Queens, a model industrial village complete with a modern factory, graded streets, sidewalks, trees, individual homes, a school, a park, a public bath, and a church. William Steinway overlooked the community from his mansion located on the crest of a hill just east of the factory.[121] Alexander Stewart constructed a planned residential community in Garden City, Long Island. Linked by railroad to Manhattan, it included homes, streets, trees, a central park, a hotel, and a railway station. By 1876 nearly one hundred homes were available for rent—Stewart would not sell them—and seven brick stores fronted the railroad station.[122]

Sadly, these two residential communities, built with private fortunes acquired in New York City, were of higher environmental quality than anything being done either privately or publicly within the centennial city itself. New York's two most distinctive planned environments dated from an earlier generation's efforts and embodied a higher level of urban idealism than that of 1876. Gramercy Park, laid out in 1831, was a handsome urban residential enclave modeled after similar developments in England.[123] But it remained an isolated private effort unrepeated in any other part of the city. An example of the area's social isolation was Samuel Tilden's home, facing the Gramercy Park, completed in 1874 by the architect Calvert Vaux, co-designer of Central Park. Governor Tilden, who understood the social realities of the city, had built into the Gramercy Park facade rolling steel doors and a tunnel to the street in back for speedy exit.[124]

The other notable environment was Central Park, designed by Frederick Law Olmsted and Calvert Vaux in 1858. By the centennial year it had won international recognition as a prototype of urban open-space planning incorporating the nation's most advanced technology. The basis of this park's physical success was meticulous planning. "Every foot of the park's surface, every tree and bush, as well as every arch, roadway and walk," wrote Olmsted, "has been fixed where it is with a *purpose*."[125] By 1875 more than 400,000 trees and shrubs had been planted at a cost of more than $1,000,000 within the park's 820 acres of land and water. Even the prehistoric gneiss-rock outcroppings bloomed with native cacti planted there.[126]

The park's social success derived from the democratic idealism of its designers. It was meant to be a harmonizing influence in the city—a space where people of all classes and ethnic groups could meet. And it became that. Olmsted wrote that it was a setting where "the poor and rich come together . . . in larger numbers than anywhere else, and enjoy what they find in it in more complete sympathy than they enjoy anything else together." During the centennial year it was estimated that as many as 100,000 persons visited the park on a single day—about 10,000,000 annually. "The one finest, grandest, and most beautiful thing yet accomplished by this [American] people," wrote one visitor, "is the *Central Park*." It was, one Englishman noted simply in his diary, "a wonderful place."[127]

The centennial year marked the decline of such public planning. Stewart's Garden City development evoked the admiration of frustrated environmentalists such as Brace and Olmsted. Brace saw this suburban affluent development as a sensible means of relieving the city of its over-crowding—as a prototype of "laborers' villages in the suburbs."[128] Olmsted viewed Stewart's effort as a miniature of his own plans for the entire city—a comprehensive scheme of integrated roads, parks, promenades, and homes. But when Olmsted presented such plans—for Staten Island and for the 23rd and 24th wards of the city—they were rejected.[129] The blame could be placed as much on the city's men of wealth as on its unconcerned public officials. The ten richest men in New York, William Cullen Bryant insisted, could, with their wealth, "sweep away the debasing tenement house system, or shatter the Tammany Ring." Instead, another critic observed bitterly, "What the money does is simply to get more money."[130]

The criticism was not entirely justified. Private philanthropy was generous enough, but not in those areas of the city's life considered of prime importance by men like Olmsted. Private wealth sustained the city's many hospitals and numerous churches and financed the construction of the new Metropolitan Opera House—to the tune of $20,000 from each of twenty patrons. The new opera house replaced the older Academy of Music, and the change was a sad manifestation of the cultural stratification of the city under the impact of new wealth. The Academy, built in 1854, had no private boxes; the Metropolitan provided such accommodations for those who could afford them. There were 122 private boxes in the completed opera house, each with a spacious parlor; the remainder of the 6,000 seats would be filled more democratically.[131]

Other institutions of high culture were more available to the city's growing population: the Metropolitan Museum of Art and the American Museum of Natural History. The former was initiated by a petition from American citizens abroad who hoped that New York City could establish a center like that in South Kensington, London, for a permanent collection of art as well as an institution for improving popular taste in design. When the museum was opened in 1879, at 82nd Street on the edge of Central Park, it was designed as part of a park/museum complex. Calvert Vaux was the architect for both the Metropolitan and its sister institution on the western side of Central Park, the American Museum of Natural History, which opened at about the same time. Under its first director, Albert S. Bickmore, a geologist and zoologist, the natural history museum vigor-ously pursued the dual objective of scientific research and public educa-tion.[132]

The new museums, it was hoped, would provide some of the whole-some forms of recreation that would divert lower-class New Yorkers from drinking and gambling. (There were in 1868-1869, it was estimated, 7,000 licensed "grog shops" in the city and 2,500 gambling places.)[133] Reformers were persuaded that alternatives were needed to divert the poor from the saloons; Sabbath-day restrictions would have to be removed in order to promote the health and welfare of the working-class population.[134] Charles Loring Brace found his model in London. It was "grand," he noted, to have the art galleries open to the public without charge, and the parks were one of London's "best moral agencies." Every art gallery and museum, in his opinion, was to be open on Sunday and every rum shop closed.[135]

New York did not entirely follow Brace's advice. The city's wide range of theaters—about twenty—included Gilmore's Garden, where light opera could be enjoyed on Sundays along with the purchase of liquor, Niblo's Garden for musicals, and Tony Pastor's for minstrel shows. There was also a German-language theater on the Bowery. Most of the theaters were located around Union Square. On the lighter side, New Yorkers until 1875 could take advantage of Phineas T. Barnum's museum and menagerie at the Hippodrome. After that date, Barnum's energies went into his new three-ring traveling circus. The sports-minded could enjoy big league baseball—already dubbed the "national game," gloves-on boxing bouts, walking races, and rifle-shooting matches. For the active sportsmen there was baseball, bicycling—the Bicycling Club of New York was organized in 1879—and ice- and roller-skating, both on rinks.[136]

Horse-racing—like polo, yachting, and football—was an upper-class sport.[137] Wealthy horseowners were organized into the American Jockey Club, formed in 1866 and located in Jerome Park at Fordham; and the Coney Island Jockey Club, organized in 1879 by a younger group of the fashionable set and located near the ocean in Brooklyn. Symbolic of the link between wealth and racing was the president of the American Jockey Club—August Belmont, one of the city's most prominent bankers. Jerome Park had the finest race track in the world, it was said; the best stables were represented at Coney Island.[138]

For the majority of New Yorkers, however, Coney Island meant not a preserve for the rich but a playground for all. Bathing and spas had been a traditional therapeutic for the upper classes, who had long sought out Saratoga Springs upstate, Rockaway and Fire Island on Long Island, Long Branch and Cape May in New Jersey, Newport in Rhode Island, and various places along the Hudson to cure ailments ranging from boils to nervous prostration.[139] By the year of the Centennial the development of Coney Island had made the seaside available to New Yorkers of lesser means. Once a hangout for toughs and hoodlums, there were in 1877 at least three modern hotels there to provide "seaside pleasure with modern improvements." Between 1869 and 1877 five railway lines were built across Brooklyn to the ocean; there were piers to receive arrivals by ferry.[140]

Those who came for the surf and the sand also could be entertained by the best orchestras and military bands in the country, by outdoor theater, and by the merry-go-round, flying swings, shooting galleries, weight-guessers, and fortune-tellers. In 1884 Coney Island opened the world's first amusement railway, and each year new manufactured magic was introduced as the hotels competed for business, adding landscaping, statuary, and electric lights, as well as yachting and boating facilities. For a splurge, families could dine at the large Victorian hotels, such as the Sea Beach Palace, which could seat 15,000 at one time. By 1882 nearly 5,000,000 persons were visiting Coney Island annually, spending $9,000,000 on its pleasures.[141]

Planners like Olmsted looked approvingly on the Coney Island development. It was for him "the only notable instance in this country in which capital has been used with . . . boldness in advance of demand."[142] It was an isolated example of private enterprise investing in a vital public need. Such planning was virtually nonexistent in the public sector. For example, when Olmsted and Vaux, as public servants, were asked in 1873 to plan a park on Morningside Heights, they resisted on the grounds that the city did not need another pastoral-type park in that location. The principal proponents were real-estate developers who had learned from the experience of Central Park the value that nearby park land gave to residential property. The planners insisted that the needs of the entire city be considered in designing for that location. Much more important than another park was a place for the study of botany, horticulture, pharmacy, or zoology. The city had made no provision for such functions—just as it was inadequately equipped for open-air markets, fairs, expositions, and civic celebrations.[143]

A direct consequence of failure to plan—to anticipate need—was the deterioration of those existing facilities that could not accommodate excessive or inappropriate use. Central Park already was being overtaxed by school athletics and civic celebrations. The problem was compounded by the inability of those who governed to appreciate or care about special conditions. The dilemma was particularly acute in relation to Tompkins Square Park on the Lower East Side, the scene of the worst social unrest of the 1870s. As Olmsted noted in an 1876 report to the Board of the Department of Public Parks, a principal physical need in this community of "crowded tenements" was an open-air refuge from the congestion of the area and the suffocating airless rooms of "women, children of tender years, invalids, and convalescents." The "statistics of mortality" demonstrated dramatically how many "nursing infants [died] during the summer months." But the park was used regularly as a parade-ground for militia practice and "athletic sports" and it was very difficult and costly—if not impossible—to combine the two functions within a ten-acre space.[144]

As the climax of the centennial year approached, however, New Yorkers forgot their problems in anticipation of the gala Fourth of July celebration that was planned. Public offices were closed from Saturday, July 1, to Wednesday, July 5. All important buildings, public and private, were decorated with flags and streamers. On the evening of the third of July, 25,000 participated in a torchlight procession from 22nd Street to Union Square, where the solid mass would make up what the *Tribune* called "the grandest spectacle of the kind ever witnessed in New-York City." At midnight, churchbells rang in the nation's second century.[145]

Concealed, however, behind the festivities was an ominous paradox. New York was the nation's social, cultural, and economic capital. Its weaknesses—like its strengths—mirrored those of the whole country; "what is true of the city is true, in effect, of all the land," the Reverend Storrs noted to his centennial audience.[146] But neither the national nor the local government seemed aware of the sources of the problems or was likely to take steps to solve them.

The enormous technological and managerial resources that went into the creation of the Centennial Exhibition at Philadelphia attested to the nation's physical capacity to solve its urban problems, but there was little reason to believe that these resources would be so employed. It was becoming increasingly apparent that the city could not adequately maintain even those few public open spaces—such as Central Park—that served as national resources for visitors from other parts of the United States and from abroad. Not many understood the full consequences of the neglect, but the country's leading environmental planner and designer, Frederick Law Olmsted, did—and better than most. His admonition to his countrymen as they embarked on their second century—drawn from his experience with the nation's largest city—was both grave and prescient:

Let what the country needs of the government of its great cities be compared at intervals with what it finds them able to perform, and on the whole the gap will always be found ominously wider.

If we must continue to let it widen, the occurrence of a grand catastrophe is plainly only a question of time. And it will be a catastrophe not merely for the republic but for civilization; for our great cities stretch their hands to all the world, and all the peoples of the world are provided through them.[147]

NOTES

1. Department of Commerce and Labor, Bureau of the Census, *A Century of Population Growth: From the First Census of the United States to the Twelfth, 1790-1900* (Washington, D. C., 1909), p. 223.
2. Ira Rosenwaike, *Population History of New York City* (Syracuse, 1972), pp. 42, 67.
3. George Townsend Fox, ms., "American journals," 4 vols., I: 9, 20-21, 24; 15 June 1868, Public Libraries, Ocean Road, South Shields, England; cited hereafter as Fox, journal.
4. Harry James Carman, *The Street Surface Franchises of New York City* (New York, 1919), pp. 5, 11, 146.
5. Richard Salter Storrs, *The Declaration of Independence and the Effects of It: An Oration Delivered Before the Citizens of New York at the Celebration of the Centennial Anniversary, July 4th, 1876* (New York, 1876), pp. 7-8.
6. The religious basis of urban reform has been developed in different ways in the following works: Aaron I. Abell, *The Urban Impact on American Protestantism, 1865-1900* (Cambridge, Mass., 1943); Carroll S. Rosenberg, *Religion and the Rise of the American City: The New York City Mission Movement, 1812-1870* (Ithaca, 1971); Raymond A. Mohl, *Poverty in New York, 1783-1825* (New York, 1971), pp. 241-58; and Albert Fein, "The American City: The Ideal and the Real," in Edgar Kaufmann, Jr., ed., *The Rise of an American Architecture* (New York, 1970), p. 80; Children's Aid Society of New York, First Annual Report (1845), p. 4–cited hereafter as CAS.
7. Quoted in William Peirce Randel, *Centennial: American Life in 1876* (Philadelphia, 1969), p. 61.
8. Ibid., p. 65.
9. There has been no full-length treatment of Tilden since Alexander C. Flick's careful and detailed biography, *Samuel Jones Tilden: A Study in Political Sagacity* (New York, 1939). Tilden's national role in reconstructing the Democratic Party is defended by Charles B. Murphy in "Samuel Tilden and the Civil War," *South Atlantic Quarterly* XXX (July 1934): 261-71. The fact that Tilden's political career had national importance was perceptively treated by Earl D. Ross, "Samuel J. Tilden and the Revival of the Democratic Party," *South Atlantic Quarterly* XIX (January 1920): 43-54. The most incisive analysis of Tilden since Flick's, demonstrating the many social and economic issues reflected in Tilden's career, is to be found in Mark D. Hirsch, "Samuel J. Tilden: The Story of a Lost Opportunity," *American Historical Review* LVI (July 1951): 788-802. Hirsch traces Tilden's political evolution from a "Jacksonian Radical" to a conservative position in the Reconstruction period. A very important analysis of Tilden as a symbol of national government is in Robert Kelley, *The Transatlantic Persuasion: The Liberal-Democratic Mind in the Age of Gladstone* (New York, 1969), chap. 7.
10. Edward Dana Durand, *The Finances of New York City* (New York, 1898), pp. 5, 112-14, 372-75.
11. Ibid., pp. 112-13.
12. CAS, Twenty-fourth Annual Report (1877), p. 3; *New York Ledger,* Oct. 7 1876; James W. Beekman to Rev. M[aunsell] V[an] Rensselaer, Nov. 27 1876, James W. Beekman Papers, New-York Historical Society, cited hereafter as Beekman Papers.
13. Herbert C. Gutman, "The Worker's Search for Power: Labor in the Gilded Age," in Howard Wayne Morgan, ed., *The Gilded Age: A Reappraisal* (Syracuse, 1963), p. 44; Ernest S. Griffith, *A History of American City Government: The Conspicuous Failure, 1870-1900* (New York, 1974), p. 18; William H. Wickham, *Message on Home Rule* (New York, 1875), p. 9; *New York Daily Tribune,* July 10 1876.

14.   *The Centennial Celebration and International Address to the People of New York by Prominent and Influential Citizens* (New York, [1876?]), pp. 6-7; *New York Ledger,* Dec. 16, 1876; James W. Beekman to Rev. M[aunsell] V[an] Rens-salaer, Sept. 27, 1876, Beekman Papers; *New York Daily Tribune,* July 1, 1876.
15.   Abram S. Hewitt to Samuel J. Tilden, Dec. 23, 1874, Samuel J. Tilden Papers, Manuscript Division, New York Public Library—cited hereafter as Tilden Papers. International Exhibition to Mayor Wickham, [?] 1876, Mayor's Papers, Municipal Archives, New York City. *The Garden: An Illustrated Weekly Journal of Gardening in All Its Branches* VI (Feb. 21, 1874), 156.
16.   Storrs, *Declaration of Independence,* pp. 5-6, 8, 63.
17.   Seth M. Scheiner, *Negro Mecca: A History of the Negro in New York City, 1865-1920* (New York, 1965), p. 17.
18.   The role of New York in almost every reform movement in the pre-Civil and Civil War Period is documented in such works as Robert H. Bremner, *From the Depths: The Discovery of Poverty in the United States* (New York, 1956), and Charles E. Rosenberg, *The Cholera Years: The United States in 1832, 1849, and 1866* (Chicago, 1962); the literary and cultural atmosphere of this reform movement is best captured in James T. Callow, *Kindred Spirits: Knickerbocker Writers and American Artists, 1807-1855* (Chapel Hill, 1967).
19.   Allan Nevins, *The Evening Post* (New York, 1922), pp. 364-66, 371; William C. Bryant to Mrs. Robert C. Waterston, Mar. 3, 1866, William Cullen Bryant Papers, New-York Historical Society, cited hereafter as the Bryant Papers.
20.   William C. Bryant to J. C. Derby, Aug. 28, 1876, Bryant Papers.
21.   Randel, *Centennial,* p. 159; Milton Plesur, "Rumblings Beneath the Surface: America's Outward Thrust, 1865-1890," in Morgan, ed., *The Gilded Age,* pp. 148-58.
22.   Benson J. Lossing, *History of New York,* 2 vols. (New York, 1884): II, 862, 527.
23.   *Report of the Joint Committee of the Senate and General Assembly of the State of New Jersey on the Encroachments upon the Bay and Harbor of New York, with the Report of Egbert L. Viele, State Topographical Engineer* (Trenton, 1855), pp. 27, 6.
24.   Bache's eminence is discussed in Robert C. Post, "Science and Technology at the New York Crystal Palace," p. 16, paper delivered to Symposium on New York Crystal Palace, 1853-54, Centennial Celebration, Department of Art History, City University of New York, Graduate Center (Oct. 25, 1974). I am grateful to Mr. Post for permitting me to read his excellent paper; State of New York Senate Document No. 40, Jan. 29, 1857, "Report of Commissioners Relative to Encroachments in the Harbor of New York," pp. 10-11; Alexander Dallas Bache, *Anniversary Address Before the American Institute of the City of New-York, at the Tabernacle,* Oct. 28, 1856 (New York, 1857), p. 38; Nevins, *The Evening Post,* p. 371.
25.   Seymour J. Mandelbaum, *Boss Tweed's New York* (New York, 1965), pp. 71, 102-103; Frederick Law Olmsted et al., "Report to the Staten Island Improvement Commission of a Preliminary Scheme of Improvements (1871)," in Albert Fein, ed., *Landscape into Cityscape: Frederick Law Olmsted's Plans for a Greater New York City* (Ithaca, 1967), p. 177. 26.
26.   *New York Daily Tribune,* July 1, 1876; Lossing, *History of New York,* II, 814-15; Randel, *Centennial,* pp. 268-69; James Parton, "The Government of the City of New York," in *Topics of the Time* (Boston, 1871), p. 380, published originally in 1866 in *The North American Review.* Parton, we can assume, saw no need to revise his judgment as the situation had grown worse, not improved.
27.   Transcript of the Proceedings of *Roberts* vs. *Balance Dock Company,* May 1, 1857, Tilden Papers, Box 64, pp. 34-35.
28.   [?] Wilson diary, Jan. 19, 1866, p. 13, Manuscript Division, Liverpool Public Library, Liverpool, England; Egbert L. Viele, *The Arcade Underground Railway* ([New York 1870?]), p. 4.

29.   Fox, journal, June 15, 1868, pp. 23-24; Robert Daley, *The World Beneath the City* (Philadelphia, 1959), p. 60.

30.   Parton, "The Government of the City of New York," pp. 383-84.

31.   Nevins, *The Evening Post,* p. 379; William C. Bryant to Governor Edwin D. Morgan, Apr. 11, 1860, Morgan Papers, New York State Library, Albany, New York, Box 3, F. 10. David M. Ellis et al., *A History of New York State* (Ithaca, 1967), p. 238.

32.   Rev. J. F. Richmond, *New York and Its Institutions: 1609-1871* (New York, 1871), p. 182. John Austin Stevens, *Greatness of New York in a Century, 1776-1876: An Address Before the New-York Historical Society* (New York, 1876), p. 62.

33.   The various alternatives available are discussed in *West Side Association, Proceedings of Six Public Meetings* (New York, 1871) and in William J. McAlpine and Egbert L. Viele, *The Opinion of Two Eminent Civil Engineers on Rapid Transit* (New York, 1876). The fact that a rational recommendation to build a subway was made by a special committee and put aside by political maneuvers is discussed in James B. Walker, *Fifty Years of Rapid Transit, 1864 to 1917* (New York, 1918), chap. 6.

34.   One such propaganda piece was Anon., *Exposé of the Facts Concerning the Proposed Elevated Patent Railway Enterprise in the City of New York* (New York, 1866).

35.   For a descriptive account of the development of the elevated trains see William Fullerton Reeves, *The First Elevated Railroads in Manhattan and the Bronx of the City of New York* (New York, 1936). For an interpretation regarding conflicting interests see Mandelbaum, *Boss Tweed's New York,* pp. 65, 123-26. On Tilden's involvement see Flick, *Samuel Jones Tilden,* pp. 275-76. Andrew Carnegie to Samuel J. Tilden, July 3, 1875, Tilden Papers.

36.   William Dean Howells, *A Hazard of New Fortunes: A Novel,* 2 vols. (New York, 1899), I, 76

37.   Frederick Law Olmsted, "The Future of New York," *New York Tribune,* Dec. 28, 1879—this quote, like all others derived from this document, is taken from the ms. version of this article in the Frederick Law Olmsted Papers, Library of Congress—cited hereafter as Olmsted Papers.

38.   Samuel J. Tilden, draft of a letter, Feb. 25, 1868, Tilden Papers.

39.   Scheiner, *Negro Mecca,* p. 174.

40.   Bremner, *From the Depths,* p. 98; Vincent P. De Santis, "The Republican Party Revisited, 1877-1897," in Morgan, ed., *The Gilded Age,* p. 108; Lawrence Grossman, "The Democratic Party and the Negro: A Study in Northern and National Politics, 1868-1892" (Ph.D. diss., CUNY, 1973), p. 259; Rosenwaike, *Population History of New York City,* pp. 76-77.

41.   Lossing, *History of New York,* II, 468-70; Scheiner, *Negro Mecca,* p. 179.

42.   John Swinton, *The New Issue: The Chinese-American Question* (New York, 1870), p. 6; Rosenwaike, *Population History of New York City,* p. 78.

43.   Rosenwaike, *Population History of New York City,* pp. 67-69; Charles L. Brace to Sir Charles Lyell, Feb. 8, 1856, in Emma Brace, ed., *The Life of Charles Loring Brace* (New York, 1894), p. 209.

44.   *The Hebrew Leader,* Dec. 22, 1876; Lossing, *History of New York,* II, 690-91; CAS, Twenty-Fifth Annual Report (1878), p. 34.

45.   Nathan Glazer, *American Judaism* (Chicago, 1957), pp. 12-42; Moses Rischin, *The Promised City: New York's Jews, 1870-1914* (New York, 1970 ed.), p. 52; Harold Philip Gastwirt, *Fraud, Corruption, and Holiness: The Controversy Over the Supervision of Jewish Dietary Practice in New York City 1881-1940* (Port Washington, N. Y., 1974); Simon Sterne to Samuel J. Tilden, Feb. 17, 1875, Tilden Papers.

46.   Samuel Gompers, *Seventy Years of Life and Labor: An Autobiography* (New York, 1943), p. 36; Gastwirt, *Fraud, Corruption and Holiness,* p. 113.

47.   John Higham, *Strangers in the Land: Patterns of American Nativism, 1860-1925* (New York, 1972 ed.), chap. 2—Higham comments on Riis, pp. 40, 67.

48.   Griffith, *A History of American City Government,* p. 7; Gompers, *Seventy Years,* pp. 47, 108; Rosenwaike, *Population History,* p. 84.

49.   Edgar Lee Masters, *The Tale of Chicago* (New York, 1933), p. 193.

50.   Storrs, *Declaration of Independence,* pp. 78-79; *New York Daily Tribune,* July 4, 1876; Howard L. Hurwitz, *Theodore Roosevelt and Labor in New York State, 1880-1900* (New York, 1943, p. 12; Blake McKelvey, *The Urbanization of America* (New Brunswick, 1963), p. 131.

51.   Gompers, *Seventy Years,* pp. 53, 58-59, 91-92.

52.   Ibid., pp. 95-96, 137-38; Norman J. Ware, *The Labor Movement in the United States, 1860-1895: A Study in Democracy* (New York, 1964 ed.; c. 1929), pp. 45, 306.

53.   As a response to the urban violence, New York City received a new Seventh Regiment Armory; its status was reflected in Tiffany's designs for its handsome interior.

54.   Hurwitz, *Theodore Roosevelt and Labor,* pp. 17-18; Gompers, *Seventy Years,* pp. 54, 57-58, 90-91; Gutman, "Worker's Search for Power," p. 63.

55.   Hurwitz, *Theodore Roosevent and Labor,* pp. 24-25; Gompers, *Seventy Years,* pp. 60-61, 112.

56.   Hurwitz, *Theodore Roosevelt and Labor,* p. 26; Thomas J. Condon, "Politics, Reform and the New York City Election of 1886," *The New-York Historical Society Quarterly* XLIV (Oct. 1960), pp. 368-69; [?] to A. J. Campbell, Feb. 15, 1876. This unsigned letter was sent to Campbell, a Republican State Assemblyman from the Fifth District, and given to Leopold Eidlitz, a prominent architect who designed— among other buildings—Temple Emanu-El. Eidlitz lent it to Frederick Law Olmsted, who made a copy of it which is in the Olmsted Papers.

57.   CAS, Nineteenth Annual Report (1871), pp. 42-43; CAS, Twenty-fifth Annual Report (1877), p. 3.

58.   Claire Brandler Walker, "A History of Factory Legislation and Inspection in New York State, 1886-1911" (Ph.D. diss., Columbia University, 1969), pp. 1, 62-63, 71-73, 93; for a discussion of the Henry George campaign see Nevins, *Abram S. Hewitt,* chap. 23.

59.   William E. Dodge, *Old New York: A Lecture* (New York, 1880), p. 57.

60.   CAS, Nineteenth Annual Report (1871), pp. 9-10; CAS, Thirty-first Annual Report (1883), pp. 8-9.

61.   The ethical quality of the reformers' goals was best captured in Walt Whitman, *Democratic Vistas and Other Papers* (London, 1888 ed.), p. 14. The essay "Democratic Vistas," written in 1867, was revised and first published in 1871. It was reissued during the centennial year as part of Vol. 2 of Whitman's *Complete Works* (Gay Wilson Allan, *Walt Whitman* [Detroit, 1969, rev. ed.]), pp. 130-32, 237.

62.   Lossing, *History of New York* II, 846-53. For a "Freudian" analysis of Comstock see Heywood Broun and Margaret Leech, *Anthony Comstock, Roundsman of the Land* (New York, 1927); for a "defense" of Comstock, see Anthony Comstock, *Frauds Exposed* (New York, 1880), pp. 5-6, and Charles Gallaudet Trumbull, *Anthony Comstock, Fighter* (New York, 1913), p. 19; Daniel Andrew Pope, "The Development of National Advertising, 1865-1920" (Ph.D. diss., Columbia University, 1973), pp. 342-49.

63.   To date the scholar who has best understood the contribution of the United States Sanitary Commission is Robert H. Bremner, *American Philanthropy* (Chicago, 1960), pp. 80-84; idem, *From the Depths,* pp. 43-45. An important critical interpretation of the significance of the Sanitary Commission is found in George M. Frederickson, *The Inner Civil War: Northern Intellectuals and the Crisis of the Union* (New York, 1965), chap. 7; for a discussion of the personalities and politics of the Commission see William Q. Maxwell, *Lincoln's Fifth Wheel: The Political History of the United States Sanitary Commission* (New York, 1956).

64.   Will Irwin et al., *A History of the Union League Club of New York City* (New York, 1952), chap. 1; Laura W. Roper, *FLO: A Biography of Frederick Law Olmsted* (Baltimore, 1973), pp. 214-15.

65. Richmond, *New York and Its Institutions,* p. 176; Lossing, *History of New York* II, 578.

66. C. W. Elliott, "Life in Great Cities: New York," *Putnam's Magazine,* XI, N.S.1 (January 1868), 95.

67. William Allen Butler, *Our Great Metropolis: Its Growth, Misgovernment and Needs; A Lecture Delivered Before the General Society of Mechanics & Tradesmen, Feb. 6, 1879* (New York, 1880), p. 43.

68. CAS, Sixth Annual Report (1859), pp. 7-8; CAS, Fifteenth Annual Report (1868), p. 7; CAS, Twentieth Annual Report (1872), pp. 25-27; CAS, Twenty-first Annual Report (1873), p. 4; CAS, Forty-first Annual Report (1893), p. 10.

69. Richmond, *New York and Its Institutions,* pp. 153-54, 347-53; Lossing, *History of New York,* II, 569, 592; CAS, Twenty-first Annual Report, p. 5; John Tracy Ellis, *American Catholicism* (Chicago, 1956), chap. 2.

70. CAS, Twenty-fourth Annual Report (1876), p. 4.

71. Elisha Harris's paper on the housing problem in which he recommended cooperatives as one possible solution was delivered to the American Social Science Association meeting at Philadelphia. The meeting and paper was reported in the *New York Herald,* June 2, 1876. Elisha Harris, *The United States Sanitary Commission* (Boston, 1967), p. 4. Maxwell, *Lincoln's Fifth Wheel,* pp. 333-34. Roy Lubove, *The Progressives and the Slums: Tenement House Reform in New York City 1890-1917* (Pittsburgh, 1962), pp. 25-28.

72. Lubove, *The Progressives and the Slums,* pp. 15-28. Lawrence M. Friedman, *Government and Slum Housing: A Century of Frustration* (Chicago, 1968), pp. 25-30. A. N. Bell, *Extract from the Ninth Annual Report of the Board of Charities of the State of New York* (Albany, 1876), p. 31. In this report a kind of massive governmental intervention in the form of "urban renewal" was suggested.

73. Nevins, *Evening Post,* pp. 368-69; Lossing, *History of New York* II, 856

74. Lubove, *The Progressives and the Slums,* pp. 28-39.

75. CAS, 25th Annual Report (1877), p. 7. Frederick Law Olmsted and J. James R. Croes, Document No. 72 of the Board of the Department of Public Parks: I. "Preliminary Report of the Landscape Architect and the Civil and Topographical Engineer, upon the Laying Out of the Twenty-third and Twenty-fourth Wards," in Fein, ed., *Landscape into Cityscape,* p. 354.

76. Olmsted, "The Future of New York," Olmsted Papers.

77. A. N. Bell, *Extract from the Ninth Annual Report of the Board of Charities of the State of New York,* p. 9. Nevins, *Evening Post,* p. 372.

78. William Rhinelander Stewart, *The Philanthropic Work of Josephine Shaw Lowell* (New York, 1911), pp. 83-85. Frank B. Sanborn, "The Work of Social Science in the United States," *American Social Science Association, New York Meeting* (Cambridge, Mass., 1874), p. 12. *The Nation,* Feb. 7, 1876, p. 116. Walter I. Trattner, "Louisa Lee Schuyler and the Founding of the State Charities Aid Association," *New-York Historical Society Quarterly* LI (July 1967), pp. 233-48

79. Elizabeth Blackwell to Barbara Smith Bodichon, March 2, 1860, Elizabeth Blackwell Papers, Special Collections, Columbia University—cited hereafter as Blackwell Papers. Elizabeth Blackwell to Barbara Smith Bodichon, June 23, 1860, Blackwell Papers.

80. Blackwell to Bodichon, June 23, 1860, Blackwell Papers.

81. *Address of the Committee to Promote the Passage of a Metropolitan Health Bill* (New York, 1865), pp. 3-4. For an important descriptive analysis of the development of a secular and professional understanding of the causes of disease see Rosenberg, *Cholera Years; New York Times,* April 7, 1860.

82. Rosenberg, *Cholera Years,* pp. 210-12.

83 A. N. Bell, *Extract from the Ninth Annual Report of the Board of Charities,* pp. 7-9; Frederick Law Olmsted, "Report of a Preliminary Survey of Rockaway Point (1879)," in Fein, ed., *Landscape into Cityscape,* p. 305; Lubove, *The Progressives and the Slums,* pp. 86, 133-34.

84. [?] Halliday, *Domiciliary Accommodations in the City of New York* ([New

York ?] , 1859), p. 20; CAS, Twenty-fourth Annual Report (1876), p. 4.

85. There is, of course, an important and serious difference of interpretation among scholars regarding the motivation and significance of New York City reformers during the centennial period. A major critical study of the civil service reform movement is Ari Hoogenboom, *Outlawing the Spoils* (Urbana, Illinois, 1961). See also his "Spoilsmen and Reformers: Civil Service Reform and Public Morality" in Morgan, ed., *The Gilded Age*, pp. 66-90. Hoogenboom's essentially critical group study should be compared with Gordon Milne's more favorable evaluation of one reformer in *George William Curtis and the Genteel Tradition* (Bloomington, 1956).

86. Griffith, *A History of American City Government*, p. 110.

87. Milne, *George William Curtis and the Genteel Tradition*, chap 13. John M. Dobson, *Politics in the Gilded Age: A New Perspective on Reform* (New York, 1972), pp. 67-68; 78-79.

88. Olmsted to Board of Park Commissioners of Central Park, March 26, 1861, Olmsted Papers.

89. Olmsted to Charles Eliot Norton, Dec. 27, 1876, Charles Eliot Norton Papers, Houghton Library, Harvard University.

90. Olmsted to Hon. W. F. Hayns (?), April 13, 1876, Olmsted Papers.

91. Frederick Law Olmsted, *The Spoils of the Park: With a Few Leaves from the Deep-laden Notebooks of "A Wholly Unpractical Man"* (Detroit, 1882), reprinted in Fein, ed., *Landscape into Cityscape*, pp. 391-440. Although this report circulated widely among civil service reformers and Olmsted was an active member of the movement, he did not consider it primarily a tract in defense of that cause. Rather, he meant it to be more a history of the difficulties encountered in managing Central Park and a plea for a redefinition of park-planning and function.

92. For a discussion of Democratic political organization see Callow, *The Tweed Ring* (New York, 1966), and Mandelbaum, *Boss Tweed's New York*.

93. Dobson, *Politics in the Gilded Age*, p. 35.

94. Durand, *The Finances of New York City*, p. 60.

95. Ibid., pp. 66-124.

96. Fox, journal, June 20, 1868, p. 33. This attitude as to the cause of corruption was wide-spread among reformer types; see, for example, Elliott, "Life in Great Cities," p. 94.

97. Durand, *The Finances of New York City*, p. 127.

98. William Wickham to the Common Council (1875), p. 17.

99. This thesis of political accommodation is convincingly argued by Thomas J. Condon, "Politics, Reform and the New York City Election of 1886," *The New-York Historical Society Quarterly* XLIV (Oct. 1960): 363-93

100. Griffith, *American City Government*, pp. 72, 82; Condon, "Politics, Reform and the New York City Election of 1886," p. 365; Florence Teicher Bloom, "The Political Career of William B. Cochran" (Ph.D. diss., City University of New York, 1970, p. 39).

101. John Lothrop Motley, *Historic Progress and American Democracy: An Address Delivered Before The New-York Historical Society* (New York, 1869), p. 4; Egbert L. Viele, *The Topography and Physical Resources of the State of New York: An Address Delivered Before the American Geographical Society* (New York, 1875), p. 21.

102. Randel, *Centennial*, pp. 278-79.

103. Roger A. Wines, "A. T. Stewart and Garden City," *The Nassau County Historical Journal* vol. XIX (Winter 1958), pp. 3-5. Philip Hone Diary, pp. 71-72, Feb. 23, 1850, and p. 158, May 31, 1850, New-York Historical Society. Richmond, *New York and Its Institutions*, p. 128.

104. George I. Juergens, "The Birth of a Modern Newspaper, Joseph Pulitzer and the New York World: 1883-1885" (Ph.D. diss., Columbia University, 1965), I, 187.

105. Ralph M. Hower, *History of Macy's of New York, 1858-1919* (Cambridge, Mass., 1943), chap. 3.

106. Fox, journal, (June 15, 1868), XXVII. Pope, "The Development of National Advertising," pp. 228-30. Lossing, *HIstory of New York*, II, 857-58.

107. Frank Luther Mott, *A History of American Magazines, Vol. III: 1865-1885* (Cambridge, Mass., 1957), pp. 25-26; idem, *American Journalism. A History of Newspapers in the United States Through 260 Years: 1690 to 1950* (New York, 3rd ed., 1962), chap. 25; Junius Henri Browne, *The Great Metropolis: a Mirror of New York* (Hartford, 1869), pp. 295-318.

108. Bache, *Anniversary Address*, p. 58. Lossing, *History of New York*, II pp. 703, 833, 863; Robert R. Roberts, "Gilt, Gingerbread, and Realism; The Public and Its Taste," in Morgan, ed., *The Gilded Age*, p. 189; Moses Forster Sweetser and Simeon Ford, *How To Know New York City* (Boston, 1888), p. 67; Phyllis Dain, *The New York Public Library: A History of Its Founding and Early Years* (New York, 1972), pp. 3-18.

109. Carl Degler, "Labor in the Economy and Politics of New York City, 1850-1860" (Ph.D. diss., Columbia University, 1952), pp. 3-4. Lossing, *History of New York*, II, 862-63.

110. [?], *Biographical Sketches of William Steinway, Henry E. Steinway, and C. F. Theodore Steinway* (New York, 1895), p. 13; James Parton, *Triumphs of Enterprise, Ingenuity, and Public Spirit* (New York, 1874), pp. 339-47.

111. Lossing, *History of New York*, II, 762-63, 706-707.

112. Richmond, *New York and Its Institutions*, pp. 127-28.

113. Lossing, *History of New York*, II, pp. 658-62, 805. Elliott, "Life in Great Cities," p. 93; McKelvey, *The Urbanization of America, 1860-1915* (New Brunswick, 1963), pp. 40, 56-57; Robert Sobel, *The Big Board: A History of the New York Stock Market* (New York, 1965) chap. 7.

114. Elliott, "LIfe in Great Cities," pp. 98-99; H. Bragg, *A Challenge Elicited by the Hon. J[ohn] Lothrop Motley's Address on Historic Progress and American Democracy* (London, 1869), pp. 55-56.

115. Gustavus Myers, *History of the Great American Fortunes* (New York, 1936 ed.), p. 333.

116. Nathan Silver, *Lost New York* (New York, 1971), pp. 120-21. Myers, *History of the Great American Fortunes*, p. 211.

117. Lossing, *History of New York*, II, 814.

118. Allan Nevins, *Abram S. Hewitt, with Some Account of Peter Cooper* (New York, 1967 ed.), pp. 175-82, 272-76.

119. David McCullough, *The Great Bridge* (New York, 1972), pp. 27-32.

120. Nevins, *Hewitt*, p. 450.

121. Vincent F. Seyfried, *The New York and Queens County Railway and the Steinway Lines 1867-1939* (?, 1950), p. 3. *Biographical Sketches of Steinway*, pp. 13-14.

122. Wines, *A. T. Stewart*, pp. 7-11.

123. Fein, "The American City: The Ideal and the Real," p. 71.

124. Norval White and Elliot Willensky, eds., *AIA Guide to New York City* (London, 1969), p. 94.

125. Albert Fein, *Frederick Law Olmsted and the American Environmental Tradition* (New York, 1972), pp. 28-29. Quoted in Henry Hope Reed and Sophia Duckworth, *Central Park: A History and a Guide* (New York, 1967), p. 2.

126. Olmsted to Board of the Department of Public Parks, March 1, 1875, Olmsted Papers. Frederick Law Olmsted, *The Park for Detroit. . . . Belle Isle Scheme* (Boston, 1882), pp. 32-33. *The Garden* II (8 June 1872): 639.

127. Frederick Law Olmsted, *Notes on the Plan of Franklin Park and Related Matters* (Boston, 1886), p. 94; Olmsted, "Public Parks," *The Garden*, VII, March 25, 1876, 299; Elliott, "Life in Great Cities," p. 95. Wilson Diary, Jan. 14, 1866, p. 11.

128. CAS, 24th Annual Report (1876), p. 14.

129. Olmsted et al., "Report to the Staten Island Improvement Commission of a Preliminary Scheme of Improvements (1871)," in Fein, ed., *Landscape into City-*

scape, p. 248. Olmsted's comprehensive plans for Staten Island and for the 23rd and 24th wards are discussed in Roper, *FLO*, pp. 324-26, 354-56; in Mandelbaum, *Boss Tweed's New York*, pp. 74-75, 114-117; and in Fein, *Frederick Law Olmsted*, pp. 49-51.

130. Nevins, *Evening Post*, p. 344. Elliott, "Life in Great Cities," p. 99.
131. Nathan Silver, *Lost New York* (New York, 1971 ed.), p. 79. Sweetser and Ford, *How to Know New York City*, p. 83. Foster Rhea Dulles, *A History of Recreation: America Learns to Play* (New York, 1965), pp. 238-39.
132. Fein, "The American City: The Ideal and the Real," pp. 84-93.
133. Elliott, "Life in Great Cities," pp. 91-95. Browne, *The Great Metropolis*, p. 244.
134. Juergens, "The Birth of a Modern Newspaper," pp. 367-68.
135. Charles L. Brace to Mrs. Charles L. Brace, June 13, 1865, in Emma Brace, ed., *The Life of Charles Loring Brace* (New York, 1894), p. 270.
136. Dulles, *A History of Recreation*, chap. 11. New York Daily *Tribune*, July 3, 1876, p. 1 col. 5; Randel, *Centennial*, p. 327. New York *Herald*, June 11, 1876, p. 6, col. 5; Sweetser and Ford, *How to Know New York City*, p. 89.
137. Juergens, "The Birth of a Modern Newspaper," 166.
138. Lucy P. Gillman, "Coney Island," *New York History, The Quarterly Journal of the New York State Historical Association* XXXVI (July 1955), 273. *New York Herald*, June 3, 1876.
139. Dulles, *A History of Recreation*, pp. 148-53. As an example of the health functions of one upper-class resort—Rockaway—see Mary de Peyster to James Beekman, Aug. 26, 1854, Beekman Papers.
140. Gillman, "Coney Island," pp. 257-59.
141. Ibid., pp. 260-70.
142. Olmsted, ms. on tourism, [nd], Olmsted Papers, Box 22.
143. Frederick Law Olmsted and Calvert Vaux, "Document No. 50 of the Board of the Department of Public Parks: A Preliminary Study by the Landscape Architect[s] of a Design for the Laying Out of Morningside Park (1873)," in Fein, ed., *Landscape into Cityscape*, pp. 334-35.
144. Fred[erick] Law Olmsted, "Report of the Landscape Architect on the treatment of Tompkins Square, with special reference to the Northwest corner of said Square," Document No. 71, Board of the Department of Public Parks, August 16, 1876 (New York, 1876), p. 6.
145. New York Daily *Tribune*, July 1, 1876; *New York Journal of Commerce*, July 3, 1876; New York Daily *Tribune*, July 4, 1876.
146. Storrs, *Centennial*, p. 64.
147. Frederick Law Olmsted, "The Beginning of Central Park: A Fragment of Autobiography (ca. 1877)," in Fein, ed., *Landscape into Cityscape*, p. 54.

SUGGESTIONS FOR FURTHER READING

GENERAL

During the past decade there have been published three books on centennial America which discuss New York City as part of the national scene. They are, in the order of their relevance for an understanding of New York City, William Peirce Randel, *Centennial: American Life in 1876* (Phil., 1969); John Brinckerhoff Jackson, *American Space: The Centennial Years, 1865-1876* (New York, 1972); and Dee Brown, *The Year of the Century: 1876* (New York, 1966). Still useful in the same way and surprisingly modern are two volumes in the series "A History of American Life" edited by Arthur M. Schlesinger and Dixon Ryan Fox: Allan Nevins, *The Emergence of Modern America, 1865-1878* (New York, 1927), and Arthur Meier Schlesinger, *The Rise of the City, 1878-1898* (New York, 1933).

For a "biography" of the city there is the magisterial effort of I. N. Phelps Stokes, *The Iconography of Manhattan Island, 1498-1909* (New York, 1915-1928). This diary-like record of significant events in the daily life of the city provides a chronological beginning-point for any student of New York City history. In a more conventional format there are two substantial histories of New York containing much social data about the decade of the 1870s: Rev. J. F. Richmond, *New York and Its Institutions, 1609-1871* (New York, 1871), and Benson J. Lossing, *History of New York* II (New York, 1884). They complement each other in a significant way: Richmond, reflecting a humanistic tradition of religion in the city, was concerned with the social problems and the institutional response to such matters as poverty, disease, and crime; Lossing was more interested in the economic, technological, and architectural growth of the city as reflected in the lives of individuals. Unfortunately, neither work is indexed. Also useful—and indexed—although less social and more political in coverage, is James Grant Wilson, ed., *The Memorial History of the City* (4 volumes, 1892). Ironically, less applicable to the centennial years is William Leete Stone, *The Centennial History of New York City from the Discovery to the Present Day* (New York, 1876). Stone's emphasis, unlike that of Richmond and Lossing, was on a description of a more distant past rather than on an understanding of the more recent—post-Civil War—city. The portraits of some of the persons discussed in this essay—R. H. Macy and A. T. Stewart—are reproduced in *Portraits from the Americans: The Democratic Experience* (New York, 1973), an exhibition catalogue "based on Daniel J. Boorstin's Pulitzer Prize-winning book."

PHYSICAL CHANGES

One of the most important and exciting characteristics of any city—and of New York in particular—is the way social, economic, and political changes are reflected in the physical fabric of the metropolis. New York's changing skyline in the 1870s—after the introduction of the Otis elevator and the elevated train—heralded a new economic and social configuration. Stokes' *The Iconography of Manhattan Island* is invaluable for the large number of maps and illustrations portraying these changes. More available (now in paperback) and, in terms of visual organization, more useful is the splendid work by John A. Kouwenhoven, *The Columbia Historical Portrait of New York: An Essay in Graphic History in Honor of the Tricentennial of New York City and the Bicentennial of Columbia University* (New York, 1953). A guide which was reprinted in 1975 is Robert Macoy, *The Centennial Guide to New York City and Its Environs* (New York, 1876).

That New York City's architecture and land-planning was influential nationally and internationally is a theme touched on in different ways in the four essays constituting Edgar Kaufmann, Jr., ed., *The Rise of an American Architecture* (New York, 1970). This work was published as part of the centennial celebration of the Metropolitan Museum of Art. As a model of how a distinctive environmental structure—the Brooklyn Bridge—can be described as part of the history of the City, see David McCullough, *The Great Bridge* (New York, 1972). The functional and aesthetic qualities of the City's other important environmental achievement—Central Park—was best described in 1869 by Clarence Cook, *A Description of the New York Central Park* (New York, 1972). Cook, a noted art and architectural critic, was a friend of the Park's designers—Olmsted and Vaux—and was guided in part in his treatment of the Park by their feelings and attitudes. The plan for the park, "Greensward," is reproduced in Albert Fein, ed., *Landscape into Cityscape: Frederick Law Olmsted's Plans for a Greater New York City* (Ithaca, 1968), pp. 63-88. Biographical detail on Olmsted is contained in Laura W. Roper, *FLO: A Biography of Frederick Law Olmsted* (Baltimore, 1973), and Albert Fein, *Frederick Law Olmsted and the American Environmental Tradition* (New York, 1972). Important for the present condition of the Park—what remains and has been changed—is Henry Hope Reed and Sophia Duckworth, *Central Park: A History and a Guide* (New York, 1967), and

M. M. Graff, *Tree Trails in Central Park* (New York, 1970).

One of the reasons why both the Bridge and the Park are so appreciated is that they destroyed very little of the existing urban fabric; rather, they enhanced the quality of life by adding to it. Unfortunately, as we are only too well aware today, urban change often means the needless loss of distinctive architectural structures and at times the obliteration of an entire section of urban tissue threatening the tradition of memory without which we have urban amnesia. Some of this loss is poignantly recorded in Nathan Silver, *Lost New York* (New York, 1971 ed.). Happily, it is now recognized that by the centennial year photography had become a socially powerful and an aesthetically effective means of recording urban life. The books by Kouwenhoven and Silver can now be complemented with photographs selected from the archives of one of the city's most important cultural institutions, The New-York Historical Society, in Mary Black, *Old New York in Early Photographs 1853-1901* (New York, 1973). As a source as to what remains from the past, nothing has replaced *New York City Guide* (New York, 1939) of the American Guide Series, prepared by the Federal Writers' Project of the Works Progress Administration. More recent is the work of Norval White and Elliot Willensky, eds., *AIA Guide to New York City* (London, 1967).

DEMOGRAPHIC AND SOCIAL CHARACTERISTICS

The demographic changes that preceded and accompanied alterations in the urban fabric are now recorded in Ira Rosenwaike, *Population History of New York City* (Syracuse, 1972). Professor Rosenwaike's work is arranged both chronologically and topically, including such subjects as birth, mortality, race, ethnicity, and religion. Although this basic work is a most valuable addition to a very tiny literature, it is only a beginning toward the sort of compilation and analysis of demographic information needed in order to have an informed understanding of the city's past. For example, we need to have in a format similar to that provided by Rosenwaike parallel information regarding changes in specific areas of the city. Demographic data regarding two groups—Jews and Negroes—living in specific communities can be found in Moses Rischin, *The Promised City: New York's Jews, 1870-1914* (New York, 1962) and in Seth M. Scheiner, *A History of the Negro in New York City, 1865-1920* (New York, 1965). Similar treatments of the Irish, the Germans, the English, and other ethnic groups are sorely needed.

The social condition of New York City always has reflected itself in the writings of some of the nation's most significant authors. This quality of life is captured in an ephemeral way by Rufus Rockwell Wilson and Otilie Erickson Wilson in *New York in Literature: The Story Told in the Landmarks of Town and Country* (Elmira, New York, 1947), and, more substantively, in a massive anthology, Esther Morgan McCullough, ed., *As I Pass, O Manhattan: An Anthology of Life in New York* (North Bennington, Vermont, 1956). The national significance of this contribution during the centennial period is analyzed in the unfinished—but published and still relevant—work of Vernon Louis Parrington, covering 1860–1920, *Main Currents in American Thought: An Interpretation of American Literature from the Beginnings to 1920* III, *The Beginnings of Critical Realism in America* (New York, 1927), and in Van Wyck Brooks's *The Times of Melville and Whitman* (New York, 1947).

The reality of the city depended at least in part on the social perspective of the author. The frozen, comical, and ultimately self-destructive snobbery of the nouveau riche is blandly articulated by the style-setter of the "Four Hundred," Ward McAllister, *Society As I Found It* (New York, 1890). Edith Wharton was fourteen at the time of the centennial and represented an older, more legitimate aristocratic group with roots in colonial America. She was able to capture some of the disintegrating elements of the city's wealthy class in *The Age of Innocence* (New York, 1920) and in four novelettes published together as *Old New York* (New York, 1924). The memories of other children of established families set down as autobiographical reminiscences contain interesting insights into the city during the 1870s. Two are: Mabel Osgood Wright, *My New York* (New York, 1926) and Edward Ringwood Hewitt *Those Were the Days: Tales of a Long Life* (New York, 1943).

Poor people generally do not leave memoirs. But New York was good to many who were poor, and some who recorded their experiences did not reject the reality of their early lives or the struggles involved in altering their condition. Samuel Gompers's *Seventy Years of Life and Labor* is a simply-written, often moving account which includes a description of his early years in the city. In the same category one can include the reminiscences of a more "radical" labor leader, John Swinton, as recorded in Robert Waters' *Career and Conversation of John Swinton, Journalist, Orator, Economist* (Chicago, 1902). Although clearly sympathetic to the plight of labor, the best literary exposition of the various ideological points of view in the city remains William Dean Howells's *A Hazard of New Fortunes* (New York, 1889). Some of the best descriptions of post–Civil War New York are to be found in Allan Nevins's *The Evening Post* (New York, 1922), and *Abram S. Hewitt, with Some Account of Peter Cooper* (New York, 1967 ed.). The first two chapters of Roy Lubove's *The Progressives and the Slums: Tenement House Reform in New York City* (Pittsburgh, 1962) offer an excellent treatment of housing conditions in the 1870s.

One of the interesting aspects of the centennial period was the extent to which New Yorkers were informed about their social conditions. Popular journalistic accounts meant for a mass audience were published, discussing, often satirically, many aspects of the city's "high" and "low" life. Among these were: *Asmodeus in New York* (New York, 1868); *High Life in New York, by Jonathan Slick, Esq., of Weathersfield, Connecticut* (Phil., 1873); Sam. A. Mackeever's *Glimpses of Gotham and City Characters* (New York, 1880); and *The Man-Traps of New York: What They Are and How They Are Worked, by a Celebrated Detective* (New York, 1881). A more serious effort to provide an understanding of and prescription for the causes of poverty and violence was Charles Loring Brace's *The Dangerous Classes of New York and Twenty Years' Work Among Them* (New York, 1872).

One can assume that the homes of the poor had little in the way of art to embellish them—but if they did, it was likely, in addition to a religious article, to be one of John Rogers's familiar sculptured groups, mass-produced and sold from New York City. The best single work dealing with popular culture during the centennial period ia a marvelous, illustrated anthology by Henry Nash Smith, ed., *Popular Culture and Industrialism: 1865–1890* (New York, 1967). Most of Nash's selections are drawn from the New York scene. The story of Rogers's extraordinary national success is told in David H. Wallace, *John Rogers, the People's Sculptor* (Middletown, Conn., 1967). The affluence of the city produced the enduring aesthetic of Louis C. Tiffany, son of the founder of the famous firm, whose contribution is discussed in Robert Koch, *Louis C. Tiffany: Rebel in Glass* (New York, 1964). Just as New York City gave the nation its most significant artists of interior design, it also produced the country's most renowned creator of public sculpture during the centennial era—Augustus Saint-Gaudens, whose biography is told in Louise Hall Tharp, *Saint-Gaudens and the Gilded Era* (Boston, 1969).

ECONOMY AND TECHNOLOGY

There is no single work on either the economic growth or the technological development of the city. The relationship between the two was best captured by James Parton in his still eminently readable *Triumphs of Enterprise, Ingenuity, and Public Spirit* (New York, 1874). Allan Nevins's *Abram S. Hewitt, with Some Account of Peter Cooper* (New York, 1967 ed.) is a most valuable analysis of the interlocking nature of technology, industry, and politics, as is McCullough's *The Great Bridge*. Gustavus Myers's *History of the Great American Fortunes* (New York, 1936 ed.), is still valuable for its data on such New York families as the Astors and the Vanderbilts.

Regarding the development of labor, there is important information on New York City in John R. Commons et al., *History of Labour in the United States* II (New York, 1918), as well as in Norman J. Ware, *The Labor Movement in the United States, 1860-1895: A Study in Democracy* (New York, 164 ed.). Howard Lawrence Hurwitz in *Theodore Roosevelt and Labor in New York State 1880-1900* (New York, 1943) provides a concise overview of conditions in the 1870s. And Samuel Gompers's autobiography is an important account of a national labor leader who lived and worked in New York City.

On the subject of public economy a most useful account is that of Edward Dana Durand in *The Finances of New York City* (New York, 1898). In Delos F. Wilcox's *Municipal Franchises* (Rochester, 2 vols., 1910-11) we have the most complete description of transportation franchises—both street and elevated railways. Wilcox's largely administrative description should be supplemented with Harry James Carman's *The Street Surface Franchises of New York City* (New York, 1919) and James Blaine Walker's *Fifty Years of Rapid Transit, 1869 to 1917* (New York, 1918).

The development of New York City as a financial capital is best recorded in Margaret G. Myers's *The New York Money Market* (New York, 1931). An interesting description of the history of Wall Street was provided by the noted poet and literary critic Edmund C. Stedman in *The New York Stock Exchange: Its History, Its Contribution to National Prosperity, and Its Relation to American Finance at the Outset of the Twentieth Century* (New York, 1905).

INSTITUTIONS: PUBLIC AND PRIVATE

Most of the city's public institutions found it difficult to maintain adequate services during the centennial era. This is documented in James F. Richardson's superb history—*The New York Police: Colonial Times to 1901* (New York, 1970). Part of the problem was the vastly increased demand, for example, for water. This story is told in Nelson M. Blake, *Water for the Cities: A History of the Urban Water Supply Problem in the United States* (Syracuse, 1956). The inadequacies of the public institutions, under State jurisdiction, to which the City's poor, mentally ill, and convicts were remanded are vividly described by David J. Rothman, *The Discovery of the Asylum: Social Order and Disorder in the New Republic* (Boston, 1971). It was not until after the Civil War that New York acquired a professional fire department, as discussed by Richard B. Calhoun in "New York City Fire Department Reorganization, 1865-1870: A Civil War Legacy," *The New-York Historical Society Quarterly* XL (Jan/Apr 1976), 7-34. The most complete discussion of the development of a Metropolitan Board of Health is provided in John Duffy's *A History of Public Health in New York City, 1625-1866.*

The importance of one particular set of Protestant institutions is described by Carroll Smith Rosenberg in *Religion and the Rise of the American City: The New York City Mission Movement, 1812-1870* (Ithaca, 1971). Dr. Rosenberg is one of a growing number of scholars to comment favorably on Brace's social work with children, which was inspired by religious impulse. The most complete analysis to date of Brace's contribution is by Joseph M. Hawes in *Children in Urban Society: Juvenile Delinquency in Nineteenth-Century America* (New York, 1971). One of the interesting aspects of Brace's work is that it served as a model for public agencies such as the Board of Education. Diane Ravitch's *The Great School Wars, New York City, 1805-1973: A History of the Public Schools As Battlefield of Social Change* (New York, 1974) is a vivid account of key episodes in the development of a public school system. Her discussion makes clear the role of "reformers" in support and defense of a public school system.

In a similar sense, continued reform of some of the city's social institutions—

such as hospitals for the poor—required the voluntary assistance of groups such as Louisa Lee Schuyler's State Charities Aid Association. This private-public relationship so essential to the humane and efficient management of social institutions is described by Walter I. Trattner in "Louisa Lee Schuyler and the Founding of the State Charities Aid Association," *The New-York Historical Society Quarterly* LI (July 1967): 233-48. The fact that the influence of Brace and Schuyler affected another generation is discussed by Walter I. Trattner in *Homer Folks, Pioneer in Social Welfare* (New York, 1968).

POLITICS

A little book on a big subject, Jon C. Teaford's *The Municipal Revolution in America: Origins of Modern Urban Government, 1650-1825* (Chicago, 1975) provides a thesis which the author extends to the present time. Teaford's major argument—with examples taken from New York City's experience—is that colonial municipal government "rested in the hands of those admitted to the commerce of the city, and this limited body of commercial participants expected the municipal corporation to devote the largest portion of its time and effort to regulating and promoting trade" (p.vi). Over time, the author reasons, in response to altered technology, trade, and ideology, the commercial functions continued to decline and the various "noneconomic duties of city government continued to expand. Municipally-financed art museums, libraries, zoos, public baths, and park systems all appeared during the latter part of the nineteenth century. By the 1890s New York City [was spending] $40,000 a year for concerts in the public parks" (p. 114). Notwithstanding this massive shift of functions, municipal government was not reorganized so as to enable it to meet its new functions.

While this thesis is too simplistic to accommodate many of the governmental problems confronting New York in the 1870s which require much more sustained research and documentation, it does underscore the constant inability of government to plan for and manage effectively those increasingly complex services required to maintain a high standard of urban life. Phrased differently, as the power of the marketplace was growing, that of municipal government was declining—yet its functions were becoming more burdensome in terms of meeting human needs. In short, government could not, within the authorized constitutional structure, at all effectively manage and call into being a more efficient political mechanism—the party—directed by a "boss."

Such a defense of New York City's "bossism" is offered by Seymour Mandelbaum in *Boss Tweed's New York* (New York, 1965). Mandelbaum defends his thesis not by an analysis of the past so much as by an application of logic drawn from a communications-and-systems theory. Mandelbaum argues that by the 1860s the economic functions of New York City's many businesses were so vast in scale that in response to their legitimate needs a more effective urban government was called into being—"boss" rule. The more controversial aspect of Mandelbaum's thesis is that in many respects the "Boss" was more "democratic" than reformers insofar as he was responding to humane needs ignored by the legitimate political structure. Alexander Callow in *The Tweed Ring* (New York, 1966) argues—albeit implicitly—to the contrary: the Tweed Ring was crooked. Regardless of the good it did, adherence to the elective system as the primary means of democratizing governmental power is possible and desirable, and there are objectively definable standards for urban governance which are violated by nongovernmental "boss" rule.

The importance of this debate among scholars must surely continue, in various ways, since the urban crisis, as epitomized in the currently grave condition of New York City, remains one of the principal concerns of the nation. Not less important is the fact that such large concepts as outlined by Teaford and Mandelbaum provide a meaningful structure within which to place so many of the excellent specific political studies of the centennial period. Among these are Charles H. Brown's *William Cullen Bryant, a Biography* (New York, 1971), which shows, among other aspects of Bryant's career, the interrelationship of the press with the political process, often in partisan fashion. Howard B. Furer, *William Frederick Havemeyer: A Political Biography* (New York, 1965), discusses in chronological and political terms the career of a man who served three terms as mayor and always as a close associate of Samuel J. Tilden. Furer's biography is limited in that it does not include the economic details of Havemeyer's career, just as is Irving Katz's *August Belmont: A Political Biography* (New York, 1968). Such data makes D. G. Brinton Thompson's *Ruggles of New York: A Life of Samuel B. Ruggles* (New York, 1946) a more satisfying analysis of one of the chief economic theoreticians of urban life in centennial New York.

For an understanding of the sustained power of the political machinery of Tammany Hall, Gustavus Myers's *The History of Tammany Hall* (New York, 1971 ed.) is still useful; but it should be supplemented with Jerome Mushkat's *Tammany: The Evolution of a Political Machine: 1789-1865* (Syracuse, 1971). The biography of the most noted leader of Tammany before Tweed, who endured as a Tilden supporter while a member of the House of Representatives in 1876, is told well by Samuel Augustus Pleasants in *Fernando Wood of New York* (New York, 1948). There is much useful material in De Alva Stanwood Alexander's third volume (1861-1882) of *A Political History of the State of New York* (New York, 1909).

RECREATION

Much of the history of recreation during the centennial era of New York City remains to be written. A starting point will remain Foster Rhea Dulles's *A History of Recreation: America Learns to Play* (New York, 1965 ed.). There is much useful material in John A. Krout and Clifford L. Lord, "Sports and Recreation," in Alexander C. Flick, *History of the State of New York* X, chap. 7: "The Empire State," (New York, 1937). Evidence of the recognition of the importance of summertime activity was the publication of John B. Bachelder, *Popular Resorts, and How to Reach Them* (Boston, 1875). Irving Kolodin's *The Metropolitan Opera* (New York, 1936) is a basic source on the origins and development of that institution. One of the most interesting aspects of the history of recreation which remains to be analyzed by historians is the development in urban centers such as New York City of all types of popular sports and games for children and adults including gambling. With notable exceptions—among them, Lucy P. Gillman's splendid article "Coney Island," *New York History* XXXVI (July 1955): 255-290, and Harold Seymour, *Baseball: The Early Years* (New York, 1960), little emphasis has been given to the subject by serious historians.

A view of lower Manhattan in 1976.

Bayrd Still

BICENTENNIAL
NEW YORK, 1976

Mid-town Manhattan in the 1970s.

The New York that celebrates the nation's bicentennial is more than 350 years old; yet in many ways this now troubled giant of a city is as new in the bicentennial era as it was when it was only a tiny cluster of dwellings hugging the tip of Manhattan Island. With a population that increased from 3.5 million in 1900 to 7.6 million seventy-four years later, bicentennial New York not only is the nation's largest city; it is the hub of the most populous urbanized area in the world—a broad metropolitan expanse, estimated, by various methods of measurement, to include from 16 to 20 million persons.[1] Since the mid-twentieth century, the outer fringe of this metropolitan cluster has been growing in population at a much faster rate than the incorporated city—one cause of the city's fiscal difficulties in the mid-1970s. During the 1960s, the population of the central city grew by less than 1.5 percent, contrasted with an increase of at least 26 percent in the population of neighboring suburbia; from 1970 to 1974 the population of the central city actually suffered a 4.2 percent decline.[2]

The physical ligaments of this broad metropolitan region are the huge bridges, underwater tunnels, and many-laned expressways—most of them products of twentieth-century technology and financing—that facilitate travel between New York and its metropolitan outskirts. Motor vehicles sustain (as well as complicate) the interrelationship of the city and its suburbs; it was estimated in 1971 that 650,000 automobiles entered Manhattan's central business district (the area south of 60th Street) daily. However, a sizable majority of New Yorkers, more than in many large cities, make their trips to work by public transportation. In the mid-1970s, on a normal business day, some eight million passengers used the subways, urban and suburban buses, and commuter railroads operated by the Metropolitan Transit Authority. The breadth of the city's commutation range extends as far as Philadelphia, from which a crack commuter train, the "Wall Streeter," departs for New York each morning at 6:33—evidence of the interlocking relationship of New York City, by the 1970s, with other major urban centers of the Atlantic Coast megalopolis.[3]

In a vertical as well as a horizontal sense, the city of the mid-1970s is a new New York. This is especially true of Manhattan where, after more than a decade of disfiguring construction, the wraps have come off scores of new skyscrapers literally transforming the appearance of parts of the lower city and sections of midtown. In 1900, church spires outreached the surrounding structures, although the 21-story Flatiron Building, completed in 1902, was then on the drawing boards. Seventy-five years later, the 110-story twin towers of the World Trade Center soar 1,350 feet, uncorniced, into the clouds, dwarfing not only New York's human inhabitants and their religious edifices but even the skyscrapers of an earlier period.[4]

Skyscrapers began to erupt in the lower city in the second decade of the 20th century, reaching a momentary peak of elevation with the completion in 1913 of the 60-story, 792-foot Woolworth Building which held the record for nearly twenty years as the world's tallest building. By the thriving 1920s the contagion of height competition had spread from the financial district of the lower city to midtown. The 1,048-foot Chrysler Building was completed in 1928, to be overshadowed two years later by the 102-story, 1,248-foot Empire State Building. In these years multi-storied commercial structures began to relieve the brownstone residential monotony of Fifth Avenue. Saks Fifth Avenue, symbolic of the avenue's fashionable department stores, was built in 1924; four years later the Bergdorf Goodman Company replaced an imposing mansion—the home of Cornelius Vanderbilt at Fifth Avenue and 58th Street—with another glamorous retail establishment. By the later 1920s, high rising hotels and office and apartment buildings had begun to proliferate in the midtown area; the 70-story RCA Building was topped out in 1932 reaching far above the spires of neighboring St. Patrick's Cathedral.[5]

The architectural novelty of Manhattan of the mid-1970s is expressed not only in the new order of elevation represented by the World Trade Center but by the increased pervasiveness of towering structures throughout the central city, creating a vertical mass unmatched in magnitude and density by any other city in the world. This broadening of the city's upward thrust resulted from a surge of office construction that began in the 1950s and peaked in the mid-1970s.[6] The 60-story Chase Manhattan Bank, completed in 1960 in the vicinity of Wall Street, spearheaded a burst of skyscraper construction that added scores of soaring structures to the lower city's already vertical conformation. At the same time, new buildings, 30 to 60 stories high, were transforming the midtown portions of Park Avenue and once-pedestrian Third Avenue and Sixth Avenue into canyons of glass, in hues of plum to bronze to charcoal, that mirror their towering neighbors and reflect the often brilliant New York sky.[7]

Two changes, the impact of which was increasingly evident by the mid-1970s, have relieved the in-depth density of Manhattan's scraperscape. One is the removal of the elevated railways, during the 1930s, 1940s, and 1950s, a change that makes endless vistas of Manhattan's grid-ordered avenues.[8] The other is the expansion of open space at the street level, the result of a sparing provision of small parks amid the skyscraping towers and the enactment of incentive zoning legislation, beginning in 1961, that encouraged builders to provide plazas and arcades at the foot of many of the new structures, in return for bonuses in height and floor space. The towers of the World Trade Center are set in a plaza larger than the Piazza San Marco in Venice. At Citicorp Center, under construction on Lexington Avenue in 1976, a 46-story tower is lifted above the street on pillars 112 feet high. The plans call for a block-long open plaza, a church geared to extensive community activity, shops, and a small park on the ground level underneath.[9]

Fifth Avenue's shining Olympic Tower, completed early in 1976, was influenced in both form and function by incentive zoning of 1971 designed not only to maximize open space, but to preserve the special quality of Fifth Avenue as a high-grade shopping district and encourage residence in the area. This 52-story multipurpose structure combines a pedestrian arcade with three floors of retail space at its base, 19 floors of office space, and 29 floors of condominium apartments.[10] A further revision of zoning rules, enacted in 1975, offers developers incentives to install chairs and benches, fountains, sculpture, book stalls, and flower kiosks in the open spaces at the foot of tall buildings. Architects and planners of the mid-1970s quite evidently are intent upon enhancing Manhattan's image on the ground as well as in the sky.[11]

Elsewhere in Manhattan and in parts of the other boroughs, huge blocks of apartments, built under both public and private auspices, exhibit the transforming influence of the high-rise revolution. The neighborhood of Lincoln Center now bristles with impressive, multi-storied structures. East Harlem boasts a Mitchell-Lama housing development—1191 Plaza—in which distinctive 30-story residential structures are integrated with retail and recreational facilities at the ground level. Co-op City, completed in 1970, gave the Bronx a residential complex, accommodating 60,000 people, that combines thirty-five high-rise towers with hundreds of two-family houses. Much of the city's public housing consists of super-blocks of tall buildings. This new construction throughout the city, encouraged by urban renewal and other government programs designed to cope with the urban crises of the 1950s and 1960s, has given large areas of the city a gigantically sculptured and imposingly finished look not as evident earlier in the century. At the same time it has tended to obscure, as indeed it helped to cause, the enclaves of physical deterioration and decay that infest the city in many places.

The most extreme examples of blighted neighborhoods are to be found in the South Bronx, Central and East Harlem, and Bedford-Stuyvesant and Brownsville in Brooklyn, even though some presentable sections exist within these areas. Close to half of the residential structures in Central Harlem are dilapidated or structurally substandard—fast deteriorating because of slipshod or nonexistent upkeep. Even buildings with presentable exteriors often are pest-ridden inside, with crumbling walls and ceilings and broken and archaic fixtures. Whole sections of Bedford-Stuyvesant have a bombed-out look. In 1970, an antipoverty group described Hunt's Point in the Bronx as "one big garbage dump." Nor is squalid living confined to the most obvious poverty areas. A resident of Manhattan's East Village described his existence there in 1971 as a life of rusty water and leaking pipes, slowly escaping gas, German roaches, American centipedes, and New York rats. "It's bars on the windows . . . police locks on the doors," he wrote, "a stink of urine in the halls . . . a view of an alley or backyard or street filled with garbage."[12]

Urban renewal unquestionably dressed up parts of the city, but the program, as administered, deepened the deterioration—the congestion, squalor, and alienation—in other sections. As it operated, the program reduced the number of low-rent units and in the process dislodged the poor, disrupted neighborhoods, and forced the dispossessed to take squatters' quarters or to add to the congestion in the superslums of the South Bronx and parts of Brooklyn. The West Side Urban Renewal Program, hailed in 1958 as a "model" for the nation, is a case in point. By 1974, when the 20-square-block section was 70 percent rebuilt, 9,500 low-income families had been displaced, and the percentage of low-income families in the renovated neighborhood had dropped from 67 to 17 percent.[13]

These adverse aspects of the urban scene help to explain the paradox that while many parts of New York in the mid-1970s are physically more imposing than ever before, its image, both at home and abroad, is far less favorable than it was earlier in the century. Conditions associated with its size—its "tightly packed structural masses" and "its hopelessly paralyzed traffic channels"—had begun to tarnish the city's image by the 1940s. These shortcomings were ascribed to the overbuilding of bridges, tunnels, hotels, and business structures, since the 1920s—developments that had encouraged population growth to what appeared to be unmanageable proportions. As early as 1959, New York journalist Marya Mannes contended that New York had become so large that it could "no longer cope with its people." In 1964, an editorial writer in the *New York Times,* deploring "the suffocating crowds, the density of automobile traffic, the congestion and inconveniences of the subways, the difficulty of being served in shopping, in eating, in accomplishing either business or pleasure," came to the conclusion that the city's "basic ill" was "size itself."[14]

Since the 1960s, however, an even more damaging facet has been added to the city's image, and that is fear. In recent years, a cumulative sense of physical insecurity has so conditioned the day-to-day habits of New Yorkers as to be like an illness one learns to live with. So widespread are the reports of muggings that pedestrians instinctively avoid deserted streets, and subway riders shun sparsely occupied cars and stations. Fearful of being robbed, apartment dwellers institute tenant patrols and install double and triple locks on their doors. During the early 1970s the city government offered block associations matching funds to purchase security equipment. In many sections of the city, storekeepers use entrance buzzers and uniformed guards for security during the day; metal barricades protect their show windows against vandalism at night. Some affluent neighborhoods employ commercial protection services, with radio-equipped cars, to supplement the police. A commentator on life in New York in 1973 reported that fear was "universally acknowledged" to be the city's "greatest single problem."[15]

Widely publicized crises such as the looting and burning in Central and East Harlem and Bedford-Stuyvesant in 1964, 1967, and 1968 have contributed to this negative aspect of the city's image; but the climate of fear is intensified by almost daily references in the communications media to crimes of violence, incidents involving knives and narcotics in the public schools, and the irresponsible behavior of drug addicts, especially blacks and Puerto Ricans. In January 1970, a poverty worker in Hunt's Point reported that during the period December 1-27, 1969, in one block alone there were eighteen assaults and robberies, one rape, one murder, and three deaths from heroin overdose. According to police reports, two single-occupancy hotels on Manhattan's West Side were the scene of 207 crimes perpetrated on the premises during the first nine-and-a-half months of 1974. In one such hotel in that area, eight elderly women were murdered in the course of the year. Methadone clinics, fast-food restaurants, and single-occupancy hotels are special targets of popular criticism as places that spawn violent crime.[16]

Statistics for 1975 show a continuing increase in all categories of crime with the exception of murder. The first six months of 1975, contrasted with a comparable period in 1974, saw an increase of 11.8 percent in robberies—the crime most feared by the public. Not that New York is unique in suffering from a high incidence of crime. National figures issued early in 1975 revealed that thirteen of the nation's large cities had a worse per capita rate for homicide than New York; and during the first six months of 1975 the over-all crime rate in the nation as a whole rose by 18 percent compared to 13 percent in New York City.[17] Nevertheless, it is a factor of New York's size that, regardless of its comparative rating, incidents are sufficiently numerous in the city to make crime seem an ever-present threat. A decline in homicide rates, beginning in 1974 and noted especially in the city's poorer neighborhoods, is a sign, according to some observers, that antipoverty programs and agencies of community control have given people a means of coping with their frustrations. On the other hand, mounting unemployment helps to explain the rise in robberies and burglaries; and a continuing cause of tension is the aggressiveness of racial and ethnic groups competing for "a place in the sun."[18]

Certainly a major factor contributing a quality of contentiousness to the urban scene in the 1970s is the volatility of the city's ethnic mix. Racial and ethnic diversity and the tensions it can produce are in the tradition of New York City; nevertheless the particular nature of the city's ethnic patterns by the 1960s and 1970s is another aspect of the urban scene that differentiates the city of the bicentennial era from what it earlier was. As late as the 1940s, Irish, Germans, Italians, and Russians, along with Anglo-American stock, were recognized to be the basic ethnic ingredients of what Mayor Fiorello LaGuardia called "our cosmopolitan metropolis," a comment he made in 1945 at a time when ethnic identity had been submerged in wartime nationalism. At the turn of the century the Irish were "still Irish, the Italians still Italians, the Germans still Germans," wrote a New Yorker who recalled the city of 1898, "not yet melted down, amalgamated, and standardized as they had become by 1948." Whatever may have been the situation in 1898 or 1948, the novelty of this aspect of the city of the 1970s is the increasing polarization, fragmentation, and assertiveness of its ethnic elements and the increased visibility of groups that were proportionately less numerous at the turn of the century, especially blacks, Puerto Ricans, and Chinese.[19]

Today, as earlier, cosmopolitanism is the most characteristic human feature of New York City, despite the fact that the percentage of foreign born in the population dropped from 37 percent in 1900 to 18 percent in 1970. The city's traditional Irishness is now less evident than in the preceding century, but there still are enclaves of heavy Irish residence as, for example, in the vicinity of Fordham Road in the Bronx and of St. Sebastian's Parish in Woodside, Queens, where Catholic churches give focus to Irish settlements. The annual St. Patrick's Day Parade—when the Irish seem to own Fifth Avenue—is still the city's most pervasively celebrated ethnic glorification. The city's German stock is now widely dispersed; even Yorkville, centering on 86th Street on Manhattan's East Side, is losing its once predominantly Teutonic flavor, with the construction since the mid-1960s of blocks of luxury apartments in the area. Czech and Hungarian travel agencies, restaurants, and newspaper offices are reminders of once sizable Central European neighborhoods nearby.[20]

Representatives of the ethnic groups that were predominant at the turn of the century, especially Italians and East European Jews, now reside throughout the city and its suburbs. Social mobility has taken New York's Jewish residents, with relative speed, from Manhattan's lower East Side to many sections of the Bronx and Brooklyn, to neighborhoods like Forest Hills in Queens, to Central Park West in Manhattan, where they were joined in the 1930s by refugees from Nazism, and to the surrounding suburbs. Communities of Hasidic Jews maintain their orthodox traditions in dress, schools, and occupations in Williamsburg, Crown Heights, and Borough Park in Brooklyn. According to an estimate made in 1973, the Jewish residents of New York City numbered more than 1.8 million, with an additional 545,000 in Nassau, Suffolk, and Westchester counties.[21]

New Yorkers of Italian stock exhibit a similar pattern of intraurban and suburban movement. Their numbers in 1970—683,000 of Italian birth or with at least one Italian-born parent—made them the city's most numerous ethnic group of recent European origin. Though their progress from working to middle class has taken many Italians to the suburbs, there are identifiable Italian communities in many parts of the city, as in Bay Ridge in Brooklyn, the Belmont section of the Bronx, Astoria and Ozone Park in Queens, on Staten Island, and in lower Manhattan. Open markets and Italian bakeries, restaurants, and coffee houses emphasize the Italianism of the historic "Little Italy" that extends from Canal Street to Bleecker Street between the Bowery and LaFayette Street and westward into the area south of Washington Square. This quality is especially evident during the annual festivals of San Gennaro and St. Anthony, when the streets are festooned with lights, parades honor the patron saint, and the aroma of Italian sausage and peppers, for sale at street-side stalls, pervades the air.

As of the mid-1970s, the Italianism of some of New York's older Italian communities was being threatened by population pressure from other ethnic stocks. By 1970, the number of Italians in the "Little Italy" of East Harlem—once the largest Italian settlement in the city—had dwindled from 150,000 to 5,000, as the construction of city housing projects dislodged Italian tenement dwellers and as Italian residents were replaced by blacks and Puerto Ricans. In 1975, a Little Italy Restoration Association was attempting to protect the lower city's "Little Italy" against the acquisition of property by Chinese purchasers. The leaders of this lower city "risorgimento" were seeking municipal support for community facilities that would encourage Italian families to remain in the area rather than move to the outlying boroughs or to the suburbs. One proposal was the conversion of the former Police Headquarters located in the neighborhood into an Italian-American cultural center where Italian film festivals, opera workshops, and exhibits of modern Italian art could be held.[22]

New Yorkers of recent Polish background, some 300,000 in 1970, cluster in several parts of the city. In the Greenpoint section of Brooklyn— 50 percent Polish at the turn of the 1970s—masses are said in Polish, school children dance the Krakowiak, and the Polish National Home is a center of efforts to preserve Polish culture. Greeks are numerous in the Astoria section of Queens and in the vicinity of Eighth Avenue and 14th and 15th streets in Manhattan, site of the headquarters of Greek fraternal organizations and newspapers. The 60,000 Greek and Cypriote immigrants in Astoria constitute the largest Greek-Cypriote community in the Western Hemisphere, with characteristic family night clubs, taverns, and catering establishments, as well as the services of the St. Demetrios Greek Orthodox Church. New York City's Cuban community totaled 85,000 in 1970—about a quarter of the number in the metropolitan area. Many reside in Queens, but the largest concentration in the city is in upper Manhattan. Here, at the corner of 181st Street and Audubon Avenue, the names of the shops and of a theater duplicate those of La Esquina de Tejas, a well-known Havana intersection.[23]

Chinese newcomers arrived in such numbers during the 1960s and 1970s as to give greatly increased visibility throughout the city to an ethnic group whose presence had first become newsworthy nearly a hundred years earlier. A change in federal law, enacted in 1965, stimulated Oriental immigration; by the mid-1970s the number of New York residents of Chinese background had ballooned from 25,000 to an estimated 60,000 to 100,000, a sizable proportion under the age of thirty. "Chinatown," in the vicinity of Mott and Canal streets, was spilling over into "Little Italy," and within the community there was tension between the Chinese Consolidated Benevolent Association, representing the establishment, and groups such as the Asian Americans for Equal Employment, the Chinatown Planning Council, and the Chinese Youth Council. Additional Oriental stocks contribute to the cosmopolitanism of New York City, as do the personnel connected with the political headquarters of the United Nations and the many students from Africa and the Far East studying at the city's several universities. Some 40,000 Japanese reside in the metropolitan area. About half of them are noncitizens, many representing Japanese business firms. A Sikh guardwara or temple, converted from a Baptist church in Richmond Hills, Queens, is a center for Indians and Pakistani, whose migration increased greatly after 1965.[24]

Though this multiplicity of nationality stocks makes New York what it always has been—a city of many tongues—the widespread use of Spanish, in both conversation and public advertising, and the inflection and idiom of American Negro speech are the most pervasive novel elements in the linguistic mix of today's New York. Subway notices warn riders that "la vía del tren subterráneo es peligrosa"; a brand of jeans, modeled by two handsome young blacks, is advertised as providing "the western look that really gets down." The census of 1970 identified nearly 1.3 million New Yorkers as of Spanish heritage; in April 1976, it was estimated that the Puerto Rican community of New York exceeded one million. A dense concentration of Puerto Ricans resides in "El Barrio" in East Harlem; there are other sizable Puerto Rican neighborhoods on the lower East Side and in the Chelsea area of Manhattan, in the Bronx—Hunt's Point, Tremont, and the South Bronx—and in Williamsburg in Brooklyn.

The rapid influx of Puerto Ricans has presented problems for the city, not so much because of a language barrier, but because of their minimal educational background, their continuing close identification with the homeland, and especially their poverty, with its negative behavioral consequences. A 1970 study showed their median income to be considerably less than that of the city's nonwhite population. As of that date, approximately 82 percent of the Puerto Ricans in the city resided in what were described as poverty areas, whereas these areas harbored only 79 percent of the city's nonwhites and less than 21 percent of its non-Puerto Rican whites. Nevertheless, they have rapidly identified with the city and increasingly assert their place in its cosmopolitan mix. Evidence of this is the annual Puerto Rican Day parade, which in 1975 drew an estimated 100,000 marchers, in contrast with the few thousand who participated in the first Puerto Rican parade in 1958. Herman Badillo, a native of Puerto Rico, served as borough president of the Bronx from 1966 to 1969, preceding his election to Congress. Chairman of the 1975 parade was Ramon S. Velez, city councilman from the Bronx, who has built a federally financed antipoverty program into a political power base and currently is rising to prominence as a Puerto Rican leader.

Puerto Ricans, like other Hispanics, have helped to bolster the number of New Yorkers claimed by the Catholic Church, whose total of reported adherents—some 2.9 million as of 1975—has not changed greatly in the past decade. As many as half of the city's Catholics are now of Hispanic background. This has posed problems for the Church, inasmuch as Hispanic Catholics tend to be more loyal to family than to church, are less concerned with religious obligations than Catholics of some other ethnic stocks, and less inclined or able to provide financial support. Also, unlike their Irish or Italian predecessors, they have not brought their priests with them. Moreover, Protestant pentecostal churches, staffed by Puerto Rican clergy, have a strong appeal for these newcomers.[25]

However much the presence of Puerto Ricans is changing the city's ethnic composition and contributing to its problems, it is the growing proportion of blacks in the central city and the interaction between this group and the rest of the population that constitutes the most significant feature of the city's ethnic conformation in the mid-1970s. This development, indeed, is related in crucial ways to many of the most serious problems in the city of the bicentennial era. According to the census of 1970, blacks numbered 1.6 million—more than 21 percent of the population—an increase from 60,000 (only 2 percent of the population) in 1900. The rapidity as well as the magnitude of this increase prompted a European commentator to report in 1973 that New York was "turning black." "In a sense," he reported, "[blacks] are the key to everything."[26] This impression has been heightened by conditions that keep the bulk of the black population in the central city. Between 1960 and 1970, the white population of the incorporated city showed a deficit in growth and an outmigration of almost a million people. On the other hand, the nonwhite population increased by nearly 62 percent, and the nonwhites who migrated to the central city exceeded in number those who left.

Unlike the situation with most other ethnic groups, increasing ghettoization has characterized the residential patterns of New York City blacks. One major concentration is in Central Harlem—since the 1920s a city within the city, extending from Central Park on the south to the Harlem River and from Morningside and St. Nicholas parks on the west to Fifth Avenue. Blacks began to move into this area as early as 1910, when overextended construction made available to Negroes apartments originally intended for whites. In 1970, more than 95 percent of Central Harlem's 180,000 residents were blacks. A similar concentration in the Bedford-Stuyvesant, Brownsville, and Crown Heights sections of Brooklyn was produced by the extension of subway connections from Harlem into this area by the mid-1930s and by the heavy migration of Negroes to New York City during and after World War II. In 1970, in one section of Bedford-Stuyvesant, 85 percent of a total of 235,000 residents were blacks.[27]

Today these areas are quieter than they were in the protest-ridden 1960s, despite the fact that much of the housing in Harlem and Bedford-Stuyvesant is still a disgrace and a larger proportion of the residents are on welfare than in most other parts of the city, with little hope of change in view of the increasingly limited employment market for unskilled workers. Nevertheless, in the city as a whole the black condition appears to be showing signs of considerable improvement. The income level of blacks has risen, as civil rights legislation has opened job opportunities in broadened areas of employment—in stores, banks, and offices, and especially in the civil service. In 1934, close to 65 percent of the transit workers in the city were Irish; by the mid-1970s, as many as 45 percent of all transit employees and a majority of those newly hired were blacks. An improved image of blacks, as presented in television and in magazine and newspaper advertising, has partly offset the popular identification of blacks with drug addiction and crime.

Agencies, both private and public, have been active in the attempt to improve environmental conditions in black communities. The Harlem Urban Development Corporation, a subsidiary of the New York State Urban Development Corporation, has sought since 1971 to encourage and coordinate improvements in housing. Municipal efforts to achieve integration in housing and public school education have given black activists some assurance that the authorities are sometimes on their side. Most importantly, neighborhood governance, instituted in the early 1970s, has been psychologically rewarding in that it has provided an opportunity for blacks to become involved in the solution of the problems of their own communities. Scores of vigorous community agencies, some of them federally supported antipoverty programs, have been working on plans and proposals to rebuild neighborhoods. In Harlem, at least, some observers detect "an unmistakable air of change."[28]

An ethnocentric attitude, increasingly pervasive among blacks since the mid-1970s, differentiates the behavior of blacks from that of earlier migrant groups to the city. Unlike the generality of newcomers from Europe, many blacks, in all economic classes and especially the young, stress separatism rather than absorption into the mainstream of the urban society as the new way to achieve a better life. Black political leaders have found it expedient to present a single voice of protest against racial repression; this has been a factor in their achievement of political recognition. Black separatism often is reflected in individuality of dress and behavior as well as in an insistence on neighborhood management of schools, hospitals, and recreational facilities. As Roy Innis, national director of the Congress of Racial Equality, wrote in June 1969: "Blacks can achieve parity with whites in a truly pluralistic society only after they have achieved control over their own institutions."[29] By the mid-1970s, New York blacks were making progress in this direction.

In recent years, Puerto Ricans have begun to emulate black solidarity as a means of achieving recognition, despite the potentially divisive color factor within this ethnic group. Puerto Ricans have made language their rallying point, arguing that the heavy dropout rate among the some 260,000 Puerto Rican students in the public schools is to be explained by the fact that from 25,000 to 100,000 speak or read little or no English. In 1972, as a result of a case brought by the Puerto Rican Legal Defense Fund and Aspira, a self-help organization, the Board of Education consented to expand its facilities for bilingual education. Critics complain that this policy will limit the traditional role of the schools in bringing about acculturation to an English-speaking norm. On the other hand, proponents of the bilingual program argue not only that it will speed the training of youth not yet equipped with English but also that knowledge of the language is essential to maintaining the cultural tradition of an ethnic group. Earlier immigrant groups have lost their heritage, Puerto Rican leaders contend. "We . . . are not going to let this happen to us."[30]

The expanding numbers and increasing assertiveness of blacks and Puerto Ricans have been paralleled by a heightened sense of group identification on the part of the city's other nationality elements. This has become evident as blacks and Puerto Ricans have moved into communities long dominated by other ethnic stocks, and especially when efforts have been made to locate public housing in middle-income white neighborhoods. It is seen, too, in resistance to Board of Education policies designed to achieve racial balance in the public schools and equalize the utilization of school buildings. Welfare has been an additional irritant. Some whites, especially in working-class areas, attribute the deterioration of municipal services in their communities to the costs of welfare, of which blacks and Puerto Ricans are the primary beneficiaries. Representatives of ethnic stocks who have "made it" through their own efforts criticize the "welfare coddling" of these most recent newcomers to the city. In 1975, the director of the Congress of Italian-American Organizations served notice on the federal and local governments that Italians must have their rightful share of the public money available for minorities and the disadvantaged.[31]

The most overt tension over housing occurred in 1971 in response to plans to build low-income public housing in predominantly Jewish Forest Hills in Queens. This proposal inspired anti-black reactions from the white ethnic group traditionally most sympathetic to the Negro's problems. Opposition was based on the apprehension that the influx of blacks, Puerto Ricans, and welfare families would increase the incidence of crime and cause the deterioration of the neighborhood. The community protest was sufficiently strong to prompt a compromise solution of the controversy. In 1972, an urban renewal project in a Polish section of Brooklyn was opposed as threatening "the systematic destruction of an ethnic community and its culture." A year earlier, Poles and Lithuanians in Maspeth, Queens, insisted that the stability of their neighborhood depended on maintaining its existing nationality structure, as symbolized in the Polish National Hall and the Lithuanian Citizens Club. Their battle cry, reportedly heard in their churches, factories, and pubs, was, "We're going to keep it this way."[32]

Busing has prompted less violent opposition in New York than in many large cities. This fortunate circumstance springs in part from the fact that many New Yorkers remove themselves from controversy. Catholic families in large numbers send their children to parochial schools. Jewish parents often respond to the increase in black enrollment by moving to the suburbs, once their children reach school age, or by sending them to private day schools. Moreover, Jewish youth are perhaps less inclined than those of some other nationalities to indulge in organized resistance. Significant, too, is the fact that as yet there has been little busing of whites into predominantly black communities. The most publicized incidents of opposition to busing have occurred in Italian neighborhoods. In 1971 an altercation between local white students and bused-in blacks in a junior high school in Ozone Park, Queens, led the Italian-American Civil Rights League to put its members on call to resist "marauders," especially blacks.[33]

In the fall of 1975, demonstrations in heavily Italian Bensonhurst, in Brooklyn, protested the existing busing of blacks from Central Brooklyn to New Utrecht High School in Bensonhurst and the assignment of sixty neighborhood youth to underenrolled James Madison High School in a section of neighboring Flatbush, which has a higher proportion, though not a majority, of black residents, and where there have been sporadic racial disturbances. One freshman girl, a graduate of a parochial elementary school, expressed the reaction of many Bensonhurst students: "This is the only white neighborhood left. If they start busing more black kids in here, there's going to be more blacks in the neighborhood, you'll be afraid on the streets, the houses around here won't be worth as much and pretty soon the whole place will be black." Adults portrayed the issue as one of "neighborhood schools for neighborhood children," arguing that the youth of the local community, virtually all of them white, should be guaranteed places in the neighborhood school. Neighborhood integrity was becoming the bastion of ethnic (and white) identity.[34]

Divisive as these attitudes may be and real as are the ingrained antagonism and apprehension in many quarters between blacks and whites, they are softened, if not countered, by a pervasive common identification with the city that seems to make all the ethnic elements in its population "New Yorkers," regardless of efforts to preserve the culture of a particular nationality group or the integrity of local neighborhoods. Modern communications facilities, especially radio and television, together with the availability of more leisure time, may have something to do with this. Certainly, most residents of mid-twentieth-century New York, regardless of where they live, identify with the city as an entity and think of themselves as part of it to a greater degree than did its residents at the turn of the century. The New York correspondent of the London *Financial Times,* writing in 1974, detected among New Yorkers what he called a broad "communal identity, a pervasive feeling that for better or worse we are all in this together." He attributed this, not to the operation of a "melting pot"—for "the separate components have refused to merge"—but to the fact that New York "seems to have room for them all, and somehow they all manage to accommodate each other." If this faculty were ever lost, he thought, it would do more to destroy New York's "unique character" than any of the "multitude of urban problems with which the city is afflicted."[35]

A potential irritant in ethnic and race relations in the city of the 1970s is the changing nature of the economy, especially the reduction in job opportunities for unskilled workers. Over the past quarter-century, the central city has solidified its position as the capital of the white-collar business world, but it has suffered a steady erosion of its capacity to provide manufacturing, warehousing, and industrial jobs, except in light manufacturing, where wage scales are only marginally above the poverty level. The New York-Northeastern New Jersey metropolitan area still constitutes the nation's prime manufacturing complex in terms of number of employees and value added by manufacture; but manufacturing within the central city has been fighting a losing battle against the attractions of the suburbs for factory production. In the central city the number of jobs in manufacturing declined from one million in 1950 to 570,000 in 1975. Where factories once provided nearly a third of New York's employment opportunities, by the mid-1970s they accounted for only a sixth. This is a change of major significance, given the correlative increase in the number of relatively unskilled workers in the population of the central city and the conditions restricting many of them to residence there rather than in the suburbs.[36]

Garment production, printing and publishing, and the manufacture of food products employ the largest numbers of New York's industrial workers. These industries flourish in part, at least, because of the size of the local market. The manufacture of electrical equipment and supplies is another major source of employment. The garment industry reflects the current decline in the number of industrial jobs (it lost some 200,000 jobs in recent years) and reveals, as well, the changes that have occurred in the pattern of production and in the composition of the work force. Within the city, garment manufacturing is more centralized than it was at the turn of the century; the Garment Center of the mid-1970s, located in lower midtown in the vicinity of Broadway and Seventh Avenue, is a city within the city. It has its own newspapers and restaurants and even its suburban fringe, made up of the fur market, the undergarment industry, the millinery market, and menswear. New ethnic elements are now numerically predominant in an industry earlier dominated, and still mostly owned, by Jewish immigrants and their sons. The International Ladies Garment Workers Union, once almost exclusively Jewish and Italian, is now Hispanic, Chinese, black, Greek, and Italian, with Jews in a substantial minority, despite their monopoly of its leadership. Chinese contractors are increasingly engaged in the industry, and Greek artisans are active in the fur business.[37]

Newspaper publication has been the victim of competition from radio and television, increased production costs, and changes in the composition of the population. Circulation figures for English dailies have not kept up with the population increase of the past twenty-five years; the *Daily News, Times, Post,* and *Wall Street Journal* are the sole survivors of a roster of newspapers that in 1951 totaled more than twice that number. As of 1975, the circulation of German and Yiddish papers had greatly declined; *Il Progresso Italo-Americano* fell slightly short of matching its 1951 circulation figure of 67,876; the only foreign-language newspaper to report a marked increase in business was *El Diario-La Prensa,* a Spanish-language daily, with a circulation of more than 67,000.

On the other hand, New York continues to have a virtual corner on the production of the leading national magazines, a fact that testifies both to the appeal of the city as a site for national white-collar enterprise and to the role of New York as a center of news and fashion dissemination. The past twenty-five years have seen a significant increase in the number of wide-circulation magazines whose offices are located in New York. A similar development has taken place in book publication, strengthening the city's role as the center of the nation's book publishing trade. Mergers within the industry have increased the concentration of management headquarters in New York City, a trend also encouraged by the presence in New York of advertising firms, review media, and literary agents, especially those concerned with the negotiation of subsidiary rights for paperback publication.[38]

Trade, commerce, and finance continue to be major props of the urban economy. In 1972, wholesale trade was valued at $80 billion and retail trade at $13 billion, despite the competition from suburban shopping centers. Traditionally, New York City has been, above all, a harbor and a port. Today, the operations of the port, though still important to the economy, are much affected by air travel and air transport. In 1974, fewer than 100,000 trans-Atlantic passengers traveled by ship from United States and Canadian ports, in contrast with an annual average of more than a million in the early 1960s. The mid-1970s marked the end of the era of the great ocean liners that for many years berthed imposingly at the Hudson River piers. The seagoing palaces of the Italian Line made their farewell voyages in 1975. On the other hand, in 1974 Kennedy, LaGuardia, and Newark airports handled more than 42 million passengers including 11.8 million overseas travelers. Despite these changes, the port still is the busiest in the nation. Customs revenues on imports by ship and aircraft for the year ending June 1974 totaled $1.3 billion, about a third of the national total and more than three times that of any other port in the United States.[39]

The presence of many of the nation's largest banks, insurance companies, and brokerage houses, as well as the concentration in the city of the headquarters of at least 140 of the nation's major corporations, provides a stabilizing influence on the urban economy. These large corporate institutions underwrote the spectacular architectural transformation of the city in the 1960s and 1970s and helped to foster the expansion of white-collar employment, which increased by at least 14 percent in the decade of the 1960s. As of the early 1970s, the city's banking institutions handled about $80 billion annually. The city's big banks have benefited from amendments to the Bank Holding Company Act of 1956 which permitted them to expand their operations beyond traditional banking functions both in the United States and abroad. As a result, they have moved into insurance, real estate, accounting, data processing, and other fields, thus broadening their profit potential. In the mid-1970s, when many businesses in the city were suffering from the effects of recession, the three largest banks—First National City Bank, Chase Manhattan Bank, and Manufacturers Hanover Trust Company—were sharply expanding their office facilities, thus bolstering the declining rental market.[40] In the summer of 1975, as we shall see, they played a not insignificant role in bringing the city's festering fiscal crisis to a head.

The novelty in the occupational pattern of New York City in the 1970s is the marked increase in the proportion of its residents engaged in skilled service activities. This change took place as the city increasingly became a front office for national and international commerce and finance, multiplied its municipal services, ministered to increasing numbers of transients from its metropolitan area and beyond, and met the often overly expanded expectations of its residents. Buckminster Fuller was quoted in 1971 as saying that New York's chief function of the moment was "the exchange of ideas and processing of paper by typewriter," an apt observation, though it overlooked the already significant role of duplicating machines. As of 1972, as many New Yorkers were employed in skilled services as in manufacturing—many more, if persons engaged in finance, transportation, and municipal government were included. By early 1975 the municipal government had become the city's largest single employer, with a payroll of close to 300,000 (by contrast with less than 150,000 in 1945). The city's fiscal crisis led to a reduction of personnel; by September 30, 1975, the number of full-time city employees had been reduced to 263,000.[41]

As of the early 1970s, service activities occupied the preponderance of workers in Manhattan, where an overwhelming proportion of the work force is employed. More than 86,000 persons were engaged in medical and other health services, testimony to the fact that activities of this kind are highly specialized in the metropolis and tend to be performed at its focal center. Suppliers of professional entertainment similarly were centered in Manhattan and to a greater degree than in years past. Persons employed in motion pictures and other amusement and recreational activities totaled more than 35,000; radio and television broadcasting occupied another 18,000. Advertising agencies accounted for nearly 30,000 employees, almost all of them located in Manhattan. Personal services were another major source of employment. Beauty parlors in Manhattan employed more than 4,000 workers, but in this more widely dispersed service, close to 2,000 persons were similarly employed in Brooklyn and more than 2,200 in Queens.[42]

These changes in the nature of occupational opportunities, coupled as they were with the increase in the proportion of unskilled persons in the population, would have seriously affected the state of the city's economy by the mid-1970s even if they had not coincided with a period of spiraling inflation and nationwide recession. The substitution of unskilled for skilled residents was bound to reduce productivity in the city, as well as demand, especially in view of the decline in the number of jobs in manufacturing, which traditionally provided employment for unskilled newcomers. Though employment in New York City was at a record high in December 1970 (some 4.1 million workers), the welfare rolls had been mounting in spectacular proportions since the mid-1960s. A distinguished economist asked early in 1964, "Can the urban economy absorb the new raw labor?" There were other signs of the instability of the economy. More than a tenth of the floor space in the city's skyscrapers lay vacant in the mid-1970s; uncollected realty taxes approached a quarter billion dollars; rent was skyrocketing, especially for New Yorkers with low and moderate incomes; and rates for electricity, a power source of vital importance to the vigor of the economy, were higher in New York than in other communities, in part because the electric utility had been encouraged to overexpand its facilities and in part because the underground distribution system used in the city was much more costly to install and repair than overhead lines.[43]

By spring 1975, the recession had wiped out the employment gains of the 1960s; in June, the job total stood at 3,373,000, the lowest since 1954. Some 380,000 New Yorkers were out of work. The average unemployment rate for the year 1975 was 10.6 percent compared with a national average of 7.5 percent. As of March 1975, more than 991,000 New Yorkers were on welfare (13 percent of the population); it was predicted that more than 1.2 million people, or 15 percent of the population, would be on the relief rolls by late 1976. Blacks and Hispanics each accounted for about 43 percent of the persons on relief; non-Hispanic whites made up only 13 percent, but the proportion in this category was increasing. In 1975, welfare grants were $258 a month for a family of four, plus heating and fuel. This sum would have been more helpful but for the fact that the New York economy was suffering from an inflation rate of at least 12 percent, the highest among the major cities of the nation. The cost of living for an average middle-income family in New York, as calculated in the fall of 1973, was $14,448—higher than the figure for any other major city except Boston.[44]

By the 1970s, efforts—both public and private—were being made to resuscitate the city's ailing economy. Since the late 1960s, the Economic Development Corporation, a municipal agency, had been attempting to encourage the location of new manufacturing enterprises within the city. Using the right of eminent domain, the city acquired property potentially suitable for industrial use in labor-populated areas and leased or sold it at advantageous prices to private industrialists, counting on the increase in the taxable value of the property to make the projects self-liquidating. The Flatlands Urban Industrial Park in Brooklyn and the Hunt's Point Food Center and Zerega Avenue Industrial Park in the East Bronx were developed in this fashion. The conversion of the Brooklyn Navy Yard to industrial use, after the city acquired it from the federal government in 1969, attracted a number of factories under temporary leases.[45] Proponents of open admission to the City University argued that widened educational opportunity would increase the pool of clerical workers, thus encouraging industrial firms to remain in the city rather than move to the suburbs.

Private effort to stimulate the economy is best illustrated in the work of the New York Convention and Visitors Bureau, which, in a burst of unabashed boosterism, in August 1975, succeeded in inducing the Democratic Party to choose New York over Los Angeles as the site for the Party's 1976 nominating convention.[46] The Bureau is a business-oriented group with a membership of 1,400, leadership of which is drawn from executives in the city's major hotels, department stores, recreational enterprises, and transportation and real estate firms. Its major activity, which receives some support from city funds, is directed toward encouraging the tourist and convention traffic. In its report for 1973, the Bureau took credit for attracting 820 conventions and giving assistance to 16 million visitors. Visitors in 1975 allegedly spent close to 1.4 billion dollars in the city, making "the visitor industry . . . the second largest in the business capital of the world." In 1974, when many New Yorkers were despairing over the city's contemporaneous image, the Bureau resurrected

"The Big Apple"—a show term meaning "the greatest"—as the city's symbol, one that allegedly would identify New York City as "the center of the universe, the place where it's at."[47]

Apart from political considerations, the selection of New York City as the site of the Democratic convention testifies to the appeal of its most impregnable asset—the abundance of cultural and entertainment fare that has prompted references to it both as "Fun City" and as "Parnassus, U. S. A." In this respect, however, New York in 1976 differs less from what is was seventy-five years earlier than in most other aspects of its urban existence. As early as the turn of the century, European visitors had praised New York not only for the variety of the entertainment it offered but for the merit of its theater, its permanent orchestra, opera "equal to the best in Europe," and an art museum that led the world "in several respects." The mushrooming profusion of its entertainment and cultural facilities, especially from the 1920s onward, only gave added visibility to this intrinsic facet of the city's urban personality.[48]

The cultural and entertainment scene of the mid-1970s, despite New York's traditional abundance of such resources, nevertheless differs in degree and configuration from the past. New York still is the preeminent theatrical center of the country and, with London, of the world; but changes have occurred in theatrical offerings, with the widespread availability of television and radio probably most responsible. Though not unique to New York City, television programs, like every other kind of entertainment, are more abundant in New York than elsewhere. By 1975, the signals of fifteen television stations could be received clearly in most of the New York area, and there were seven city-based high frequency TV outlets. Radio stations are even more numerous; at least fifty-seven FM stations, several operating twenty-four hours a day, offer music from rock to classical and news and talk shows in a wide variety of languages.[49]

The competition of radio and television, together with the suburban dispersal of the middle-class theater-going population, has reduced the number of major playhouses in the city to hardly more than half the number operating in the peak season of 1927-1928. Live theater now is concentrated in Manhattan in a cluster of houses in the vicinity of Broadway and the forties and fifties or in the lofts, basements, night clubs, and converted halls and churches that constitute the "off" and "off-off" Broadway theater. No longer do Broadway offerings play limited runs at the Harlem Opera House, the Brooklyn and Majestic theaters in Brooklyn, the Bronx Opera House at 149th Street east of Third Avenue, or the Shubert and Broad Street theaters in Newark, as they did earlier in the century. Because of opportunities in television, fewer performers of star quality are available for Broadway than there were fifty years ago. This competition for talent, as well as the round-the-clock entertainment offered by television, may also explain the virtual disappearance of the big vaudeville houses that provided continuous live entertainment in the first half of the century, not only on Broadway but in the outlying boroughs and in Newark. Burlesque theaters, the businessman's delight of the earlier era, have declined in number as the legitimate theater and the movies, in the sensual seventies, deal more openly with sex.[50]

The state of the ethnic theater mirrors the changing population patterns in the contemporary city. Gone is the once flourishing German language repertory theater, victim in part of the cultural consequences of two world wars. Productions in Yiddish by one or two professional groups are all that remain of the Yiddish theater, in marked contrast to the situation in the 1920s, when as many as eleven theaters and two vaudeville houses provided professional performances in Yiddish. By the 1940s, production costs and the diminished use of the Yiddish language had inaugurated the decline of a cultural institution in which a number of actors, ultimately distinguished on Broadway, had gained a start. The Folksbeine Players still give a season of weekend performances at the Central Synagogue Theater. They are the descendants of the Folksbuehne, organized by the Workmen's Circle in 1915 to present the best of Yiddish dramatic literature as a means of acquainting Jewish newcomers with the riches of their cultural inheritance.

On the other hand, blacks and Hispanics are exerting an increasing impact on theatrical activity in the city. Several off-Broadway theaters present, in limited seasons, weekend performances of serious Spanish drama, not to mention the large number of motion picture houses featuring films in Spanish. Blacks are much more evident than earlier not only as actors and playwrights but as audience, in both the Broadway and off-Broadway theater and in plays dealing with non-black as well as black themes. The widened exposure of blacks in the New York theatrical scene is in part a consequence of the efforts of blacks during the 1960s to develop in Harlem and other off-Broadway localities a theater that would interpret black culture to black audiences. The Negro Ensemble Company is one of several black groups with this goal. Plays originally produced in the off-Broadway black theater ultimately have reached Broadway where they have given broadened visibility to black actors and playwrights. A case in point is Leslie Lee's *The First Breeze of Summer,* designed to puncture some of the myths concerning black family life. It originally was produced as a one-act play by the Negro Ensemble Company, at its off-Broadway theater, and later moved to Broadway where it played to award-winning acclaim. This trend is likely to have a more lasting effect on theatrical offerings in New York than productions that depend for their appeal upon a foreign-speaking audience.[51]

Motion pictures are far less at the center of the entertainment scene in the New York of the 1970s than they were in the generation following the introduction of talking films in 1927. The newer theaters are functional in design, not the ornate movie "palaces" of the era of the Roxy Theater and Radio City Music Hall. Some of the newest are built into skyscrapers, a development encouraged by a change in building ordinances granting builders a bonus in floor space for including a theater in the structure. Fewer motion pictures have Broadway premieres than in the past; more theaters in midtown Manhattan specialize in art films and pornography. Film distributors now provide a film fare common to both the central city and the metropolitan area. Today the city's chief contribution to film production is in the realm of film as an art form and in providing professional training in film making as in the cinema program at New York University's School of the Arts.[52]

In the broad spectrum of entertainment available to New Yorkers, spectator sports continue to have a wide appeal. Even though the Brooklyn Dodgers have defected to the West Coast, the Mets and Yankees attract a wide following from baseball fans, vying for the patronage of sports enthusiasts with topflight performers in professional football, the Giants and Jets; the Knicks and the Nets in professional basketball; the Islanders and the Rangers in hockey; racing at Aqueduct and Belmont Park; and tennis at Forest Hills.

The city's many night clubs, supperclubs, discotheques, and cafes offer fewer name entertainers than in years past. Superstars like Barbra Streisand, Frank Sinatra, and the Rolling Stones now attract sold-out audiences at Madison Square Garden and Carnegie and Avery Fisher halls or draw tens of thousands to free concerts in the parks. As rock appears to be passing the peak of its popularity, there are signs, in the mid-1970s, of an increasing enthusiasm for jazz, both as entertainment and as an art form. Jazz entertainers figure in the resurgence of cabaret singing; on February 18, 1975 Mary Lou Williams performed a jazz Mass at St. Patrick's Cathedral. An annual ten-day jazz festival held during the summer months is scaled to the seating capacity of Avery Fisher and Carnegie halls, Radio City Music Hall, and the Nassau Veterans' Memorial Coliseum. Among the performers are the nation's leading jazz groups and singers. "Pop music" in New York City is not "quite like Mozart," as one critic observed, but it is "music making of a high and vital order."[53]

Quality is not novel in the city's more traditional musical fare, but the quantity of such music as of the mid-1970s, has reached virtually indigestible proportions. What Cecil Beaton wrote of the New York musical scene in 1947 continues to characterize it thirty years later: "In Winter there is almost too much good music. . . . Foreign pianists, conductors, and singers are continually arriving and departing. The symphony concerts are of the highest quality. . . . New York audiences are the most enthusiastic and critical in the world."[54]

Today two opera companies of international stature, the Metropolitan and the New York City Opera, present extended seasons of this most costly musical entertainment. The New York Philharmonic plays four performances weekly from late September to mid-May, competing with subscription series offered by the Boston and Philadelphia symphony orchestras and with the concerts, on shorter visits, of nearly every major orchestra of the United States and Europe. A galaxy of smaller musical ensembles and recitalists of international repute vie nightly for the patronage of New York's music-loving public, along with scores of neighborhood orchestras and a proliferation of opera workshop groups that attract more aspiring opera singers to New York than to any other city in the world.

The construction of Lincoln Center during the 1960s, an architectural complex that includes a new Metropolitan Opera House, the New York State Theater, Philharmonic (later Avery Fisher) Hall, the Vivian Beaumont Theater, and the Juilliard School, has given New York a luminous, if somewhat earthbound, shrine to its resources in the performing arts. The concert scene reflects the counterpoint between core and neighborhood in the city of the 1970s. Lincoln Center and Carnegie Hall are the major focal points of musical entertainment; but "star" series, promoted in a variety of localities—such as at the Brooklyn Academy of Music, the 92nd Street Young Men's Hebrew Association, Hunter and Brooklyn colleges, and Iona College in Westchester—give some neighborhoods subscription concerts of a quality equivalent to what is offered at Lincoln Center and Carnegie Hall.[55]

Mounting production costs have forced the performing arts to look increasingly to sources of subsistence beyond box office receipts and the gifts of wealthy donors, their chief support in the past. By 1975, for example, the annual operating budget of the Metropolitan Opera Association had reached $24 million; deficits of $8 and $9 million, before contributions, became customary, despite ticket prices that ranged from $4.50 to a $35 top. The philanthropic foundations constitute a relatively new source of financial aid; the Metropolitan lists among its patrons some seventy-five foundations, trusts, and major corporations; but the potential of their gifts has been limited by the shrinkage in the value of investments that occurred in the mid-1970s. The city supplies subsidies of a limited sort; and like other performing companies, the Metropolitan shares in the more than $34 million voted by the State Legislature in support of the arts. In 1975 the Metropolitan also benefited from contributions made by more than 300 corporations and business institutions to the Lincoln Center Consolidated Corporate Fund. The necessity of relying on this kind of support reveals the dependence of the performing arts upon the skill of professional money raising agencies and upon the commitment of a concerned citizenry made effective through patrons groups such as the Metropolitan Opera Guild.[56]

The designation of the New York State Theater as the home of the New York City Ballet recognized the recently achieved stature of the most newly popular ingredient of the New York entertainment scene. An explosion of dance activity, anticipated no earlier than the 1930s and accelerating greatly during the 1960s, has made New York the dance capital of the world. The city now boasts an array of New York-based dance companies that includes not only the New York City Ballet but the American Ballet Theater, the Joffrey Ballet, the Alvin Ailey Ballet, the Martha Graham Company, the Paul Taylor Company, the Dance Theater of Harlem, the Jose Limon Company, the Alwin Nikolais Dance Theater, and many others. Sold-out houses attest to the appeal of visiting companies, such as the Bolshoi, Royal, Canadian, and Stuttgart ballets, that play long engagements; it is not unusual for as many as three major companies to be performing in the city on the same night. To theater-going New Yorkers, ballet no longer is an esoteric art; New York City of the mid-seventies has become a balletomane's paradise.[57]

Painting and sculpture are other areas of creative effort in which New York City in the bicentennial era has a preeminence not enjoyed early in the century. Since the 1950s, for the first time in the American experience New York artists have been playing a leadership role in contemporary painting throughout the non-Communist world. The abstract expressionists of the New York School, who began to find themselves during the Depression of the 1930s and to exhibit in the 1940s, contributed to this development, as did the European modernists who sojourned here during the war years of the 1940s. The new activity also was inspired and fostered by the presence of the Museum of Modern Art, organized in 1929, and the Solomon R. Guggenheim Museum of non-objective art, established in 1937. Arshile Gorky exhibited each year from 1945 to 1948 at the Julien Levy Gallery. Jackson Pollock's first one-man show was held in 1947 at Peggy Guggenheim's Gallery. Willem de Kooning held his first one-man show at the Egan Gallery in 1948. Franz Kline had his first exhibition in 1950. The proliferation of commercial galleries during the 1950s and 1960s attests to the number of artists active in the city, its role as a collectors' market, and the growth of popular interest in contemporary art. In 1925, the *New York Times* made reference in notes and advertising to fewer than 25 local commercial galleries. An international index to galleries, published in June 1975 listed more than 250 galleries and 50 one-man shows in New York, by contrast with 15 in San Francisco, 13 in Chicago, 9 in Boston, and 9 in Philadelphia.[58]

The creative vigor of the New York City art scene of the mid-1970s is best exhibited in SoHo, a neighborhood of studios and galleries that began to develop in the 1960s at the northern edge of lower Manhattan. Young artists found that the cavernous lofts and warehouses of the area provided sufficient space, originally at reasonable rentals, to permit them to produce the huge canvases and massive metal sculpture that reflect the prevailing interest in experimental and conceptual art, in a wide variety of media and often scaled to the monumental dimensions of the urban environment. The lofts and warehouses also are spacious enough for the display of works too large to be exhibited in the uptown galleries. By 1975, there were more than twenty-five galleries in SoHo. Many of the residents have found in SoHo the "general ambiance of a small town," inhabited by artists intent upon making a living through serious experimental work, but as rents have increased and the area has become a tourist attraction, some have moved to Williamsburg and other points in Brooklyn or south of SoHo in Manhattan.[59]

The democratization of art—"to bridge the gap between art and life"—and a concern for the urban environment figured significantly in the art discourse of the 1960s and 1970s in New York City. Interest in the environment led to the creation and installation of large-scale outdoor public sculpture, as in the work of Isamu Noguchi, in the Chase Manhattan Plaza and at 140 Broadway, and to the activities of City Walls, a cooperative artist group that embellished the walls of many buildings with bold and colorful geometric designs. The democratization of art is reflected in the prevailing, though perhaps waning, interest in pop art and photorealism, but especially in the efforts of the city's many museums to organize exhibits that would attract popular interest and give the museum a central role in the New York cultural scene. This is true of the Museum of Modern Art, the Whitney Museum of American Art, the Solomon R. Guggenheim Museum, the Pierpont Morgan Library, the Frick Museum, the New-York Historical Society, the Museum of the City of New York, the American Museum of Natural History, the Brooklyn Museum, and especially the Metropolitan Museum of Art, whose policy by the mid-1970s was described as being directed toward "a dynamic and unremitting program of events to capture public attention." However, despite such efforts to give broad popular appeal to its collection, the Metropolitan has been criticized for a construction program at its Fifth Avenue site that will further concentrate the city's art treasures rather than disperse them to outlying neighborhoods.[60]

A concern for neighborhood identity and control, albeit within the larger municipality, figures significantly in the attitude of New Yorkers toward the municipal government in the mid-1970s. The emphasis by the later 1960s on decentralization of decision-making marked a departure from the centralization that generally had characterized the government of New York since 1898, when the Greater City came into being. The concept of a "greater" city had had proponents as early as the mid-nineteenth century when New York already was recognized to be the hub of a metropolitan cluster comprising portions of counties in the vicinity of the city, as well as Brooklyn, then a large city in its own right. In 1868, Andrew H. Green, while a member of the New York Park Board, presented a plan for consolidating this population cluster into a Greater New York, with boundaries approximating those realized in 1898.

It took Green thirty years to achieve his objective, despite its growing popular appeal. Two developments ultimately overcame the legislative delay that was his chief obstacle. One was the apprehension, after the publication of the census of 1890, that Chicago might replace New York as the nation's most populous city. The other was the support of Thomas C. Platt, long-time leader of the state Republican Party, who presumably saw the enlarged city as offering political advantage for himself and his party. After a series of legislative complications, a charter—the work of a commission of which former Secretary of the Navy Benjamin Tracy was chairman and Green was a member—was adopted and signed by Governor Frank Black on May 4, 1897. The newly created Greater New York, which became a reality on January 1, 1898, included the boroughs of Brooklyn, the Bronx, Manhattan, Queens, and Richmond (later designated the Borough of Staten Island).[61]

The charter of the enlarged city created a strongly centralized municipal administration, reflecting the desire of its proponents to weaken government at the ward level which, in their opinion, had spawned the boss and the machine. Power was concentrated in central agencies—the mayor, chosen by a citywide electorate, a bicameral municipal legislature, and numerous boards and commissions often dependent upon central authority. Each borough had an elected president, but there were no borough or county councils. In 1901 and 1936, charter changes creating and later strengthening the Board of Estimate and Apportionment momentarily broadened the role of the borough presidents at the center of city government, weakened the leadership role of the mayor, and substituted borough politics for the ward politics which the creators of the Greater City had sought to minimize. But the charter of 1961 tipped the balance again in the direction of centralization. It gave the mayor a broader and less restricted role in budget making and enhanced his potential for leadership through the power to organize administrative agencies. All remaining administrative functions of the borough presidents were transferred to central city agencies, thus confirming the centralized character of the city's administrative system. The mayor's leadership role theoretically was strengthened by the administrative streamlining achieved by Mayor John V. Lindsay, in the late 1960s, when forty separate departments and agencies were grouped into ten inclusive "administrations."[62]

The familiarity of one's neighborhood has been a cliché of the New York City scene for many years, but the concern for neighborhood governance and the implementation of it at the turn of the 1970s were the product of attitudes that first found vigorous expression in the mid-1960s—the growing conviction that New York City had become too large for centralized management; the belief of blacks and Puerto Ricans that community control was the key to the achievement of equal rights; the resistance of white ethnic groups, especially in lower-middle and middle-class neighborhoods, to policies designed to achieve citywide racial integration; the physical insecurity that prompted reliance on one's neighbors for protection; disillusionment with urban renewal as destructive of neighborhood identity; and support for programs such as Model Cities (1966) that conceived of broad neighborhoods as appropriate units for comprehensive social rehabilitation. Criticism of the mayor, in connection with the city's fiscal difficulties in the mid-1970s, further strengthened arguments for transferring decision-making from central to borough or neighborhood authorities.[63]

By the later 1960s, community organizations were springing up everywhere throughout the city. By 1976, close to 10,000 block associations were in operation, with their building captains, security patrols, sanitation committees, and beautification boards. These urban grass-roots groups financed their activities with the returns from block parties and fairs, supplemented by small subsidies from private corporations—as in "Operation Better Block"—and from the city, which provided matching funds for the purchase of crime prevention equipment. Equally pervasive were the more widely gauged community organizations, such as the Park Slope Civic Council, spokesmen for an Irish and Italian community in Brooklyn; the South Bronx Community Corporation; the Civic Association of Maspeth, Queens, largely Polish and Lithuanian in membership; and the Inwood Civic Council in upper Manhattan, originally organized in opposition to plans for locating a marine garbage transfer facility in the neighborhood. A local Catholic church sponsored the activities of the Sunset Ridge Organized

Community in Bay Ridge in Brooklyn; the Bronx Chamber of Commerce donated 1,400 police whistles to the Fordham-Bedford Community Coalition Security Program that served the residents of a forty-block community in the Bronx.[64]

Since the mid-1960s, the federal government has involved the residents of some localities in decision-making at the community level. For example, elected representatives on the boards of Community Action agencies, under the federal antipoverty program, have participated in determining how millions of dollars in federal and city funds would be spent in their own localities on programs involving health, housing, job training, and the like. However, as of the mid-1970s, neighborhood governance finds its most regularized expression in the activities of the local planning boards and community school boards.[65]

The local planning board, in each of the city's sixty-two planning districts, includes the members of the City Council from the planning district, those elected at large in the borough, and not more than fifty persons— usually neighborhood "activists"—appointed by the borough president. They constitute the "voice of the neighborhood" in making recommendations on local issues having to do with zoning and other land use regulations and, since 1973, in initiating proposals for consideration in the preparation of the capital budget. In 1974, the City Planning Commission organized a series of community planning workshops to prepare the members of the sixty-two boards for their new responsibility. In making proposals for the capital budget, the boards submit their priorities, based on local hearings, and these are circulated to the interested agencies for their consideration in making recommendations to the Planning Commission.

In recent years, landmark and neighborhood preservation has figured prominently in the policies of the City Planning Commission, headed by John E. Zuccotti, who stands high in the counsels of Mayor Abraham D. Beame. Planning today is less a matter of implementing a preconceived master plan for the city than of fostering adjustments, on a day-to-day basis, in response to citizen efforts to improve the quality of life in the city and its neighborhoods. In housing, programs aimed at maintaining the "fabric of the neighborhood community" through low-rise, infill housing and the rehabilitation of existing housing stock have replaced the earlier large-scale redevelopment of blighted areas through the use of high-rise construction. Rehabilitation is not a new idea in New York. The city's first public housing project, First Houses, built on the lower East Side in 1935, represented the rehabilitation of old-law tenements, with light and air secured by demolition of every third structure.[66]

Decentralized management of the elementary and junior high schools was achieved in 1969, with provision for community school boards (32 in

1976), totaling not less than seven nor more than fifteen in membership and elected for two-year terms by the registered voters and parents of children attending school in the district. These boards hire the district superintendent and are responsible for the physical condition of the schools, for operating extra-curricular and recreational facilities, and for proposing new schools, suggesting sites, approving design, and expediting construction. The move to decentralize was triggered in the later 1960s by black protest when the Board of Education failed to live up to its promise to integrate a new Harlem school. It was furthered by a Ford Foundation plan to experiment with locally administered schools and by the belief of the Lindsay administration not only that decentralization was appropriate but that it would provide a means of increasing state aid for local education.

As of the early 1970s, New Yorkers were about equally divided in their reactions to community control of school management. A survey made in 1973 showed the chief support came from blacks and Puerto Ricans and from the parents of children in school. Performance has not greatly improved; some districts have experienced financial mismanagement and racial tension; but blacks and Puerto Ricans (whose children make up almost two-thirds of the total enrollment) are much more numerously represented in supervisory posts; and dissidence, as well as management, has been decentralized, thus reducing the incidence of boycotts and strikes that plagued the schools in the 1960s.[67]

The continuing pressure for neighborhood "input" in city management is exhibited in broadened powers for local planning boards, proposed by a state charter revision commission, and endorsed by the electorate in the fall of 1975. Charter changes scheduled to take effect on July 1, 1976, give these community boards authority over land-use changes and power to review the city's expense and capital budgets. The grant of wider authority over municipal services, with the exception of police, in the districts, was authorized, but its implementation in newly defined districts, in which municipal services will be realigned for administrative purposes, is likely to be postponed until 1977. It was argued that this "administrative decentralization," anticipated by an experiment in neighborhood government inaugurated during the Lindsay administration, would reduce costs and make the provision of urban services more responsive to the desires of the localities. Opponents of the proposals, including some of the city's most prestigious civic groups, thought it likely that such decentralization would increase costs, encourage patronage abuses, excite competitive ethnic tensions, and impose an additional layer of government at a time when the city needed a cohesive approach to its problems.[68]

The provision of urban services is at the heart of the question of New York's fiscal integrity, which became a burning issue in the mid-1970s when the difficulty of raising funds for the day-to-day operations of the municipal government led to the threat of default and municipal bankruptcy. Urban services—in an order of magnitude far beyond what other major American cities provide—have long been a tradition in New York City. These services include not only what is customarily expected of cities in police and fire protection, street cleaning, waste removal, and public welfare—all made more costly for New York because of the large number of transients and commuters it has had to serve and the particular nature of its population—but also a wide range of educational, cultural, recreational, and medical amenities which, when supplied at all in other cities, are subsidized to a greater degree by the state and federal governments.

Its municipal generosity is an aspect of New York's personality that stems from many sources: the achievements of generations of altruistic reformers, supported by the philanthropic benevolence of men of wealth who made their fortunes in New York; the liberal inclinations of the very sizable Jewish ingredient in the city's population; the multiplication of parks, playgrounds, and health facilities built under federal auspices during the depression of the 1930s and the federally funded programs of the "Great Society" of the 1960s; the continuous presence of large numbers of dependent newcomers creating problems that demanded municipal solutions; the power in numbers and political potential of organized pressure groups in the city; and the magnitude of the city itself, which encourages bold and expansive action. By the inflated 1970s, however, the wide range of city services was costing more than the city had the funds to supply, both because of the abundance of the services and the costly nature of their administration.[69]

One of the most expansive, as well as expensive, city services is the provision of public education in a school system distinguished for its many specialized programs and unique in its extension to free college training for all high school graduates. In 1974-1975 more than a million students were enrolled in New York City's 950 public elementary and secondary schools, some of which, as in the case of the high schools of science, music and art, and the performing arts, offer unusual opportunities for the gifted youth of the city. School expenditures for 1974-1975 totaled nearly $2.3 billion, of which the city contributed more than 60 percent, the state 30 percent, and the federal government the remainder.

Municipal expenditures for education spiraled in 1970 with the introduction of open admission in the City University, a move that made all high school graduates eligible to enter one of the City University's two-year or four-year colleges, the selection depending on high school grades. Between 1969 and 1971, admissions to the city colleges doubled—from about 19,000 to more than 39,000. Space shortages contributed to the increased expense, as did the cost of remedial training for unprepared students. In 1975, some 79 percent of the city's 1974 high school graduates were enrolled in college compared to 47.5 percent of the 1974 high school graduates in the nation at large. By this date, the City University system was larger than the university systems of forty-three states. The budget for higher education increased from $6 million in 1933 to a request (later reduced) for more than $660 million in 1975-1976.

By 1976 it had become evident that without augmented state or federal support the city could not continue to provide its residents with relatively free college education (a tradition of long standing for qualified students) and at the same time maintain its broad open admission policy —symbol of the expansiveness of the city's services and of its effort to encourage the upward mobility of the needy youth (largely from minority families) in its population. The city's fiscal crisis brought the issue to a head, as of May 1976, when funds were not available to meet faculty and staff payrolls. Despite opposition from a congress representing 17,000 faculty and staff and from a student senate speaking for 270,000 students, it seemed likely that some modification of the free tuition-open admission practices of the City University would be instituted and that the state would assume a more influential role in the organization and administration of the university.[70]

The mushrooming growth of the City University is contributing to the problems of the city's close to fifty privately supported colleges and universities, already suffering from inflated operational costs, reductions in support from foundations and from the federal government, and a decline in out-of-city enrollment, the result not only of high tuition but of the city's negative image. For many years, Columbia University, New York University, and Fordham University—beneficiaries of only minimal state support—have been among the cultural ornaments of New York City, with a heavy investment in library and technical equipment for scholarly research. In June of 1973, these and other privately supported institutions granted more than 18,000 M. A., Ph.D., and M. D. degrees, by contrast with less than 6,300 (predominantly M. A.) degrees granted by the City University. Some of the smaller private colleges have suffered seriously as the open admission policy of the City University has deprived them of the students they once served. If the city's duplication of services in higher education threatens the continued achievement of the long established privately subsidized institutions, this is a development which, quite apart from its bearing upon the city's financial crisis, the city can ill afford.[71]

Health services constitute another area of expense that exhibits the corporate benevolence of New York. Its nineteen municipal hospitals, in contrast to Chicago's one, are only part of a traditionally broad health-care program that includes child-health stations, neighborhood family care centers, and public health nursing. Medical services of this kind contribute significantly to the cost of welfare and welfare supplements which, since 1968, has become the largest item in the city's expense budget. In having to make heavy outlays for welfare, New York City is the victim of state legislation requiring local communities to pay 25 percent of their welfare costs. This requirement imposes a burden on New York that large cities in many other states do not have to carry. The states of Massachusetts and Pennsylvania, for example, require no local contribution; Illinois exacts only 1 percent. At the same time, New York City continues to be the mecca of often dependent immigrants from all parts of the nation, and the city has no statutory means of impeding the flow. In the ten years from 1964 to 1974, the annual costs of maintaining the poor mounted from less than $500 million to more than $2.5 billion. This almost insuperable obstacle to the city's solvency has prompted pleas that the welfare burden be wholly assumed by the federal government which now contributes only 44 percent of the over-all costs for all types of welfare.[72]

Municipal contributions in support of libraries, museums, and cultural and recreational programs, which help to foster New York's image of abundance in these areas, totaled more than $96 million in 1974-1975. Shakespeare in the parks and music from rock to classical, including performances by the New York Philharmonic and the Metropolitan Opera, provide New Yorkers with free summer entertainment of a quality not matched in other cities. On July 29, 1975, the New York Philharmonic drew an audience of 150,000 to a free concert in Central Park, the first of a dozen concerts to be played in the parks of the five boroughs and produced at a cost of $400,000. The city contributed about $135,000 to this cost; the remainder was met by the Philharmonic itself, by state and federal agencies, and by private corporations, especially the Schlitz Brewing Company, a major donor over the years. Borough arts councils, funded by the city, sponsor a year-round program of art, musical, and dramatic events and workshops for youths and senior citizens. Added to these are such city-supported recreational facilities as beaches, pools, skating rinks, boxing rings, tennis courts, and golf courses. Municipal support of transit fares has a bearing on the city dweller's ability to enjoy these recreational opportunities, as well as on other aspects of his existence. Though bus and subway fares were raised from 35 to 50 cents in September 1975, as part of the city's austerity program, the increase still did not meet the cost of an average subway ride, which was estimated at 73 cents.[73]

By the 1970s, the expansion of services, the increase in the number of people taking advantage of them, and the toll imposed by inflation pushed costs to the point that the expense budget proposed for the fiscal year

1975-1976 totaled $12.8 billion, plus a capital budget slightly under $2 billion. New York City was living beyond its income, as it had been during the past decade, despite a contribution of 45 percent from state and federal funds, by contrast with a contribution of 25 percent from these sources in 1963-1964. One cause of the spiraling costs was the huge increase in the number of municipal workers—from about 150,000 in 1945 to 330,000 in May 1975—and the results of their unionization, reflected not only in salary increases but in pension agreements that promised to cost an estimated $1.1 billion in 1975-1976 and $1.7 billion in 1980. Another expensive charge on the budget was the cost of servicing a debt that by May 1975 had reached $13.3 billion in bonds and notes outstanding. In August 1975, it was determined, with considerable difficulty, that the deficit accumulated in the past five years was $3.3 billion.[74]

In previous years, city administrations had obscured the widening gap between income and outgo by short-term borrowing and by budget gimmickry that entailed, among other types of manipulation, overestimating income and underestimating costs and hiding daily expenses in the capital budget. By May 1975, however, apprehensions concerning the city's credit were such that a group of influential bankers, after a decade of floating bonds and notes to patch the city's budgets, warned that their banks could no longer purchase or market the issues of bonds and notes necessary to cover current payrolls and debt financing. When the city was unable to obtain the needed funds from either Washington or Albany or sufficient additional taxing power from the state legislature, it was forced, during the summer months of 1975, to surrender control over its financial affairs to a state-dominated agency, promise to reform its budgetary and management procedures, and impose an austerity program which resulted in cutbacks in library, museum, educational, park, medical, garbage collection, and subway services and a reduction in the municipal payroll, to which the first reaction was a sit-in by policemen on the Brooklyn Bridge, a sick-out by firemen, and a 100 percent effective "wild-cat" sanitationmen's strike. Ultimately the unions involved agreed to accept graduated wage freezes.[75]

The city's "crisis of borrowing" nevertheless deepened, making it evident that the only alternative to municipal bankruptcy was more drastic therapy, including loans from the federal government. President Ford refused to support aid of this kind until the city and state took steps that, in his words, showed the willingness of New Yorkers to "bail themselves" out of their difficulties. By late December, 1975, a package of financial devices amounting to $6.8 billion had been achieved by federal, state, and city action, in the hope of giving the city time to reform its fiscal practices so that investors would feel safe in lending it money. In the hard-won package were provisions for refinancing the existing debt; loans from the federal government totaling $2.3 billion on a short-term basis over a two-and-a-half-year period; and new tax revenues including an increase in the personal income tax of New York City residents to an average of 25 percent. The city agreed to balance its budget, which means ending a $72.5 million operating deficit by 1978, with further reductions in payroll and services. Whether these are more than stop-gap measures only time will tell. For the moment the city's fiscal behavior is strictly circumscribed by a watchdog panel, the state Emergency Financial Control Board, on which the Governor exerts a strong influence.[76]

It seems ironical that as the United States reaches the bicentennial of its independence, its largest city—one of the chief cultural and commercial ornaments of the nation's achievement—should be less independent, more unsure of its future than at almost any time in its recent history. Traditionally indomitable New York seems to be boxed in by conditions of its own and the nation's making—a resident population disproportionately burdened with dependents; a commuter population out of reach for financial support of the services with which the city provides it and unavailable to supply the civic leadership which resident business and professional men and women once gave the city; a fiscal relationship with Washington and Albany that fails to bring aid commensurate with the magnitude of the city's financial and social contribution to the state and nation and that threatens its much cherished pride in home rule; a city government limited in effectiveness by bureaucracies "historically adapted to thwarting action" and subject to the pressures of municipal employees accustomed to costly benefits and militantly organized to achieve and preserve them; a municipal plant badly in need of modernization; and a tradition of the ultimate in services—in a city with the most of everything—that is difficult to separate from its image as a world metropolis.[77]

Compelling considerations argue for the survival of New York City if realistic means can be found for imposing more of the costs of essential urban services on the suburbanites who benefit from them; if the state and federal governments will help the city cope with the problems of the dependent elements in its population; and if New Yorkers themselves can devise and accept substitutes (and this has political as well as social implications) for some of the services the municipal government has performed in recent years. The United States needs the contribution New York City makes as the cultural capital of the nation—the place where artists, actors, musicians, dancers, and writers come together to make American culture happen. The nation needs New York's magnitude and dynamism as a commercial and financial center. Despite some migration of business and industry, New York City still houses three times as many corporate headquarters as its nearest competitor, Chicago; and there is promise of expanded economic growth for the city in its role as the center of the nation's knowledge industries—advertising, publishing, merchandising and marketing companies, art galleries and art centers, theater and dance production, universities, colleges, special health facilities, and business services.[78]

Whatever the future holds for New York City, as the nation copes with the dilemmas of another century in its history, to the average New Yorker it seems unbelievable that the New York he knows will not survive. For all the city's difficulties and shortcomings, of which New Yorkers are the first to complain, its residents still contend, according to a scientifically drawn attitudinal profile, that "New York is more beautiful, has better stores and restaurants, and offers more cultural opportunities and better job prospects; [is] a better place than its sister cities to meet interesting people, to obtain a free higher education, to enjoy free entertainment and to find good medical care." To an eminent visitor to New York, it is "a tonic city—life giving, life enhancing," however "violent, criminal, teetering on bankruptcy, and impossible to govern" it may be. A Queens housewife expressed the characteristic ambivalence of mood—difficulties, yes, but the potential to enable the city to prevail: "New York is going down. . . . I was mugged in a department store. . . . Too much free money has been given out to people who didn't work. They should have let them sweep the streets. The city is filthy. . . . We hate the thought of moving. I love New York. If I want to go to the Stuttgart Ballet on Wednesday afternoon, I'm in. They're moving by the hundreds to Florida. How much swimming can you do? How much walking in the sands? Florida has no soul. This is the city. It's beautiful."[79]

NOTES

1.   New York City had a population of 7,567,100 as of July 1, 1974, according to a Census Bureau estimate. *New York Times,* July 20, 1975. As of the Census of 1970, the New York–Northeastern New Jersey Urbanized Area had a population of 16,206,841. This urbanized area (defined as a central city or cities and the surrounding closely settled territory) includes Bronx, Kings, New York, Queens, and Richmond counties and parts of Nassau, Putnam, Rockland, Suffolk, and Westchester counties in New York, and Essex, Hudson, and Union counties and parts of Bergen, Middlesex, Monmouth, Morris, Ocean, Passaic, and Somerset counties in New Jersey. U. S. Bureau of the Census, *Census of Population: 1970,* Vol. 1, *Characteristics of the Population,* Part 34, *New York,* Section 1 (U. S. Government Printing Office, Washington, D. C., 1973), Table 11, pp. 34-37 to 40. The land area in the "urbanized area" totaled 2,425.1 square miles in 1970; the land area of New York City was 299.7 square miles. The Regional Plan Association defines the New York Metropolitan Area as New York City and the surrounding twenty-six counties in New Jersey, New York, and Connecticut. A study made by the Regional Plan Association, reporting 19.8 million persons in this 13,000 square-mile area as of January 1975,

asserted that population growth in the metropolitan area halted in 1974 for the first time since colonial days. *New York Times,* Jan. 12, 1975; Wallace S. Sayre, "New York," in *Great Cities of the World,* eds. William A. Robson and D. E. Regan (Beverly Hills, Calif., 1972), pp. 693–94.

2.   See Ronald B. Conners, *Manhattan's West Side: a Demographic Study* (Roosevelt Hospital, New York, 1974), p. 25; *New York Times,* Mar. 23, 1975. According to census figures issued in July 1975, there were 507,800 births and 372,100 deaths in New York City between 1970 and mid-1974. The resulting natural increase was more than offset by a net out-migration of 464,000. Ibid., July 20, 1975. It was predicted, after a survey made in 1976, that by the year 2000 the city's population would drop to 6.8 million. Ibid., Feb. 23, 1976.

3.   Ibid., May 13, 1973. As of 1970, some 56 percent of the persons going to work in New York's five boroughs used public transportation. Ibid., Dec. 17, 1973.

4.   Ibid., Mar. 13, 1971.

5.   Ibid., Oct. 4, 1970, Dec. 3, 1972, May 31, 1974.

6.   The *New York Times* reported in November 1972 that the postwar building boom produced more than 250 major office buildings in midtown and the lower city. Eighteen were completed in 1971 and another 18 in 1972. Ibid., Nov. 8, 1972.

7.   Ibid., Dec. 6, 1970, Jan. 11, 1973, Mar. 23, 1975. The 1970s saw increasing examples of a new style in skyscraper construction deviating from the sheer towers with glass and metal or glass and concrete facades that set the fashion in the 1960s. The new style was distinguished by a tower that widens rather than narrows toward the top and by the chamfered (cut off) corner. Typical of the new style were Waterside, the four-tower project at 24th Street and the East River, the Ruppert Brewery housing complex in the East 90s, and Riverbend in Harlem. Ibid., Mar. 12, 1975.

8.   Ibid., Jan. 19, May 6, 1941, June 3, 1962, Apr. 18, 1965, Oct. 4, 1970. Mayor LaGuardia commented in 1945 that the elevated—"that wonder of our youth"—had all but vanished. Ibid., Sep. 30, 1945.

9.   Ibid., July 22, 1973, April 13, 1975.

10.   Ibid., May 31, 1974, Jan. 12, 1975.

11.   Ibid., Apr. 17, 1975. The ordinance was enacted on May 21, 1975.

12.   Ibid., Sep. 24, 1969, Jan. 14, 1970, June 19, 1971.

13.   Natalie Becker, "Housing the City Poor," ibid., July 10, 1974.

14.   Ibid., June 16, 1945, Feb. 6, 1949, Sep. 11, 1964; Marya Mannes, *The New York I Know* (Philadelphia, 1961), p. 9. This is a reprint of articles that originally were published in 1959 in *The New Yorker.* Richard J. Whalen's *A City Destroying Itself* (New York, 1965) verbalizes the disillusionment and frustration that characterized the attitude of many New Yorkers toward the city in the mid-1960s. A more favorable image of the city is found in Gilbert Millstein, *New York: True North* (Garden City, N. Y., 1964). Air pollution, in part a consequence of the city's size, was becoming a widely publicized threat by the 1960s. *New York Times,* Sep. 27, 1967, May 25, 1975.

15.   Ibid., June 3, 1969, Apr. 8, 1973; [London] *Sunday Times Magazine,* Mar. 4, 1973. According to a survey published in the *New York Times* in January 1974, New Yorkers called crime "far and away" the number one problem of the city; drug addiction was thought to be the next most serious problem. *New York Times,* Jan. 16, 20, 1974.

16.   Ibid., June 3, Sep. 24, 1969, Jan. 14, 1970, Jan. 6, Nov. 15, 1974. In January 1974, Percy Sutton, borough president of Manhattan, characterized as exaggerated an article in the Paris daily *Aurore* warning travelers of the dangers in certain areas of the city. Ibid., Jan. 24, 1972. On several occasions, the humorist, S. J. Perelman, criticized New York as dirty, disorderly, and violent. Ibid., Sep. 27, 1967, Sep. 20, 1972.

17.   Ibid., Mar. 23, May 13, Aug. 3, 1975.

18.   Ibid., June 3, 1969, Jan. 1, 22, 1972, Mar. 23, 1975. Of all the commentators on modern New York City, Soviet visitors have been the most critical. Nikita Khrus-

chev, speaking in 1960, called it "repulsive," indicative of the "ugliness and degeneracy of capitalism." Ibid., Oct. 21, 1960. See also Jan. 3, 1947, Jan. 24, 1965, June 22, 1969. George Feifer wrote in the [London] *Sunday Times Magazine*, Mar. 4, 1973: "Violence in New York has become a cliché; its statistics are so appalling that they defeat the imagination." A condition with possible bearing on the incidence of crime was the marked increase between 1960 and 1970 in the number of youths under 18 living with only one parent or with neither parent. Nearly half of the youths in this category were blacks. *New York Times*, Feb. 1, 1973.

19.   Ibid., Dec. 21, 1944, Sep. 30, 1945, Mar. 26, Aug. 31, 1948. According to a public opinion poll taken in November 1973, a majority of whites were of the opinion that racial polarization had increased; a majority of blacks and Puerto Ricans saw it as unchanged or possibly less evident. Ibid., Jan. 20, 1974. As of 1970, the ethnic breakdown of the population of the city was as follows: white, 5,306,171 (67.2%); black, 1,612,066 (20.4%); other non white, 164,782 (2.1%); Puerto Rican, 811,843 (10.3%). A total of 741,218 Puerto Ricans (91.3%) reported as white, 70,625 (8.7%) as non white. There were 35,000 third-generation Puerto Ricans. Abraham C. Burstein, *A Demographic Profile of New York City* (City of New York Human Resources Administration, New York, September, 1973), p. xiv.

20.   *New York Times*, Apr. 18, 1968, Mar. 11, 1970, Jan. 6, 1974. The St. Patrick's Day parade drew 1.5 million spectators on March 17, 1975. Ibid., Mar. 18, 1975. On the Irish, see Nathan Glazer and Daniel P. Moynihan, *Beyond the Melting Pot* (Cambridge, Mass., 1964), pp. 254-62. On Germans, see New York City Planning Commission, *Plan for New York City, 1969*, IV, *Manhattan* (Cambridge, Mass., 1969), p. 106; *New York Times*, Oct. 2, 1968, Jan. 12, 1975.

21.   Ibid., Apr. 18, Aug. 15, 1968, Oct. 8, 1969; *American Jewish Yearbook, 1973* (New York, 1973), LXXIV, 313; Glazer and Moynihan, *Beyond the Melting Pot*, pp. 137-80; New York City Planning Commission, *Plan for New York City, 1969*, III, *Brooklyn* (Cambridge, Mass., 1969), pp. 122, 130; N. Y. C. Planning Commission, *Manhattan*, p. 44; *New York Times*, Aug. 13, 1972 (migration to Bronx).

22.   Ibid., Oct. 15, 1968, Mar. 27, 1970, Dec. 6, 1971, Apr. 26, 1974; *The Villager*, Mar. 27, 1975; N. Y. C. Planning Commission, *Manhattan*, pp. 33-34, 144; Glazer and Moynihan, *Beyond the Melting Pot*, pp. 186-208; Raanan Geberer, "Italian East Harlem Hangs On—Barely," *Our Town*, Sep. 26, 1975.

23.   *New York Times*, Aug. 23, Dec. 24, 1969, Jan. 14, 1972 (Polish); May 16, 1970, Mar. 25, 1975 (Greeks), Feb. 25, 1975 (Cubans).

24.   Ibid., June 28, 1967, Aug. 1, 1969, June 16, 1970, Dec. 2, 1974, Feb. 18, 1975; N. Y. C. Planning Commission, *Manhattan*, p. 43. The new visibility of the Chinese was exhibited in the use of Chinese men as models in clothing advertisements in general-circulation newspapers, beginning in 1975. Ibid., Apr. 27, 1975.

25.   Burstein, *A Demographic Profile of New York City*, p. xiv, tables 17, 19; Joseph P. Fitzpatrick, "Puerto Ricans in Perspective: The Meaning of Migration to the Mainland," *International Migration Review*, New Series, II (Spring 1968), 7-19; Glazer and Moynihan, *Beyond the Melting Pot*, pp. 86-136; Oscar Lewis, *A Study of Slum Culture: Backgrounds for La Vida* (New York, 1968); *New York Times*, Feb. 13, June 9, Aug, 18, 19, 1975, Apr. 15, 1976.

26.   [London] *Sunday Times Magazine*, Mar. 4, 1973.

27.   Conners, *Manhattan's West Side*, p. 25; N. Y. C. Planning Commission, *Manhattan*, pp. 134-50. For the evolution of the black community in Harlem, see Gilbert Osofsky, *Harlem: The Making of a Ghetto: Negro New York, 1890-1930* (New York, 1966), Seth M. Scheiner, *Negro Mecca, a History of the Negro in New York City, 1865-1920* (New York, 1965), and Glazer and Moynihan, *Beyond the Melting Pot*, pp. 24-85. On Bedford-Stuyvesant, see N. Y. C. Planning Commission, *Brooklyn*, pp. 40-52; Harold X. Connolly, "Blacks in Brooklyn from 1900 to 1960" (Ph.D. dissertation, New York University, 1972).

28.   Motormen's wages were to be $15,025 annually as of April 1, 1975. John J. O'Connor, "Good Times for the Black Image," *New York Times*, Feb. 2, 1975;

"Manhattan Model Cities," in N. Y. C. Planning Commission, *Manhattan,* pp. 114–22. For a positive view, see *A Profile of the Harlem Area: Findings of the Harlem Task Force, December, 1973,* published by The Harlem Urban Development Corporation, pp. 5, 12, 155–57; *New York Times,* June 7, 1967. For a negative view see the contention that the increase in blacks and Puerto Ricans would inevitably lower the level of quality in New York. "Even if the antagonisms are somehow softened . . . and the pervading atmosphere of cynicism, despair, and disgust lifted, the good things cannot be the same because the inhabitants are very different." [London] *Sunday Times Magazine,* Mar. 4, 1973.

29. *New York Times,* June 7, 1969, Dec. 6, 1970.

30. Ibid., Feb. 13, Mar. 12, Apr. 9. 1975. Following the example of blacks and Puerto Ricans, members of the fast-growing Chinese community concluded by May, 1975, that they should submerge their internal tensions in the interest of presenting a united front as a minority group. Goaded by the Asian Americans for Equal Employment, who claimed that the Chinese establishment was not being sufficiently militant in fighting for the community's rights, Man Bun Lee, president of the Chinese Consolidated Benevolent Association, emphasized the need for the differing factions within Chinatown to present a united front: "If we do not unite, other people are not going to take us seriously." Ibid., May 30, 1975. Police raids on gambling, controlled by two tongs, were a cause of tension in Chinatown. For fifty years, the Chinese community had tolerated this activity as "a viceless form of recreation." Chinese youth contended that the police were using such raids as an excuse for brutality. Ibid., June 8, 1975.

31. Ibid., Mar. 22, 1968, Jan. 24, 1970, Aug. 27, 1971, Mar. 10, 1974, Feb. 6, 1975.

32. Bayrd Still, *Urban America: A History with Documents* (Boston, 1974), pp. 439–40. The number of units in the Forest Hills development was reduced from 840 to 430 and the height of the buildings from 24 to 12 stories. It was agreed that the housing would be available only to residents of Queens, but provisions for renting to blacks and low-income residents were retained. Of the first residents, 70 percent were white, 30 percent black. *New York Times,* June 10, 1975. See also ibid., Oct. 20, 1971; [New York] *Village Voice,* Feb. 15, 1973. On the background of black–Jewish relations in New York City, see Steven Bloom, "Interactions between Blacks and Jews in New York City, 1900–1930, as Reflected in the Black Press" (Ph.D. dissertation, New York University, 1973).

33. *New York Times,* Dec. 6, 1971.

34. Ibid., Sep. 21, 1975.

35. Guy de Jonquieres, *New York Times,* Jan. 6, 1974. Speaking on May 22, 1975, at the opening of New York City's observance of the nation's bicentennial, the scientist René Dubos found a virtue in the tendency of New Yorkers to retain their cultural identity, rather than to be the products of a "melting pot." He saw the "coexistence of multiple cultural groups" as leading to the "emergence of self-contained, competitive units" whose activity has enhanced the social, economic, and cultural strengths of the city as a whole. Ibid., May 22, 1975. W. H. Auden, writing in 1972, praised New York as "not only a metropolis. It is also a city of [ethnic] neighborhoods." Ibid., Mar. 18, 1972. Blacks now found their entertainment throughout the city; 125th Street in Harlem was far less the hub of black entertainment than in the 1920s.

36. *New York Times,* May 13, 1975; U. S. Bureau of the Census, *Annual Survey of Manufactures, 1970 and 1971* (U. S. Government Printing Office, Washington, D. C.), pp. 12–13.

37. U. S. Bureau of the Census, *County Business Patterns, 1972, New York* (U. S. Government Printing Office, Washington, D. C., 1973), passim; *New York Times,* May 13, 1975; *New York Post,* Nov. 22, 1974.

38. See sections on New York City in *N. W. Ayer & Son's Directory, Newspapers and Periodicals,* 1951 (Philadelphia, 1951) and *1975 Ayer Directory of Publications*

(Philadelphia, 1975). *Jewish Daily Forward* reported circulation figures of 80,064 (1951), 41,850 (1975); *Staats-Zeitung und Herold*, 24,703 (1951), 10,850 (1975). These figures do not include Sunday circulation.

39. *New York Times*, Nov. 10, 24, 1974, Mar. 2, Apr. 17, 1975.

40. Ibid., Apr. 13, 1975.

41. Ibid., Mar. 13, 1971. The figure of 263,000 full-time employees does not include employees of the Housing Authority, the Transit Authority, or the Triborough Bridge and Tunnel Authority. Conversation with Mr. Edward Silverman, Bureau of the Budget, Oct. 31, 1975.

42. *County Business Patterns*, 1972, passim.

43. *New York Times*, Dec. 6, 1970, May 14, 1975; Barbara Ward, "The City May Be as Lethal as the Bomb," ibid., Apr. 19, 1964, VI, 100. In May 1975, a member of the City Planning Commission contended that the high electric rates in the city resulted in part from the fact that since the potential profits of the utility company were geared to the value of plant investment, the company was encouraged to overbuild rather than to buy power at cheaper prices or cooperate in the development of a national grid that would enable it to share and level out peak load demands. Ibid., May 17, 1975.

44. Ibid., Sep. 21, 22, 1974, Jan. 12, Feb. 10, Apr. 29, 1975, Mar. 14, 1976. In January 1976, unemployment rose from 11.5% to 12.2%.

45. Ibid., Dec. 21, 1969, May 13, 1975.

46. Ibid., Apr. 4, 20, May 6, Aug. 28, 1975.

47. Preston R. Tisch, *A Report on the Year 1973*, published by New York Convention and Visitors Bureau, Inc., unpaged, undated; Jack MacBean, "Increase in NYC's Tourism for 1973 Puts a New Glow on 'The Big Apple'," press release of New York Convention and Visitors Bureau, Inc., dated April 18, 1974; Paul C. Friedlander, "Salesmanship Shines New York's Image," *New York Times*, Oct. 14, 1973; David Winder, "New York polishes its image as it adopts 'big apple' emblem," *Christian Science Monitor*, Jan. 31, 1974. "We're still the Big Apple," was Mayor Beame's response to news that New York had been selected as the convention site. "[The selection] reaffirms the city's role as the center stage in the American drama. It also comes as a timely gesture of confidence in our common effort to strengthen this city at a time of national crisis." *New York Times*, Aug. 28, 1975, May 4, 1976.

48. Hugo Munsterberg, *The Americans* (1904), quoted in Still, *Urban America*, pp. 241–42; *New York Times*, May 23, 1975. Commentators of the 1920s contended that New York had a "keener intellectual life than London," was "possessed of more and better theaters than a dozen Londons," was "loaded with art to the gunwales," and in libraries and museums was the "refuge of Western culture." Bayrd Still, *Mirror for Gotham: New York as Seen by Contemporaries...* (New York, 1956), pp. 273–74. According to Clive Barnes, drama critic of the *New York Times*, there were 250 theaters in New York in late 1975 to 60 in London and 50 in Paris. Radio speech, WQXR, Oct. 9, 1975. On cultural scene, see *Cue*, Dec. 6-12, 1975, passim.

49. *Cue*, June 1, 1975, pp. 37, 43.

50. See Mary C. Henderson, *The City and the Theatre: New York Playhouses from Bowling Green to Times Square* (Clifton, N. J., 1973), pp. 177–99. Experimental off-Broadway theater was threatened in 1975 by the inflation and recession that increased costs and curtailed audiences for all but hit shows. In May 1975, Joseph Papp announced that he was converting the off-Broadway Public Theater into off-off Broadway workshops. By contrast, Broadway appeared to be in good health despite the recession. Managers reported the theater business as "the best we have had in six or seven years." They attributed this not only to the merit of the plays but to "the fact that in a recession era people travel less and seek entertainment near home." *New York Times*, May 11, 27, June 6, 15, 1975.

51. David S. Lifson, *The Yiddish Theatre in America* (New York, 1965), pp. 47, 164, 214, 217, 222, 567, 569. The Compania de Teatro Repertorio Espanol announced productions from Spain's great theater heritage, its Golden Age theater, and the new theater of Latin America. This company has support from federal, state,

and business sources, including the Venezuelan Mission to the United Nations and the Consul General of Spain in New York. For information on the black theater, I am indebted to Robbie McCauley of the Faculty of the School of the Arts, New York University. See also, "Spotlight on Leslie Lee," *Essence,* VI (October, 1975), p. 9.

52. For a comparison of entertainment offerings, see *New York Times,* Feb. 4, 6, Nov. 3, 1900, Nov. 7, 8, 1925, Feb. 1, 1950, Feb. 1, 1975; *Cue,* Nov. 18-24, 1974, May 26-June 1, 1975, passim.

53. *New York Times,* June 1, 6, 1975; William Livingstone, "Jazz in the Big Apple," *Stagebill,* II (June 1975), pp. 13-15, 25.

54. Still, *Mirror for Gotham,* p. 313.

55. Managerial problems as well as production costs plagued the Metropolitan Opera. It was rumored that tax demands on the part of the United States government discouraged some major European stars from signing contracts with the Metropolitan. On the status of the New York City Opera in the 1970s, see Dale Harris, "The Identity Crisis of the City Opera," *New York Times,* May 4, 1975, section 2, and Julius Rudel, "The City Opera's 'Identity Crisis' Is Progress," ibid., June 1, 1975, section 2.

56. Ibid., Nov. 22, 1974; Amyas Ames, "The State and the Arts," *Stagebill,* II (March 1975), pp. 11-12, 34-38.

57. Edmund White, "What Makes Dance Our Most Vital Art Form?" *New York Times,* June 1, 1975.

58. Dore Ashton, *New York* (New York, 1972), pp. 146-55; Alfred H. Barr, Jr., in Millstein, ed., *New York: True North,* pp. 179-82; *The Art Gallery Scene, June, 1975* (Ivoryton, Conn.: Hollycroft Press, 1975), passim; *New York Times,* Nov. 8, 1925.

59. The heart of the SoHo neighborhood is the block on West Broadway between Spring and Prince streets, though the term SoHo is an acronym for "South of Houston Street." See Wendy Schuman, "SoHo a Victim of Its Own Success," *New York Times,* Nov. 24, 1974, section 8; Julian Weissman, "Standoff in SoHo," *Art News,* LXXIII (November 1974), pp. 92-94.

60. Some New Yorkers questioned the appropriateness of having most of the major art repositories in the center of Manhattan where they rarely were accessible to the city's many ghetto residents. Brooklyn's Children's Museum (MUSE) was praised for combining exhibition space and workshop facilities in a densely populated, seriously blighted area. Ashton, *New York,* pp. 192-201; *New York Times,* May 25, 1975. For support of the policies of the Metropolitan Museum, see Richard M. Clurman, "We Should Take Pride in Hoving's Met," ibid., June 8, 1975, section 2.

61. John A. Krout, "Framing the Charter," in Allan Nevins and John A. Krout, eds., *The Greater City: New York, 1898-1948* (New York, 1948); Sayre, "New York," in *Great Cities,* eds. Robson and Regan, pp. 696-697.

62. Sayre, "New York," pp. 697-702, 712-15. For extensive treatments of the government of New York City, see Wallace S. Sayre and Herbert Kaufman, *Governing New York City: Politics in the Metropolis* (New York, 1960), and Thelma E. Smith, *Guide to the Municipal Government of the City of New York* (New York, 1973).

63. *New York Times,* Nov. 16, 1969, Mar. 23, 1975. The British economist Barbara Ward saw in the new emphasis on neighborhood the possibility of restoring "the human scale that the skyscraper city has destroyed." Ibid., Apr. 19, 1964. But E. B. White asserted in 1960 that the privilege of being "unneighborly" was "the thing that makes New York tolerable to many." Ibid., Nov. 30, 1960.

64. Ibid., Jan. 30, Feb. 11, 27, Oct. 28, 1970, Oct. 30, 1971, May 23, 1974, Feb. 2, May 18, 1975. Recognition of the growing assertiveness of and interest in neighborhoods, as of the late 1960s, is exhibited in the fact that in the fall of 1968, the *New York Times* began a continuing practice of publishing feature stories on the city's neighborhoods.

65.   In 1972 the Bedford-Stuyvesant Community Corporation was the largest of these agencies. It had an overall annual budget of $5.5 million. *New York Times,* July 30, 1972.

66.   Ibid., Sep. 22, 1974; Paul Selver, "Community Boards Meet a Vital Need," ibid., Dec. 1, 1974. On planning by compromise, see ibid., June 25, 1972, Nov. 29, 1974, Mar. 23, May 15, 31, June 6, 1975. See "Restoring Housing" in *The Livable City,* a publication of the Municipal Art Society of New York, II (May 1975), p. 2. *New York Times,* May 16, June 9, 1975.

67.   Smith, *Guide to the Municipal Government of . . . New York,* p. 252; Diane Ravitch, "School Decentralization and What It Has Come To," *New York Times,* June 30, 1974. See also ibid., June 6, 1969, Jan. 19, June 30, 1974, Apr. 28, May 20, June 15, 23, 1975.

68.   Some members of the charter commission favored stopping decentralization at the borough level. One favored even greater authority for the district councils, arguing that true local participation could not exist without resorting to a decentralized budget. Ibid., Mar. 10, 1974, Feb. 4, 7, 9, June 17, 1975. A survey taken in November 1973 showed strong support for city control of the police, the hospitals, and garbage collection. Ibid., Jan. 19, 1974. See also July 23, Aug. 13, Sep. 19, 22, 26, 28, Oct. 10, 1975, Mar. 27, 1976.

69.   As of January 1, 1973, the number of actual full-time paid employees in the Police Department was 31,656; in the Fire Department, 14,689; and in refuse collection, 14,902. International Management Association, *The Municipal Yearbook* (Washington, 1974), p. 175. See also Alan K. Campbell, Roy W. Bahl, and David Greylak, *Taxes, Expenditures, and the Economic Base: Case Study of New York City* (New York, 1974).

70.   *New York Times,* Dec. 30, 1974, Apr. 8, May 20, 30, 1975. In June 1975, a member of the Board of Higher Education criticized the academic program of the City University as unsuited to the new "mold" of student produced by open admission. Ibid., June 23, 1975. The state contributed $2,500 per student in the state system, $1,100 per student in the city system. See also ibid., Feb. 19, 1974, Apr. 17, 27, July 30, Dec. 17, 1975, May 22, 28, 29, 1976.

71.   Regents Advisory Council, *New York City Regional Plan for Higher Education: Report from New York City* (New York, June 9, 1972), pp. 3, 4, 6, 123-25.

72.   *New York Times,* Oct. 27, 1974. A total of 531,000 persons were on relief in January 1966; as of May 1, 1975, the number exceeded a million. *New York Post,* June 2, 1975; *New York Times,* Dec. 31, 1973, May 19, Aug. 11, 12, 1975.

73.   Ibid., Mar. 7, May 12, 13, 17, 30, July 29, 30, 1975; *New York Post,* May 24, 1975. As of 1975, for example, the city operated 35 outdoor public pools, at a fee of 10 cents for children and 50 cents for adults. Ibid., May 17, 24, 1975.

74.   *New York Times,* Oct. 27, 1974, Mar. 14, 19, 22, 24, 30, Apr. 8, May 17, June 12, 13, 16, 22, Sep. 24, 1975. For a brief chronological digest of the city's financial crisis, see ibid., July 28, 1975.

75.   The expense budget that finally was agreed upon for 1975-1976 totaled $12,087,000,000. *New York Times,* Nov. 26, Dec. 31, 1974, May 12, 31, June 10, 11, 15, 20, July 11, 22, Aug. 11, 15, Sep. 13, 1975. The identification of the mayor with the fiscal crisis contributed to the support, in the charter revision commission, for giving the City Council and citizens at the neighborhood level more influence in the budget-making process. For observations on the role of the banks and the unions in the fiscal crisis, see ibid., July 29, 1975.

76.   *New York Post,* Sep. 15, 1975; *New York Times,* May 19, Aug. 4, Sep. 15, 26, Oct. 12, 1975. A spokesman for Chase Manhattan Bank asserted: "It can be safely assumed that any failure by either New York or New York City to meet maturing obligations will further erode the national market for municipal securities and cause vital government programs at the state, county, and local level to go unfunded through the nation." Ibid., Sep. 28, Nov. 30, 1975, Feb. 1, 6, 15, 1976.

77.   Richard Reeves, "The Changing City: Power Is Limited," ibid., June 8, 1969;

August Hecksher, *Alive in the City: Memoir of an Ex-Commissioner* (New York, 1974), p. 100. Hecksher concluded that the administrative changes of the Lindsay administration made the city work better "within its immovable framework of bureaucratic and political checks," but that Lindsay created expectations that the city could not fulfill because of the cost and the obstruction of the bureaucracy. *New York Times,* Jan. 2, 1974. The Patrolmen's Benevolent Society responded to the threats of layoffs by waging a "fear campaign," in which a pamphlet entitled "Welcome to Fear City" and illustrated with a shrouded skeleton was distributed to visitors; 24 unions of the uniformed services called a rally urging popular opposition to the proposed cuts and playing on the fear theme. Ibid., June 10, 13, 17, 1975. In March 1975 it was announced that $225 million in federal, state, and local funds would be spent annually for the next six years rehabilitating the subway system. Ibid., Mar. 24, May 19, June 12, 1975. For the views of eighteen urban specialists, see ibid., July 30, 1975.

78. *New York Times,* Apr. 5, 8, May 16, 1976; *Cue,* Dec. 6-12, 1975, p. 3. The increasing linkage between the suburbs and the central city is seen in the fact that between 1960 and 1970 the number of New York City jobs held by commuters increased by nearly 29 percent. Most of these were in high-paid fields. An employee of Union Carbide, commenting on the company's proposed move to Connecticut in 1976, said, "You can't afford to stay in a sinking city, and this city definitely is sinking. The advantages of New York will still be available when we move, but we won't be taken down when the city goes under." *New York Times,* Mar. 30, Apr. 8, 1976. In the opinion of a specialist at Brookings Institute, "the city can never be on a sound basis unless the welfare load is borne by the state or nation." Ibid., Sep. 15, 1975.

79. Ibid., Sep. 2, 1973, Jan. 1, 1974, June 9, 1975.

SUGGESTIONS FOR FURTHER READING

DEMOGRAPHIC DEVELOPMENTS

Useful statistical and descriptive detail on New York City in the 1970s can be found in the following books and official reports drawing on data from the census of 1970: Abraham C. Burstein, *A Demographic Profile of New York* (City of New York Human Resources Administration, September 1973); Ronald B. Conners, *Manhattan's West Side: A Demographic Study* (New York, 1974); Andrew Hacker, *New Yorkers* (New York, 1975); New York City Planning Commission, *Community Planning District Profiles,* part I, "Population and Housing" (New York, 1973), part II, "Socio-Economic Characteristics" (New York, 1974); New York City Planning Commission, *Community Planning Handbook*—one of these is published for each Community Planning District; Ira Rosenwaike, *Population History of New York City* (Syracuse, 1972)—chapters 5 and 6 deal statistically with all aspects of population change from 1900 to 1970, less fully for 1970 than for earlier years. A wealth of descriptive, historical, and statistical data (with many maps and photographs) is available in *Plans for New York City, 1969: A Proposal,* published in 1969 by the New York City Planning Commission—a volume on critical issues and one for each of the five boroughs.

CONTEMPORARY DESCRIPTION AND EVALUATION

For the comments of eye-witnesses, see Bayrd Still, *Mirror for Gotham: New York as Seen by Contemporaries from Dutch Days to the Present* (New York, 1956) –chapters 5 and 6 for the period 1900-1955. Representative titles for the later period include Meyer Berger, *Meyer Berger's New York* (New York, 1960); Helen Hayes and Anita Loos, *Twice over Lightly: New York Then and Now* (New York, 1972); Marya Mannes, *The New York I Know* (New York, 1959); Gilbert Millstein, *New York: True North* (Garden City, N. Y., 1964); V. S. Pritchett, *New York Proclaimed: New York, 1964-65* (New York, 1965); and Richard T. Whalen, *A City Destroying Itself* (New York, 1965).

THE ECONOMY

Eli Ginzberg, *New York Is Very Much Alive: a Manpower View* (New York, 1973); Jane Jacobs, *The Death and Life of Great American Cities* (New York, 1961); Raymond Vernon, *Metropolis, 1985* (Cambridge, Mass., 1960)–origins of the metropolitan economy and its characteristics in the mid-20th century and summaries of the findings of the other publications of the New York Metropolitan Region Study. These include Edgar M. Hoover and Raymond Vernon, *Anatomy of a Metropolis* (1959); Roy B. Helfgott, W. Eric Gustafson, and James M. Hund, *Made in New York* (1959)–the garment, printing, and electronic industries; Martin Segal, *Wages in the Metropolis* (1960); Benjamin Chinitz, *Freight and the Metropolis* (1960)–the port; and Sidney M. Robbins and Nestor E. Terleckyj, *Money Metropolis* (1960)–the New York money market.

THE PEOPLE

The best inclusive volumes on this topic are Nathan Glazer and Daniel P. Moynihan, *Beyond the Melting Pot: the Negroes, Puerto Ricans, Jews, Italians, and Irish of New York City* (rev. ed., Cambridge, Mass., 1970) and Oscar Handlin, *The Newcomers* (Cambridge, Mass., 1963)–the experience of blacks and Puerto Ricans set against a brief survey of earlier immigrant elements. For treatment of individual ethnic groups, the following are useful: Gilbert Osofsky, *Harlem: the Making of a Ghetto: Negro New York, 1890-1930* (New York, 1966); Seth M. Scheiner, *Negro Mecca, A History of the Negro in New York City, 1865-1920* (New York, 1965); Claude Brown, *Manchild in the Promised Land* (New York, 1965); Ralph Ellison, *Invisible Man* (New York, 1952); Allon Schoener, *Harlem on My Mind: Cultural Capital of Black America* (New York, 1968)–pictures; Howard Brotz, *The Black Jews of Harlem: Negro Nationalism and the Dilemmas of Negro Leadership* (New York, 1964, 1970); Maurice R. Berube and Marilyn Gittell, eds., *Confrontation at Ocean Hill-Brownsville; the New York School Strikes of 1968* (New York, 1970); Glenn Hendricks, *The Dominican Diaspora: from the Dominican Republic to New York City: Villagers in Transition* (New York, 1974); Lawrence R. Chenault, *The Puerto Rican Migrant in New York City* (New York, 1938); Joseph P. Fitzpatrick, *Puerto Rican Americans; The Meaning of Migration to the Mainland* (Englewood Cliffs, N. J., 1971); Oscar Lewis, *La Vida: a Puerto Rican Family in the Culture of Poverty* (New York, 1966); Patricia C. Sexton, *Spanish Harlem: An Anatomy of Poverty* (New York, 1966); Piri Thomas, *Down These Mean Streets* (New York, 1967)–the Puerto Rican experience in East Harlem; Leonard Covello, *The Social Background of the Italo-American School Child* (Totowa, N. J., 1972); D. Y. Yuan, "Chinatown and Beyond: the Chinese Population in Metropolitan New York," *Phylon*, XXVII (Winter 1966), pp. 321-332; Joseph P. Lyford, *The Airtight Cage: a Study of New York's West Side* (New York, 1968).

THE ARTS AND ENTERTAINMENT

Dore Ashton, *New York* (New York, 1972) discusses trends in art and architecture, with appendices describing galleries, museums, and historic buildings and listing painters, sculptors, and architects; Brooks Atkinson, *Broadway* (New York, 1970); Mary C. Henderson, *The City and the Theatre: New York Playhouses from Bowling Green to Times Square* (New York, 1973); Ada Louise Huxtable, *Four Walking Tours of Modern Architecture in New York City* (New York, 1961) and *Will They Ever Finish Bruckner Boulevard?* (New York, 1970)—reprint of articles, many on New York City architecture, that originally appeared from 1963 to 1970 in the *New York Times*; Lincoln Kirstein, *New York City Ballet* (New York, 1973); Russell Lynes, *Good Old Modern: An Intimate Portrait of the Museum of Modern Art* (New York, 1973); and Calvin Tomkins, *Merchants and Masterpieces: the Story of the Metropolitan Museum of Art* (New York, 1973).

GOVERNMENT AND POLITICS

The most extensive survey of the structure of the city government and its operation is Wallace S. Sayre and Herbert Kaufman, *Governing New York City: Politics in the Metropolis* (New York, 1960). A useful handbook detailing administrative changes is Thelma E. Smith, *Guide to the Municipal Government of the City of New York* (New York, 1973). Aspects of the problems of governing the city are revealed in the following: City of New York Commission on State-City Relations, *The New York Metropolitan Region: problems of growth; proposals for change* (New York, 1972); Alan K. Campbell, Roy W. Bahl, and David Greylak, *Taxes, Expenditures, and the Economic Base: case study of New York City* (New York, 1974); Edward N. Costikyan and Maxwell Lehman, *Restructuring the Government of New York City: Report of the Scott Commission Task Force on Jurisdiction and Structure* (New York, 1972); August Heckscher, *Alive in the City* (New York, 1974)—his experiences as Commissioner of Parks, Recreation, and Cultural Affairs; Theodore J. Lowi, *At the Pleasure of the Mayor* (New York, 1964); and Twentieth Century Fund Task Force on Prospects and Priorities of New York City, . . . *A Nice Place to Live* (New York, 1973). Useful books dealing more particularly with political developments are the following: Allan Nevins and John A. Krout, *The Greater City: New York, 1898-1948* (New York, 1948) and Cleveland Rodgers and Rebecca Rankin, *New York: the World's Capital City* (New York, 1948)—written by two persons active in the municipal government in the 1930s; Jewell Bellush and Stephen David, eds., *Race and Politics in New York: Five Studies in Policy Making* (New York, 1971); Robert A. Caro, *The Power Broker: Robert Moses and the Fall of New York* (New York, 1974); Edward N. Costikyan, *Behind Closed Doors: Politics in the Public Interest* (New York, 1968); Charles Garrett, *The La Guardia Years: Machine and Reform Politics in New York City* (New Brunswick, N. J., 1962)—emphasis on the years 1933-45; Barry Gottehrer, *The Mayor's Man* (Garden City, N. Y., 1975)—Lindsay administration; Arthur Mann, *La Guardia, a Fighter against His Times, 1882-1933* (Philadelphia, 1959) and *La Guardia Comes to Power* (Philadelphia, 1965); Robert Moses, *Public Works: a Dangerous Trade* (New York, 1970).

THE GREATER CITY:
NEW YORK AND
ITS SUBURBS, 1876–2076

Kenneth T. Jackson

A view of Levittown, a Long Island suburb.

As New York City enters the last quarter of the twentieth century, its citizens have ample reason to be apocalyptic in their thinking. The vast transit system, persistently overcrowded and badly in need of modernization, has raised fares and reduced service; the schools, once the pride of public education, are suffering from racial tensions, ineffective discipline, and vandalism; the housing stock, predominantly rent-controlled and unprofitable to landlords, is being reduced each year by thousands of abandonments; the unemployment rate, even by the widely distrusted official count, exceeds 9 percent. According to columnist Mary McCrory, the "Big Apple" is becoming the "Big Trouble."

Symptomatic of Gotham's difficulties is its well-publicized fiscal crisis. Reduced to its simplest dimension, the city had been living beyond its means by spending more for salaries and services than it could collect in taxes and in federal and state grants.[1] For ten years the increasing deficits were effectively hidden by paying current expenses out of the capital budget and by floating billions of dollars of tax-exempt municipal bonds. In no other American city did borrowing grow by such leaps and bounds; in no other American city did the ratio of debt to taxable real estate rise so high. By 1975, investor confidence in New York had collapsed, and it was unable to stave off default without federal assistance.

New York is not alone in its predicament. Cities and towns all over the United States are laying off workers, reducing services, and paying higher interest rates on their bonds. And also in 1975, Rome, the Eternal City, was so far in debt that 45 percent of its expenditures went for interest payments on municipal obligations and repayments of old loans. But New York is a special case, not only because it is responsible for an incredible 30 percent of all the short-term notes issued by all states, cities, and counties in the nation, but also because it has so far tottered closer to bankruptcy than any other important city. The irony is particularly sharp because Manhattan Island has been synonymous for generations with wealth and power. Its very streets are symbolic—Seventh Avenue for style and fashion, Broadway for the world of theater, Wall Street for banking and high finance, Park Avenue and Fifth Avenue for elegance, and Madison Avenue for commercial and subliminal tastemaking. That this home of the biggest corporations, the most important news organizations and television networks, not to mention six of the world's ten largest banks, could be threatened with bankruptcy has been enough to shake the nation's entire credit system.

Paradoxically, it was New York's reputation for size and ostentation—as well as chicanery and profligacy—that contributed to its difficulties in securing help either at the federal level or from the individual investor. President Gerald Ford, confident that his views were shared by millions of Americans west of the Hudson River, commented on both sides of the Atlantic Ocean, that the city was getting just about what it deserved. One director of the Municipal Assistance Corporation—a state body designed to market the city's securities—remarked: "I couldn't believe the animosity around the country toward New York." Another commented that "there was this sadistic urge to see pain inflicted on the city."[2]

The national debate about the resolution of the New York City bond crisis has focused on the short-term future of the Promethean metropolis and especially on such immediate questions as the size of the municipal bureaucracy (currently about 300,000), the range and cost of social services (currently the most extensive in the nation), the imposition of tuition at the City University (currently the third largest institution of higher education in America), and the number of public hospitals (currently eighteen compared to only one each in Chicago and Los Angeles). Obviously, the future of New York will be shaped by the resolution of such problems and indeed by many other decisions and policies of the present. But the purpose of this essay is to consider long-term regional and metropolitan demographic trends in order to provide a framework for speculation about the condition of New York in 2076. The author does not possess a crystal ball and does not presume to suggest that the existence of a trend is any guarantee that it will continue. As Graham S. Finney has observed, however, we are on a moving train of history and it would be wise to look around its cars for clues.

The most basic fact about New York is its immense size. In 1970, the city alone contained about eight million inhabitants, or approximately as many as Chicago, Los Angeles, Houston, and Pittsburgh combined. In addition, Gotham's 13,000 square mile suburban region housed another twelve million. Together, these twenty million people represented about a tenth of the entire United States population. In all the world, only Tokyo and London rivaled New York, and in most respects even they paled in comparison.[3]

Since 1960, when French geographer Jean Gottmann completed his seven year study of *Megalopolis*, New York City has also been recognized as the center of America's urbanized northeastern seaboard. Fifty-seven million people lived in the vast agglomeration between Boston and Washington (Boswash) in 1970, and by most measures they were the wealthiest, best-educated, and most technologically-advanced group anywhere. According to the Commission on the Year 2000, the same area (then to be called PortPort in recognition of its new spread from Portsmouth, New Hampshire, to Portsmouth, Virginia) will contain eighty million persons at the turn of the twenty-first century, or about one-fourth of the national population.

The future of New York City cannot be understood in isolation from this larger regional setting any more than its past successes can be attributed solely to good fortune or to aggressive entrepreneurship. Throughout the nineteenth century, when New York firmly established itself as the first city of the Western Hemisphere, its hinterland was disproportionately inventive and productive, and its rail and water transportation network was unsurpassed even by Chicago. While the rival Boston and Charleston regions suffered because of their peripheral locations and their relatively depleted farming areas, Gotham was surrounded by fertile lands and by such busy industrial towns as Paterson and Passaic in New Jersey, Bridgeport and Danbury in Connecticut, and Poughkeepsie and Yonkers in New York. For a century and a half following the adoption of the Constitution of the United States, New York and the Northeast prospered.

Since the end of World War II, however, the Northeast has suffered a relative decline as the South and the East have registered impressive gains both in population and in per-capita income. In fact, the recent growth of Houston, Los Angeles, and Atlanta has been a reflection of the prosperity of the geographic areas of which each is the respective nerve center.

Whether other sections will continue to "catch up" with the Northeast and with New York City over the next century will depend very largely on federal policies. Defense spending, for example, has traditionally benefited California and the southern states at the expense of New York. Very little armaments manufacture takes place anywhere in the region (Grumman Aircraft on Long Island being a notable exception), which is also dramatically underrepresented in terms of military bases. Even the Brooklyn Navy Yard, for almost two centuries the largest and most important in the United States, was closed in favor of installations in the South. Similarly, "pork-barrel" legislation has recently been aimed primarily at such items as flood control projects in Arkansas and Oklahoma rather than at mass transit improvement in Manhattan. Upper limits on Federal Housing Administration (FHA) mortgage insurance loans similarly discriminate against New York, as does the policy of reimbursing 80 percent of Mississippi's low level welfare aid and only 50 percent of New York's expenditures. Barring a sudden swing in Congressional attitudes, however, New York is likely to continue to send more money to Washington in taxes than is returned in federal aid. The result will be a narrowing of the population and income gap in the United States into the twenty-first century, and a continuation of below-average growth for the Northeast.

Although the New York region is unlikely to grow at the national average in the next century, its tremendous size means that even a smaller percentage increase will result in substantial population gains. The glamour of Manhattan, which has for more than a hundred and fifty years exercised a pull on the ambitious, the talented, the artistic, and the unusual from other places, will continue to attract those who want to share its bustle, its movement, its variety, its fluctuations, and above all to be part of the tumble and the tide. Where there is so much of everything, newcomers have long thought, there is a chance of taking a part. And not without reason. More than any other city yet examined by historians, New York provided an avenue for upward mobility, a place where talent, ambition, and hard work often combined to good result.[4] Even Theodore Dreiser, who did not always love New York, conceded the powerful effect of the great metropolis. Looking at it from afar, he said, was always to see it "in its first wild promise of all the mystery and beauty in the world."

The vision and the motivation of in-migrants have perhaps remained the same, but their ethnic makeup has changed considerably over time. Between 1830 and 1890, the Irish and the Germans represented the dominant strain; between 1890 and 1925 the shift was toward Italians and East European Jews; since 1925, in-migrants have frequently been black or Puerto Rican. And throughout American history, the nation's rural population has moved toward New York and other cities. But the prospect for the next century is somewhat different. The United States farm population (in 1975, less than 5 percent of the national total) is so low that it can no longer furnish the disaffected youth who earlier accounted for so much urban growth. Similarly, blacks have found that stronger civil rights laws have removed their primary incentive for leaving the South. Only Hispanic migration to New York, which has been especially noticeable since the expansion of airline service to the Carribean in the 1950s, is likely to continue at a high rate. In the next century, therefore, the likelihood is that New York's population will be more stable than it has been since the presidency of George Washington.

Several years ago, Columbia University sociologist Herbert J. Gans wrote that in an unpredictable world nothing could be predicted quite so easily as the continued proliferation of suburbia. His prognosis would appear to be especially accurate for New York City, which was the first community in the United States to spawn residential neighborhoods made up predominantly of commuters. By 1920, soon after Robert Fulton had established a steam ferry across the East River, Hezekiah Beers Pierrepont had begun to attract Manhattan businessmen to his genteel suburban subdivision on Brooklyn Heights. As Pierrepont explained to prospective purchasers in 1819: "Families who may desire to associate in forming a select neighborhood and circle of society, for a summer's residence or a whole year's cannot anywhere obtain more desireable situations." By 1823, his appeal to commuters was even more direct: "Gentlemen whose business or profession require daily attendance into the city, cannot better, or with less expense, secure the health and comfort of their families than by uniting in such an association."

Brooklyn gained so rapidly in prestige and population that in 1849 an important New York newspaper expressed concern over "the desertion of the city by its men of wealth." If that condition has a peculiarly modern ring, consider the description of Walt Whitman, whose office at the *Brooklyn Eagle* overlooked the Fulton Ferry slip, of rush hour commutation of mid-century:

> In the morning there is one incessant stream of people—employed in New York on business—tending toward the ferry. This rush commences soon after six o'clock. . . . It is highly edifying to see the phrenzy exhibited by certain portions of the younger gentlemen, a few rods from the landing, when the bell strikes . . . they rush forward as if for dear life, and woe to the fat woman or unwieldy person of any kind, who stands in their way.

Metropolitan sprawl in the nineteenth century was encouraged by innovations in land as well as water transport. The city's first railroad, the New York and Harlem, was in full operation to 125th Street by 1837 and to White Plains by 1844. Lines up the Hudson River and along the Connecticut shore were opened by 1850, and by 1875 there was better commuter service from Greenwich and Stamford than there would be a century later. Meanwhile, the first horsecars were in regular service before the Civil War, and in the late 1870s elevated lines were built up on Second, Third, and Ninth avenues toward upper Manhattan and the Bronx. Each new innovation expanded the boundaries of previous settlement and extended the commuting zone outward. As early as May 6, 1871, in the caption to a pictorial map, *Harper's Weekly* indicated how distant the true edges of the urbanized area really were:

> In the centre he will see the great metropolis, with its busy marts and wharves, its splendid Park, and the surrounding islands. On the right, the city of Brooklyn, and the towns lying eastward as far as Jamaica and Hempstead, and northward as far as New Rochelle, with the railroads that make them suburbs of New York, and the islands and headlands of the Sound. On the left he will see Staten Island, with its picturesque villas, Jersey City, Newark, and all the pleasant suburban villages and towns of

New Jersey as far south as Perth Amboy, westward to West Orange and northward to Caldwell and Paterson.

The long-term nature of New York's suburban trend has not been widely recognized because many of Manhattan's early suburbs were absorbed into the city as part of the consolidation of 1898. As Bayrd Still has noted in the previous essay, the addition of Brooklyn, Queens, Staten Island, and those parts of Westchester County which were later to be known as the Bronx, increased the size of the Greater City from 40 to more than 300 square miles and insured New York's twentieth-century role as one of the world's two or three dominant cities.

Although one purpose of the Greater City movement was the amalgamation of the entire metropolitan population under one government, the extended municipal boundaries soon proved inadequate to the task. Especially among middle and upper-middle class New Yorkers, the verdant suburbs beyond the city's legal rim proved irresistible. Among attorneys practicing in Manhattan, for example, only 2 percent lived outside the borough in 1835. By 1908, that proportion had jumped to 38 percent, and by 1973, it was up to about two-thirds. Similarly, a Manhattan lawyer's average journey to work which was less than one mile in 1835, increased to seven miles in 1908 and to fifteen in 1973.

The motivation of the attorney was simple and not so different from that of other prospective suburbanites. He wanted a house, and he wanted that house to be in a clean, healthy neighborhood that offered superior schools for his children. In the suburb, the spirit of individualism and exclusivity reigned; in the city, there was more emphasis on community. New York, in a sense, exchanged its private front yards for monumental municipal parks where recreation could be had in common. The suburb, on the other hand, carved up the natural land and parceled it out to private entities to ensure that each family would be able to relax in quasirural seclusion. The yard, especially, was held up as the image of all that made suburban living an attractive alternative to congested New York.

No large residential area anywhere promised better-kept lawns or more affluent neighbors than the several hundred square miles of hills and lakes above the northern border of the Bronx known as Westchester County. In the first third of the twentieth century, the population of the county tripled as old, established communities like Yonkers, New Rochelle, Rye, White Plains, and Mount Vernon, as well as newer, more-elite areas like Scarsdale, Larchmont, and Chappaqua, were inundated by newcomers. Bronxville, in particular, became synonymous with status and prestige. Located on a craggy, breathtaking square mile, 28 minutes by train from Grand Central Station, this community of Italianate, Romanesque Revival, and Tudor estates was the brainchild of William Van Duzer Lawrence. A Gilded Age millionaire who could buy pretty much what he wanted, Lawrence reasoned that Westchester was directly in the path of New York's growth. In 1889, he decided to develop an exclusive preserve of the very prosperous and the very artistic on a rugged, 86-acre estate near the house of his in-laws. He ordered his road builders to follow the cow paths and construct curvilinear streets rather than the more familiar grid ones.[5] He retained the raw slabs of rock, the fruit trees, and the wildflowers; forbade the use of fences; and insisted on architectural diversity, if not elegance. The success of "Lawrence Park" was immediate and its expensive standards soon enveloped the whole village. Within a generation, Bronxville had earned a reputation as "a suburb endlessly copied and never matched."

Although Westchester County suburbs, and those of Connecticut's adjacent Fairfield County, owed their initial prosperity as bedroom communities to their positions along one of the four main trunk railroads operating out of New York City to the north, their reliance on the trains weakened after 1925 as the metropolitan area initiated the nation's most extensive express highway projects. The Bronx River Parkway, begun in 1906 and completed in 1923 between Bruckner Boulevard in New York and White Plains, was the first major highway in the United States to eliminate intersecting traffic by lifting all crossroads above or below a carefully landscaped right of way. It was followed by the Hutchinson River Parkway, the Saw Mill River Parkway, and the Cross County Parkway, all within the next ten years. The Henry Hudson Parkway along the upper west side of Manhattan was begun in 1934 as the first "urban expressway" in the United States. Meanwhile, Connecticut opened the scenic and noncommercial Merritt Parkway in 1938 in order to relieve congestion on the Boston Post Road and to make it easier to reach places like Greenwich, Stamford, Cos Cob, New Canaan, and Darien by car. Each of the new private automobile-oriented projects demonstrated the economic stimulus of highways to land values, local revenues, and future suburban growth. As Jay Downer, Chief Engineer of the Westchester County Park Commission, noted on April 18, 1927,

A recent investigation of values of land situated within 500 feet of the Bronx River Parkway in Westchester County shows an average increase ranging from 600% near the New York City line to an average of 1100% in the Scarsdale and White Plains sections, or a general average increase in values along the parkway of more than 800 per cent during the ten years since the Commission purchased the land for the parkway.

No man was more active in building roads and thus in shaping the future of the New York metropolitan area than Robert Moses. The greatest builder and most powerful non-elected public official the United States has yet produced, Moses conceived and executed public works costing 27 billion pre-1968 dollars. Between 1924 and 1968 his was the dominant influence in the city and state of New York, an arena that included Alfred E. Smith, Fiorello LaGuardia, Franklin D. Roosevelt, W. Averell Harriman, Herbert H. Lehman, Thomas E. Dewey, Robert Wagner, John Lindsay, and Nelson Rockefeller, not to mention the sachems of Tammany Hall or the money changers of Wall Street. Indeed, in the field of public works, Robert Moses's impact was as great as all the rest of them combined. In addition to most of the parks and virtually every parkway, expressway, and public housing complex in the metropolitan area, his projects included the Brooklyn-Battery Tunnel (he had hoped for a bridge there instead); the Henry Hudson, Bronx-Whitestone, Cross Bay, Throgs Neck, Verrazano Narrows, and Triborough bridges; the United Nations buildings, Lincoln Center; Shea Stadium; and the 1964 World's Fair. As Robert A. Caro observed in *The Power Broker:*

> Other great builders left their mark on physical New York. But the achievement of even the greatest—a Zeckendorf or a Helmsley or a Winston or a Lefrak, the Rockefellers of Rockefeller Center—is dwarfed by the achievement of Robert Moses. . . . He was a shaper not of sections of a city but of a *city.* He was, for the greatest city in the Western world, the entire city shaper, the only city shaper. In sheer physical impact on New York and the entire New York metropolitan region, he is comparable not to the works of any man or group of men. . . . In the shaping of New York, Robert Moses was comparable only to some elemental force of nature.[6]

No matter how much one may question Moses's obsession with the private automobile, his disregard of mass transit, or his contempt for opinions at variance with his own, no one can deny that New York in 2076, like New York in 1976, will be shaped in part by his vision and his decisions. Long Island is a particularly important case in point. As a young man, Moses was struck by the island's natural beauty and vast coastline. He observed that the best land, particularly along the rolling North Shore, was owned by the barons of Wall Street and American business—families like the Morgans, Vanderbilts, Fricks, Whitneys, Phippses, and Woolworths. Their great manor houses, usually set on fifty or a hundred acres or more and equipped with every luxury that Western civilization could provide, reverberated to the sound of their horses' hooves and the bay of their hounds. F. Scott Fitzgerald caught one aspect of their sumptuous life style in *The Great Gatsby.*

Moses was an idealist, and he dreamed of opening the beauty of Long Island to the crowded millions of New York City. Each of the boroughs had at least one great park—Central in Manhattan, Prospect in Brooklyn, Van Cortlandt in the Bronx—but they were not sufficient. And yet the rich families of the North Shore were fiercely determined to keep their world for themselves.

Over the extended legal and political objections of these entrenched interests, who fought every road or park improvement on the theory that they would open Long Island to New York's poor, Moses began in the 1920s to intrude on the privacy of the land barons by building a series of parkways—first the Northern State, later the Southern State, Wantagh State, Cross Island, and Bethpage State Parkways—across the length and breadth of Nassau County. Moses intended that his roads be passports to recreation: Sunday drives with the family to the country or holiday trips to the shore. Instead, the new automobile right of ways had their greatest impact on the weekday journey to work. The Southern State Parkway, for example, gave motorists a route clear across western Long Island without a single traffic light or intersection. Designed as a highway eastward to Jones Beach, it found its greatest use as a rush hour artery in the direction of Manhattan, so much so that by 1957 it was one of the most heavily traveled highways in the world.

If Robert Moses lacked interest in the residential implications of his controlled access parkways, other men took notice. Even before the outbreak of World War II, comfortable subdivisions for the well-to-do were being carved from the elaborate estates of Oyster Bay, Great Neck, Glen Cove, and Roslyn. But the most spectacular instances of metropolitan sprawl involved the cutting up of Long Island's potato farms into "cookie-cutter" lots for the middle class. In this regard, William Levitt provided the prototype not only for New York and the east coast but for the entire United States.

The first Levittown opened in September 1947. Located in the Town of Hempstead, 25 miles east of Manhattan, the four thousand acre development was especially attractive to the new families which had been formed during and just after the war. In fact, the new homes were originally limited to veterans. With no down payment, no "hidden extras," and no closing costs, more than seventeen thousand Cape Cod (priced at $6,900) and ranch style (prices at $9,500) houses were sold by 1951. Levitt, who disposed of homes as quickly as other men disposed of used cars, sweetened the deal by including kitchen appliances in the purchase price. Architectural critics complained that Levittown (others were later built in New Jersey and in Pennsylvania) was degraded in conception and impoverished in form, but it served the popular dream house market at close to the lowest prices the industry could attain. More than 82,000 people lived in this single development by 1960.

Levittown was unusual for its size, but hundreds of similar developments were completed in the generation after World War II, not only in Nassau and Westchester counties, but far to the west, beyond New Brunswick and Englishtown in New Jersey, and north toward Rockland, Putnam, and even Dutchess counties in New York. On suburban Long Island, the population quadrupled between 1940 and 1970 to a new total of 2.54 million and official recognition as the ninth largest metropolitan area in the United States.[7] Everywhere in the metropolitan area the drift was outward as hundreds of thousands of families traded their walk-up apartments for their own little piece of earth.

Their choice was made easy because the federal government was the silent partner of every real estate developer and builder. Not only did Washington largesse assist with the cost of sewerage, water facilities, airports, law enforcement, and other amenities which made suburban living attractive, but it also directly underwrote single-family home ownership through its mortgage insurance, income tax writeoffs for interest payments and expressway programs.

Federal home loan policies have been especially detrimental to older cities like New York which have not had large, developable parcels of land within their municipal boundaries. During the 1930s, President Franklin D. Roosevelt and Congress became concerned over the high foreclosure rate as thousands of unemployed family heads proved unable to make their monthly mortgage payments. The New Deal responded with federally sponsored mortgage insurance and incentives for building. Congressional support for the long-term, low-interest mortgage increased even more after 1945 when the government adopted the position that the veteran should own his own home. Through the G. I. Bill, former servicemen were able to purchase dwellings with a one dollar down payment. By 1975, such programs had enabled the federal government to aid more than twelve million homeowners, most of them in large subdivisions outside the troubled cities.

Important provisions in the FHA legislation have worked to the disadvantage of congested, older neighborhoods in Manhattan, Brooklyn, and the Bronx. Home improvement loans, badly needed in such areas, were difficult to get, and then only for short periods at high interest. New home loans, by contrast, were available under more favorable, longer-term conditions. Families were thus encouraged by the United States government to buy newer homes rather than to repair older ones or to move to rental housing.

Guidelines not in the legislation but established by the FHA bureaucracy and the real estate industry also stimulated suburban growth. The agency was run as if it were a private business. To protect its loans, the FHA rated neighborhoods according to the presumed safety of housing investments made there. Four categories were established, and each rating was translated into a color, which was then placed on secret maps in FHA offices around every metropolitan area. Every block in every city had a rating and a color. High ratings were given to homogenous and new neighborhoods, such as those in Westchester and Nassau counties, that were well away from the problems of Harlem and the South Bronx. The lowest rating, red, was assigned to communities which contained such "adverse influences" as smoke, odor, or "inharmonious racial and nationality groups." The presence of older properties and slums dramatically lowered the rating of any area and, because of limited funding, practically insured that a neighborhood would be ineligible for federal funds. Such a predicament faced dozens of square miles of New York real estate. As urban renewal critic Jane Jacobs has noted, such credit blacklisting maps were accurate forecasts because they were self-fulfilling prophecies.

More direct and important federal subsidies came in the form of income tax deductions for two items large in the budget of any homeowner—property taxes and interest charges on the mortgage loan. According to economist Richard Muth, this policy alone reduces the relative price of housing by at least 25 percent to homeowners. The large renting population of New York City receives no such subsidy.

Because federal housing policies virtually guarantee that suburban families will need two cars to get back to the cities to earn enough money to afford the suburbs and the new cars, it is not surprising that national transportation funds favor automobiles over subways and buses. The Federal Road Act of 1921, which designated 200,000 miles of pavement as "primary" and thus eligible for federal subsidies on a fifty-fifty matching basis, was the first of a series of public encouragements to cars and trucks. The biggest stimulus came in 1956, when Congress passed the Interstate Highway Act and thus initiated the largest public works project in history. Financed by federal gasoline taxes which flowed into a self-perpetuating Highway Trust Fund, the 42,500 mile, 95 billion dollar road network included a number of urban expressways which made commuting easier from distant suburbs.

The big roads not only encouraged everyone from attorneys to policemen literally to head for the hills, but they also demonstrated that a highway, like a river or a railroad siding, can influence the location of industry. Prior to 1910, factories tended to cluster toward the centers of cities, largely because it was easier to move people in and out of the core by public transit than it was to move freight by horses and wagons. New York City's long-time specialty, the loft building, where raw materials went in at the top and finished products came out at the bottom, was well suited for that type of operation. Indeed, the advantages of a Manhattan location were so overwhelming that Edward Ewing Pratt of the New York School of Philanthropy was desperately seeking ways to reduce industrial congestion in the first decade of the twentieth century. He worried about the tendency toward concentration but was heartened by the results of his research on the places of work and residence of Italian-Americans in New York. He decided that if the government could regulate the location of factories, essentially forcing them out of the city, then a large proportion of the workers would themselves relocate to suburban locations.

Even as Pratt propagandized, however, the introduction of electric motors was altering the technology of manufacture by making it more efficient to operate highly-automated, single-level factories utilizing forklift trucks than multi-story plants utilizing elevators. And as motor trucks became more dependable and more powerful, particularly after 1920, highway transport created a new inducement for peripheral industry that was not matched by similar improvements in inner city forms of transit. Taken together, these technological innovations altered the basic spatial structure of the New York metropolitan area by accelerating the suburban trend of manufacturing activity. For example, since 1915, virtually all new industrial construction in the region has taken place outside Manhattan. Northern New Jersey has captured many of Gotham's heavy machinery and wood industries, several of its jewelry and precious metal manufacturers, and hundreds of warehousing and distribution activities involving food, meat, and dairy products. Nassau County and parts of the South have similarly boomed at the city's expense, especially since 1960 when interstate highways began to weaken the importance of immediate proximity to markets. Not surprisingly, Kenneth Patton, former head of New York City's Economic Development Administration, estimated a loss of two hundred thousand manufacturing jobs between 1950 and 1970.[8] In the earlier year, industrial employees in the five boroughs had represented almost 7 percent of the nation's manufacturing work force; by 1975, this figure had dropped to barely 3 percent. By 2076, it is not likely that the proportion will exceed 1 percent.

Retailing activities have followed population and industry to the New York suburbs. Although mid-town Manhattan remains the location of many of the world's largest and most fashionable stores, a deconcentrating trend began in the 1920s with the establishment of branches in outlying areas. And since 1945, the metropolis has spawned a number of prototypical shopping centers. The first was opened in 1949 at the intersection of the New York Thruway and the Cross County Expressway in Yonkers. An even larger concentration, the Roosevelt Field Shopping Center, opened in Nassau County in 1950 on the site of a former military installation. By 1975, more than one hundred air-conditioned malls and regional centers ringed the city. A typical example of their impact came in 1969, when Stern Brothers, after 102 years in Manhattan, closed its big flagship store on 42nd Street and announced its intention to concentrate its future operations exclusively at suburban locations west of the Hudson River. The suburban trend has even tarnished New York's reputation as the headquarters city of major American and international corporations. In 1966, of *Fortune* magazine's one thousand largest United States industrial companies, 198 maintained their home office in Manhattan. Ten years later the list had dropped to 120. A few have gont out of business and some have merged, but 55 of these major corporations have actually left the city. Not surprisingly, most of these firms have chosen locations within fifty miles of Times Square—in New Jersey, Westchester County, or especially in Stamford, Connecticut, which now ranks third—behind New York and Chicago—as the home of the most corporate headquarters in the nation. Arguing that "it's an altogether more pleasant way of life for all," Pepsico, International Business Machines, Doubleday, Prentice-Hall, General Telephone and Electronics, American Cyanamid, Olin, General Electric, and Continental Oil, among many well-known companies, have built spacious, low-slung campuses surrounded by acres of trees and free parking. New York City's airports, advertising agencies, and banks are close at hand, and yet the new offices are far removed from crowded streets and towering skyscrapers. If the transition has not always been smooth, executives who have relocated to suburbia nevertheless regard such transportation arteries as the Penn Central and the Connecticut Thruway as the Scylla and Charybdis of their former lives.

Perhaps the suburban exodus from New York City will continue on such a scale that Manhattan, like conquered Carthage, will be plowed with salt by 2076. Who can know? Who could have predicted in 1876 the shape of things in our own time, what with radio and television, the automobile and the airplane, or even the notion of a city budget, not yet on the horizon? But predictions for the distant future at least have the great advantage of being unassailable. Thus most futurists engage in technological fantasies regarding possible (not usually probable in my view) developments in their own fields. Transit experts wax enthusiastic about electrically-powered people capsules, which will follow programmed routes on automated guideways at great speeds and with considerable safety. All the driver will have to do is dial his destination on a sequence of number buttons. Similarly, architectural projections usually involve speculation about futuristic housing configurations. R. Buckminster Fuller's geodesic dome idea is perhaps the most famous, but linear cities, underground cities, and high-rise cities are among the possibilities frequently discussed. Lacking the precision of an engineer, the imagination of a science fiction author, or the assurance of a soothsayer, I shall confine my observations about New York in 2076 to those changes which seem to be both possible and politically, socially, and technologically feasible. My prognostication is essentially conservative and optimistic—conservative because I believe that the miracles of machine technology are mostly behind us and optimistic because I believe that the late twentieth century decline of American cities is a temporary phenomenon caused by misguided federal policies, unusually severe racial antagonisms, and the profligate use of energy.

ONE. The suburban trend, so long a characteristic of New York, will end within the next half century. Although this reversal will be due to the interaction of many factors—among them a decline in the birth rate, a rise in the real cost of housing, a new system of tough, environmental controls (particularly in sewage disposal and utility use), a drying up of rural sources of urban in-migration, and mounting political opposition to continued suburban growth—the basic cause will be the scarcity and price of fuel. Natural gas is already in critically short supply, and developing nations are rapidly pushing up the cost of oil to the American consumer. In 1976, the United States, with less than 6 percent of the earth's population, consumed about 35 percent of its non-renewable energy. Even the most optimistic jingoist must concede that the national proportion of world fuel usage will decline in the next century.

TWO. An important result of expensive oil will be a lowering of the private automobile in the pantheon of national values and an increased commitment at all levels of government to public transportation. In most parts of urban America, there is insufficient "mass" to support "mass" transit. In 1970, the average population density in American central cities was only 4,464 per square mile; for urbanized areas in general, it was only 2,627. But the New York region, with a density of about 35,000 in the city (almost 70,000 per square mile in Manhattan) and about 5,000 per square mile in the suburbs, has the requisite degree of concentration. Moreover, the radial arrangement of homes, jobs, schools, and hospitals in the New York area is especially well suited to rail and bus operations. Long before the year 2076, all of Manhattan will be closed to private traffic, while in outlying suburbs whole streets will be converted to pedestrian malls.

THREE. As the suburban trend comes to an end, so also will the socio-economic gap between New York City and its adjacent areas be reversed by 2076. Exclusionary zoning practices are already being dismantled by the courts, and the process will be complete by the end of this century.[9] The new rulings will require all communities—especially the elite suburbs—to provide housing for a cross section of society, not just the very white or the very rich. Such racial and economic integration by judicial fiat will undercut suburbia's reputation as a haven from social unrest as well as erode some of the financial and educational advantages of single-family residence. Even in the outer suburbs, new construction will emphasize land intensive apartments, condominiums, and row houses.

FOUR. Suburbia will encounter greater physical as well as social problems within the next century. Just as the Bronx and Brooklyn were once lush preserves of the good, solid middle class, so also will the leafy suburbs of the twentieth century discover that they also are subject to cycles of prosperity and despair and that obsolescence and decay are not respectful of urban boundaries. The problem will be most severe where post World War II growth was most rapid. There the jerry-built houses and standardized motels, fast food outlets, and gas stations will give in to shoddiness at approximately the same time, overwhelming the ability of any local government to arrest the resulting blight. Older, non-mall type shopping centers will often be abandoned as new downtown-style shopping districts develop in regional centers like Bridgeport, Stamford, White Plains, Paterson, Brooklyn, New Haven, and Poughkeepsie.

FIVE. In twenty-first century New York City, by contrast, the quality of the housing, like that of the air, water, and streets,[10] will be much improved, in part because rent control will have been consigned to the junk heap of well-intentioned policies that did more harm than good. Most importantly, there will be a new popularity for high-density living, where the use of an automobile will not be required for mundane chores like the purchase of cigarettes, and a fresh appreciation of the richness of the city's physical past. The middle class will repopulate many inner neighborhoods, especially those like Harlem, Bedford, and Washington Heights that offer both solid, restorable buildings and easy access to transit facilities. Young professional people between the ages of 23 and 40, for whom population density will provide opportunity for specialization and advancement, will be in the vanguard in this steady upgrading of older areas.

SIX. In the coming century, the economy of New York City will continue in the direction of office functions, tourism, and personal services and away from manufacturing. Even in the garment trades, so long a staple of Gotham's employment market, the city's function will be that of style-setter rather than fabricator, as those jobs that do not shift to the

South are taken in the Far East. The dominance of the New York and American Stock Exchanges will be threatened by the complete computerization of securities transactions, but investment banking will continue to be centralized on Wall Street, which will retain its position as the fulcrum of national and international finance. Similarly, the rising cost of energy will probably stop the corporate move to the suburbs. Scattering offices across the countryside and putting nearly all employees in their own cars is obviously not the most efficient way to conserve energy. For this reason, and because the communications, advertising, and publishing industries seem to feed on each other, Manhattan will remain the preferred location for major business headquarters in 2076.

SEVEN. So far as the city government is concerned, municipal default will not be a threat in 2076. For one thing, the proportion of New Yorkers requiring public assistance will decline as the suburbs absorb a larger percentage of the needy and as the city attracts more of the middle class. For another, the federal government will absorb the entire cost of many functions—such as welfare, education, and public health—that are now carried at least partially on the municipal budget. Finally, the city will benefit from the creation of regional authorities in fields like water supply, pollution control, transportation, and public housing. Although suburban and upstate fear of an expanded New York City will probably be sufficient to prevent an 1898 style consolidation with Nassau, Suffolk, Westchester, and Rockland counties, the more extensive sharing of regional revenues will serve to counteract any gross imbalances in welfare and minority distribution.

EIGHT. Regardless of the physical and social changes that will take place in New York over the next one hundred years, the basic character of the city will not undergo significant modification. Gotham has always been more open, more permissive, and more unusual than other places. As early as the 1840s, it was becoming famous as a city of frenetic energy and bustle, a place where the streets were busy at all hours of the day and night. Even then it was distrusted and feared.

Although New York has remained a metropolis of ineradicable fascination and drive, as well as the nation's top tourist attraction, it has not been and will not become popular in the nation as a whole. Most Americans will continue to regard it as a mismanaged ant heap, unfit for human habitation. Their suspicion will remain correct that New York is not a particularly pleasant or agreeable spot and that individuals seeking comfort or ease can find a better haven elsewhere.

Great cities, however, have always been noted for their effervescent vitality, their variety of choices, their tolerance, and their opportunities, and not for their comfort or ease. More than just the sum of a hundred Dubuques or a dozen Atlantas, the east coast giant has a magic such that once caught by it, men cannot forget or long leave it. Thomas Wolfe, the ebullient North Carolina writer who used to dash out of his Brooklyn room after long sessions of work to celebrate by dumping pitchers of beer over his head in a nearby bar, wrote that New York "lays hand upon a man's bowels; he grows drunk with ecstasy; he grows young and full of glory; he feels that he can never die."

Stereotypes of the decline of New York are false. No other city on earth—not London or Paris or Tokyo or San Francisco or Chicago, and certainly not Los Angeles or Houston—can match the intensity, the mysteriousness, or the prodigious mass of New York. Alternately loved and hated, the "Big Apple" will be alive and well in 2076.

NOTES

1. Except for the federal government, New York City has had the largest governmental budget in the nation throughout this century. In 1975, considerable dispute arose over the question of responsibility for the fiscal crisis. Those who faulted the city's political leadership pointed to the fact that in ten years, welfare costs increased six-fold to $2.4 billion. Salaries and wages tripled to $6.5 billion, including $1 billion in pensions. By 1975, municipal employees, who in the 1950s made less than private employees, were earning 25 percent more than those in the private sector. The city's many free or "discount" services, like tuition-free college education and the country's most extensive municipal hospital system, all further swelled the operating budget.

Those who defended New York City and its leaders tended to emphasize that the troubled metropolis provided many public services that elsewhere were paid for by a county or state government.

2. This is not to suggest that New Yorkers have not on occasion been obnoxious, arrogant, and condescending in their dealings with residents of what are presumed to be the hinterlands. The essential difference is that the people and the government of the City of New York have always been unusually generous with their resources in dealing with the less fortunate. Indeed excessive public generosity was often cited as the most important single factor in the budget crisis.

3. Although Tokyo is technically the largest city in the world at this time, its total metropolitan population is generally considered to be slightly smaller than that of New York. London is a distant third.

4. Thomas Kessner's forthcoming book, *The Golden Door*, will provide massive evidence that occupational mobility was much higher in the period between 1880 and 1915 in the nation's biggest city than it was in Boston, Omaha, Atlanta, Los Angeles, and Norristown, Pennsylvania. Such comparisons have been made possible by the imaginative and pioneering work of Sidney Goldstein, Stephan Thernstrom, Howard Chudacoff, Richard Hopkins, Clyde Griffen, and Peter R. Knights.

5.   The notion of the curving residential street was actually pioneered in Llewellyn Park (West Orange), New Jersey in the 1850s, and in Riverside and Lake Forest, Illinois in the next quarter century.

6.   Robert A. Caro, *The Power Broker: Robert Moses and the Fall of New York* (New York, 1974), p. 830.

7.   Prior to the taking of the 1970 Census, Nassau and Suffolk counties were detached from the New York metropolitan area on the official Census Bureau charts. Such an action bears no relation to reality, inasmuch as a county which actually borders the City of New York and whose economy is heavily dependent and interrelated with the municipality is defined as being outside the metropolitan area. Similarly, Jersey City and Hoboken, which are literally in the shadow of the World Trade Center, are counted in a separate metropolitan area with Newark.

8.   Despite this pattern in 1970, New York City retained a higher percentage of its metropolitan area jobs than the average of the fifteen largest metropolitan areas. In that year, the typical big city had only 52 percent of metropolitan jobs. In New York, the proportion was about two-thirds. The most important recent trend, both in New York and elsewhere, is a massive increase in the number of workers who both live and work in the suburbs.

9.   In a landmark decision that was sustained by the United States Supreme Court in October 1975, the New Jersey Supreme Court ruled on March 24, 1975, that the zoning regulations of Mount Laurel Township, a developing suburban community serving Camden and Philadelphia, excluded housing for poor and moderate-income families and thus was unconstitutional. The case was important for its affirmation that "regional" rather than "local" needs should be paramount. Thus, the Mount Laurel decision ruled that communities have a legal obligation to provide housing opportunities for various income groups where there is a regional need for such housing.

10.   In 1975, the United States Environmental Protection Administration reported that Los Angeles had smog in excess of the health limit 15 percent of the time; New Haven 13 percent of the time; Sacramento 10 percent; Denver 7 percent; and San Francisco 4 percent. By comparison, New York City air violated the smog health standard only 1 percent of the time. The New York City water system also compared quite favorably with that of other important cities in 1975. The streets, however, were decidedly inferior in terms of cleanliness and road surface to those elsewhere.

SUGGESTIONS FOR FURTHER READING

DEMOGRAPHIC PATTERNS

The best general treatment of the northeastern region remains Jean Gottmann's monumental, *Megalopolis: The Urbanized Northeastern Seaboard of the United States* (Cambridge, 1961). Joseph R. Passonneau and Richard Saul Wurman, *Urban Atlas: 20 American Cities* (Cambridge, 1968), contains a wealth of statistical information which makes comparisons possible among large urban areas. The six volume *Plan for New York City,* published in 1969, includes both future projections and historical information, as well as hundreds of aerial photographs and maps. Herbert J. Gans, "The White Exodus to Suburbia Steps Up," *New York Times Magazine,* January 7, 1968; and Kenneth T. Jackson, "The Effect of Suburbanization on Cities," in Phillip C. Dolce, ed., *Suburbia: The American Dream and Dilemma* (Garden City, 1976), are also useful.

HISTORY OF SUBURBANIZATION

An excellent study of the deconcentration of manufacturing activity in one of the numerous industrial cities ringing New York City is James B. Kenyon, *Industrial*

Location and Metropolitan Growth: The Paterson-Passaic District (Chicago: University of Chicago Department of Geography Research Paper No. 67, 1960). A statistical study that is focused on northeastern suburbanization is Kenneth T. Jackson, "Urban Deconcentration in the Nineteenth Century: A Statistical Inquiry," in Leo Schnore, ed., *The New Urban History: Quantitative Explorations by American Historians* (Princeton, 1975). A more general treatment is Kenneth T. Jackson, "The Crabgrass Frontier: 150 Years of Suburban Growth in America," in Raymond Mohl and James F. Richardson, eds., *The Urban Experience: Themes in American History* (Belmont, Calif., 1973), pp. 196–221.

AUTOMOBILES AND HIGHWAYS

The most informative and readable book ever written on the history of New York is Robert Caro, *The Power Broker: Robert Moses and the Fall of New York* (New York, 1974). Caro relates more than the biography of one man; his book is an exhaustive analysis of the reasons why modern New York developed as it did. In particular, Caro points out the importance of automobile-related decisions to build roads instead of subways, and he documents the decline of the mass transit system in the twentieth century. An equally critical, but less exhaustive, study of the rubber-tire mentality is contained in Bradford C. Snell, "American Ground Transport: A Proposal for Restructuring the Automobile, Truck, Bus, and Rail Industries," presented to the Subcommittee on Antitrust and Monopoly of the Committee on the Judiciary, U. S. Senate, Feb. 26, 1974, 93rd Cong., 2nd Sess. Snell offers a brief account of the takeover of the New York City trolley system by General Motors subsidiaries in the 1930s and its conversion to buses. More general accounts of the influence of the automobile on metropolitan growth are John Burby, *The Great American Motion Sickness* (Boston, 1971); James L. Flink, *The Car Culture* (Cambridge, 1975); and Flink, *America Adopts the Automobile* (Cambridge, 1971).

NEW YORK SUBURBAN PATTERNS

A long, detailed, and sophisticated analysis of residential development is Marion Clawson, *Suburban Land Conversion in the United States: An Economic and Governmental Process* (Baltimore, 1971). The standard analysis of the suburban price system is Richard F. Muth, *Cities and Housing: The Spatial Pattern of Urban Residential Land Use* (Chicago, 1969). Scott Donaldson, *The Suburban Myth* (New York, 1969) is an attack on the anti-suburban bias of intellectuals. Richard E. Gordon, et. al., *The Split-Level Trap* (New York, 1960), is a study of emotional problems in one of the suburbs in Bergen County, New Jersey. Unfortunately, it substitutes sensationalism for careful analysis. Nancy Mayer, "Westchester: The Land of Let's Pretend," *New York Magazine*, February 9, 1970; and Mel Ziegler, "Diary of a Suburban Rabbi," *New York Magazine*, January 18, 1971, are among the best pieces on New York suburbia in recent periodical literature.

THE FUTURE OF NEW YORK CITY AND ITS SUBURBS

The best publications on the future of New York come from the Regional Plan Association. Other publications are less useful and, in my view, less perceptive. I have found both Raymond Vernon, *Metropolis 1985* (Cambridge, 1960); and Dennis P. Sobin, *The Future of the American Suburbs: Survival or Extinction* (Port Washington, N. Y., 1971), to be disappointing. Herman Kahn and Anthony J. Wiener, *The Year 2000: A Framework for Speculation on the Next Thirty-three Years* (New York, 1967), is thoughtfully done, but its focus is not on metropolitan concerns. Moshe Safde, "Beyond the City Limits," *Saturday Review World*, August 24, 1974, pp. 54–57, is a prediction of urban America in the next half century. Reflecting Safde's background as an architect and planner, the focus is on housing and the prediction is for a revitalized city. Daniel Jack Chasan, "An Answer to City Traffic May Be a Horizontal Elevator," *Smithsonian*, July, 1973, pp. 47–52, is a futuristic account of the possibilities of "personal rapid transit."

Milton M. Klein

EPILOGUE:
TOWARD THE
TWENTY-FIRST CENTURY

Painting by Joseph Stella, Newark Museum, Newark, New Jersey

Historians, as one of the best of the breed, Carl Becker, once observed, are keepers of the ancient myths, much like storytellers and minstrels, to whom society has entrusted the task of perpetuating the traditions by which it lives. History is the collective memory of a people; its utility lies in orienting them to where they are because they know where they have been. Few historians have dared to use history as a guide to the future. The historian as prophet does not have a very distinguished record. Yet, unless the past is to be studied for mere antiquarian interest, its message must have some relevance for the present—and the future. History is a continuum; every generation is permitted the luxury only of a fleeting glance at a brief portion of the moving pageant. If historians are no better at prophecy than the ancient soothsayers, at least they are no worse; and as our view of the present shapes our perception of the past, so does the past inform the present.

In any case, "the future cannot be predicted, but futures can be invented."[1] What purpose can such inventions serve? As history provides the legends by which individuals explain and justify their living present, so invented futures offer the ideals by which the present shapes its tomorrows:

We create our literary myths, legends, and epics of the future, not so that some day we shall find our golden age, but because in the creation of utopian standards we have created forms which make present action possible. For an image of a future is preparation for action. . . . Every form of action makes use of ideals, as fictions in science, heavens in religion, utopias in politics, or completely fulfilling acts in art. We . . . thus create a means, a model, a standard, by which we determine the efficacy of present action.[2]

Where will New York City be at the Tricentennial of American independence? If the changes of the past several hundred years are any guide, the integral elements of the city's past may well endure into the twenty-first century: a rich diversity of population; a metropolis linked in dynamic fashion to its continental hinterland, on the one hand, and to the non-American worlds outside, on the other; a fascinatingly changing landscape, adroitly accommodating itself to the demands of its social and economic environment—a city constantly in the process of rebuilding itself; and always—however resented and distrusted—a microcosm of what the United States is and will be. A modern Rip Van Winkle, returning to New York City in 2076, would nevertheless be as astonished as his eighteenth-century counterpart by the transformation of his native Gotham during his absence.

Futurists, as Kenneth Jackson has indicated in his essay, are inclined to foresee the next century largely in physical and technological terms. Surely, New York City in 2076 will be part of a more advanced technological civilization than the America of the Bicentennial Era. Surely, industry, transportation, communication, and even farming will be heavily computerized. Satellites in the skies will link the city even closer to the events of the rest of the world than do our instant forms of communication today. News of far-away places will be available not only to the formal media but at the finger tips of researchers, students, and interested ordinary citizens. Householders will be able to employ far more sophisticated means of communication than hand-written letters or voice telephones to make instant contact with friends and relatives everywhere. The world will be literally in reach by the touch of an electronic button.

Buildings and transportation, too, will bear the imprint of advanced design, made possible by new construction methods and materials but also by the use of fuels which are already almost within our grasp: atomic power and solar energy. If the private automobile will become a luxury beyond the reach of most New Yorkers, the loss will be more than made up by the availability of novel and sophisticated forms of alternative transportation: movable sidewalks; high-speed trains, overhead or beneath the surface; non-polluting buses; and air-lifted commuter boats. Manned by a variety of automated devices, these transportation services will relieve New Yorkers of the tensions of navigating themselves through the complex arteries of the new city but will also allow them greater energy for leisure and creative work. The business of making a living itself will be limited to monitoring the machines for short periods of time; spaced-out work will again create a large reservoir of leisure time. Computerized banking and finance will remove still another of the complicated demands imposed on Bicentennial New Yorkers; and shopping will be moneyless, as Gothamites will have their earnings and spending automatically recorded and computed by machine.

With increased leisure time, New Yorkers will undoubtedly spend more time on recreation and on continuing self-education. Formal entertainment will be available as much by remote forms of presentation as by live versions; "books" will be talking as well as viewing; and libraries will be information centers from which New Yorkers will retrieve by remote inquiries the knowledge required for their education, work, and recreation.

Disease will not have been conquered, but certainly life spans will be longer, resulting from advances in the transplant of vital organs and successes in the treatment if not the cure of heart disease, artereosclerosis, hypertension, and even cancer. Despite the longer life span, the self-control of human reproduction will cause New Yorkers to live in a city and a country with a relatively stable population. Families will be smaller, and the city not much larger than the New York of the Bicentennial. The suburbs, however, will be larger and closer; and they will be peopled by New Yorkers who have not moved very far from their original homesites.

The political process will mirror the technological and physical transformation of the city. The blurred lines between city and suburb will make practical—even essential—regional government; and it is unlikely that even the Greater New York of the Tricentennial will be expected to be financially self-supporting. National planning and centralized fiscal management will leave New York with the responsibility for managing its resources but not for securing them. Despite perennial fears of centralization, the nation's governance and financing will be more closely integrated than ever; and no locality—not even New York—will be expected to go it alone. Nevertheless, the advantages of national and regional government will be balanced by an increasing devolution of responsibility for designing and operating local facilities—for recreation, education, housing, and social living—to local neighborhoods and communities.

The paradoxes that have shaped New York City's past will continue to confound observers even in the era of the Tricentennial. The city will be a scene of hustle and bustle, but it will be a place of loneliness for many despite its crowds; it will be filled with cynics but also with sentimentalists; it will be the heart of America yet occupied by a continuing flow of strangers to its shores, as residents, transient workers, and visitors. Much of its physical configuration will be unchanging, yet it will be in its traditional process of rebuilding. And while then, as now, New York will be for most simply their homes and places of business, from which they will not budge very far or very often, the city of 2076 will be to the outer world what it seemed to Washington Irving in the 1850s: "It is really . . . one of the most racketing cities in the world and reminds me of one of the great European cities . . . in the time of an annual fair. Here it is a Fair almost all the year round."[3]

Fair or Fun City, Tricentennial New York, with whatever impressive physical grandeur it may possess, and despite its constant energy and wealth as the continuing commercial, financial, entertainment, communications, and transportation capital of the country, will have to face the question so starkly put by a visiting Englishman to the United States of 1876:

I cannot say that I am in the slightest degree impressed by your bigness, or your material resources, as such. Size is not grandeur, and territory does not make a nation. The great issue, about which hangs a true sublimity, and the terror of overhanging fate, is what are you going to do with all these things? What is to be the end to which these are to be the means?[4]

Consciously or unconsciously, New Yorkers in 2076 will respond as they have responded for three centuries: the city will continue to be the "Babel on the Hudson" which critics called it almost from its birth, when it already had a population so heterogeneous that no one could readily say just what a New Yorker was. Even then a magnet for the dispossessed of Europe, the city became the symbol of the American dream, the "Mother of Exiles," the land of promise and hope for the "wretched refuse" of the older world. Rightly or wrongly, people from everywhere came to the city on the Hudson not to become part of the "melting pot"—a dish that was never really brewed except in the imaginations of myopic nativists—but to live their own lives in freedom, the freedom to maintain their own cultural identities while they contributed to the larger mosaic that had become the real America. For countless millions, Gotham was not merely a place in which to achieve material comfort but also a haven of peace—from the cruel impositions of an older world which valued uniformity more than diversity. The constant strain in the city's three-hundred-and-fifty-year history is diversity. In this, the city early foreshadowed the pluralism of the nation that was to be. Diversity created tensions; but tension is the source of energy, creativity, and fulfillment. And diversity compelled tolerance, not as a theoretical principle but as the pragmatic requirement for survival. When E. B. White remarked some twenty years ago that "it is a miracle that New York works at all," he was thinking of its congestion, its snarled arteries, its frenetic pace of living, and its impossible government; but the true miracle escaped him: the capacity of New Yorkers to maintain both individual and cultural identities in an awesome crowd.

The challenge is even greater today than it was three centuries ago; and it will continue to challenge New Yorkers in 2076. The means to meet the test will not be found in a technology that has enabled humans to fly in the skies faster than birds or to swim under water more easily than fishes but in the resources of the human spirit which alone will make it possible for men and women to walk the earth in peace. New York has survived because it has recognized, vaguely and inchoately, the quintessential spirit of the American Revolution whose Bicentennial we now observe—the commitment to human equality as an inalienable right and the foundation of that "happiness" of which Jefferson wrote in 1776. In this realization lies the remedy for the crisis of New York in the year 1976 and the promise of the city of 2076.

NOTES

1. Dennis Gabor, *Inventing the Future* (New York, 1963), pp. 207–208.
2. Hugh D. Duncan, *Language and Literature in Society* (New York, 1961), p. 15.
3. Washington Irving to Mrs. Van Wart, c. 1855–1859, quoted in Andrew B. Myers, ed., *The Knickerbocker Tradition: Washington Irving's New York* (Tarrytown, N. Y., 1974), p. 123.
4. Thomas H. Huxley, the famous biologist, quoted in Dee Brown, *The Year of the Century: 1876* (New York, 1966), p. 295.

THE CONTRIBUTORS

Thomas J. Archdeacon, Assistant Professor of History at the University of Wisconsin, Madison, is the author of *New York City, 1664-1710: Conquest and Change* (1976).

Albert Fein, Director of Urban Studies at the Brooklyn Center of Long Island University, is the author of *Landscape into Cityscape: Frederick Law Olmsted's Plans for a Greater New York City* (1967), "The American City: The Ideal and the Real" in *The Rise of an American Architecture* (1970), and *Frederick Law Olmsted and the American Environmental Tradition* (1972).

Kenneth T. Jackson, Professor of History and Chairman of Urban Studies at Columbia University, is the author of *The Ku Klux Klan in the City, 1915-1930* (1967), and co-editor of *American Vistas* (1971, rev. ed., 1975) and of *Cities in American History* (1972). He has written numerous articles on the suburban experience in the United States.

Milton M. Klein, Professor of History at the University of Tennessee, Knoxville, is the author of *The Politics of Diversity: Essays in the History of Colonial New York* (1974), *New York in the American Revolution: A Bibliography* (1974), and general editor (with Jacob E. Cooke) of *A History of the American Colonies*, 3 vols. (1973-).

Bayrd Still, Professor Emeritus of History at New York University, is the author of *Milwaukee: The History of a City* (1948, rev. ed., 1965), *Mirror for Gotham: New York as Seen by Contemporaries from Dutch Days to the Present* (1956), and *Urban America: A History with Documents* (1974).

Bruce M. Wilkenfeld, Assistant Professor of History at Hunter College of the City University of New York, is the author of "The New York City Common Council, 1689-1800," which appeared in *New York History*, July 1971, and was awarded the Kerr Prize as the best article to be published in that journal during the year.

INDEX